ENCOUNTER
WITH
GOD

ENCOUNTER WITH GOD

by

DUNCAN FORRESTER
JAMES I. H. McDONALD
and
GIAN TELLINI

T. & T. CLARK LIMITED

59 GEORGE STREET
EDINBURGH

First published by
T. & T. Clark Limited
59 George Street
Edinburgh EH2 2LQ

First Printed 1983
Reprinted 1988

ISBN 0 567 29346 7

Typeset by C. R. Barber & Partners (Highlands) Ltd., Fort William, Inverness-shire

Printed by Billings, Worcester and London

CONTENTS

PREFACE

'Are you interested in Liturgy?' an old woman asked Dean Inge. 'No, Madam, neither do I collect butterflies,' the Gloomy Dean replied. But if liturgy properly understood focuses and interacts with the whole of life it cannot be only the esoteric hobby of a few, and if worship indeed is a central activity of the Church, the study of worship should have a significant place in departments and faculties of theology and in seminaries and centres of ministerial formation. Since theology, like worship, is a function of the whole Church rather than the preserve of an elite, Christians who take their faith and its practice seriously should constantly be reviewing and discussing their worship as part of the ongoing interaction between theology and practice which is integral to the Christian Faith. This introductory textbook is offered in the hope that it will stimulate, provoke and encourage profitable study and reflection on worship, rooted both in theology and practice, on the part of theological students and seminarians, clergy and lay people of various traditions.

The writing of this book was stimulated by the experience of teaching worship to lively, responsive and varied groups of students in the ecumenical context of Edinburgh University's Faculty of Divinity. Most, but not all, of these students were preparing for the ministry of Presbyterian or Anglican churches, but students from other traditions and with different motivations leading them to the study of worship also made distinctive and valuable contributions to the discussions out of which this book has arisen. We wish to thank our students for comments, challenges, questions and suggestions which have played no little part in carrying forward our thinking on worship and shaping this book.

Encounter with God has three particular emphases. In the first place, it is written with the conviction that the study of worship today must be ecumenical. The modern convergence in the theology and practice of worship is based on the realization that the major ecclesiastical traditions share more in terms of the principles and structure of worship than was commonly realised when the various traditions were studied and practised in virtual isolation from one another. Now we can, and must, take a broader view which is full of possibilities for the renewal of worship and the restoration of Christian unity.

Secondly, we have made the complementarity of Word and Sacrament the pivot of our argument. In the past even when the theological principle was affirmed, practice often denied it. For example, in churches which gave to their ministers great freedom in the conduct of worship, much attention was devoted in theological education to homiletics while the principles of worship were often given perfunctory treatment. As a consequence worship sometimes degenerated into nothing but the preliminaries to the sermon, and sacramental life became impoverished. In churches of the 'catholic' tradition, on the other hand, it was not uncommon for seminaries to devote a major part of their time to liturgy but to inculcate the view that preaching and the ministry of the Word were little more than appendages. This unhealthy polarization is clearly reflected in many textbooks. We have tried to do something to redress the balance and hope we have suggested some ways in which this fundamental principle of the theology of worship may be more adequately expressed in practice.

In the third place, we believe that worship should be studied primarily theologically. Karl Barth was right to say of the adage *Lex orandi, lex credendi*, 'this saying is not simply a pious dictum, but one of the most intelligent things that has ever been said about method in theology.' It is as important for theology that it takes seriously both worship and the questions it generates as it is that the study of worship should understand itself as a theological discipline. Some may feel that we have given too little attention to the history of liturgy, but we have restricted the space devoted to historical matters advisedly, because we feel it necessary to stress that the study of worship is not a form of antiquarianism – and, besides, the necessary historical information is easy to come by elsewhere.

The three authors brought varied experience and background to teaching in Edinburgh and the writing of this book. Tellini was a Roman Catholic priest working on eastern liturgies in Rome before becoming an Anglican and teaching in various theological colleges. He now divides his time between teaching, in Edinburgh University, serving as a parish priest, and working on the Scottish Episcopal Church's Liturgical Commission. McDonald was a parish minister of the Church of Scotland before teaching Religious Education in a college of education and developing special expertise in New Testament and in homiletics. Forrester was ordained in the Church of South India where an interest in worship was aroused which he further developed while chaplain of a new English University. It should not be beyond the capacity of a moderately competent textual critic to work out which author has had primary responsibility for which parts of the book. Each section has been revised after discussion, but we have not sought uniformity of style and although we have substantial agreement on our approach to the theology of worship, we are still debating vigorously among ourselves some of the positions presented in these pages. We hope that those who read and use this book will join in the debate, recognising its importance for the future vitality of the worship and theology of the Church.

Duncan Forrester
James I. H. McDonald
Gian Tellini

New College,
University of Edinburgh

Easter, 1983

CHAPTER 1

IN MANY AND VARIOUS WAYS

Primitive stone circles, ancient tombs, ruined temples in the jungles, wayside shrines and standing crosses, basilicas in Ravenna, mosques in Cairo, gothic cathedrals – all remind us of the strange pertinacity with which people have worshipped all down the ages, and of the importance they allocated to their worship. Things to do with worship were made to last, whereas ordinary life, being regarded as of comparatively little importance, has left scant trace behind.

The oldest archaeological evidence suggests that worship in some form or other occupied a central place in the activity of people from the dawn of history. We cannot find an age or a culture when people disposed of their dead like so much rubbish; always there is some ritual accompaniment to burial or cremation, suggesting not just the awareness of a transcendent order, but a worshipful attitude towards it.

And it is not only the past that supplies evidence that people have worshipped; the contemporary world is full of shrines, temples, mosques, churches, gospel halls, meeting houses: places where activity relating to the holy, what Rudolph Otto speaks of as the *mysterium tremendum et fascinans*, takes place. The little, plain and forbidding corrugated iron church in a remote glen in the Scottish Highlands, the Pentecostal shopfront in Harlem, and the glorious gothic splendour of Chartres cathedral with its vibrant stained glass windows are all places of worship.

But is it not true that in the West, at least, society has become secular, worship has less and less of a recognised place, and fewer and fewer people seem to take part in any recognizable form of it? There is force in the argument, let that be admitted. But although the formal expressions of Christian worship may play a less significant role in western societies than once they did, these very societies are not as free from worship as might appear at first sight. There are, of course, nations in the West where Christian worship continues to hold a central place, as if to mock the sociologists' generalizations about secularization – Poland and the United States are good examples. And even where few seem to attend worship frequently, an amazing number of people feel the need to mark the great turning points of life – birth, maturity, marriage, death – with Christian rituals, or 'rites of passage', which give meaning to these transitions and allow them to be understood in the context of eternity. This may be residual Christianity, or it may be something more. It has become customary for clergy to be supercilious about the 'Four-wheelers' – people who come to church in a pram to be baptized, in a limousine to be married and in a hearse when they are dead – but the conviction that the great moments of celebration, fear, grief and mystery in life can best be marked by Christian worship should not be dismissed as sheer superstition or slavery to tradition. It suggests some continuing relationship to the Christian faith and the worship of the church which must be taken seriously.

The worship of civil religion is also alive and well. Crowds come to church on Remembrance Sunday who are not seen again for another twelvemonth. Long queues continue to shuffle past the embalmed body of Lenin in his mausoleum in Red Square in a strange ritual of communist civil religion. In East Germany they hold Marxist 'confirmations' to try to wean the young away from the church. And Hitler had a multitude of rituals to confirm and express loyalty to the state and the perverse ideology of Nazism. Folk religion also continues to flourish and influence not just baptisms and weddings, but above all that great modern feast, the Harvest Festival. And alongside all this, there is the proliferation of sects which worship or meditate or dance through the streets in ways which seem strange and somewhat disconcerting to the more conventional Christians – the Hari Krishna folk, the Moonies, and the devotees of countless eastern gurus.

As if this were not enough, in secular societies, so called, there are plentiful surrogates for worship to which people for whom the teaching and the worship of the Church no longer hold any meaning turn for solace and significance. Consider the parallels between pornography and the old fertility cults, think of the potent, if ineffably banal, myth of Superman, remember the continuing fascination with the occult, if you still believe that a secular age has in fact set aside worship as childish play inappropriate for man come of age.

Worship continues, in a multitude of forms, some of them bizarre, others but 'vain repetitions' of rituals which seem to have lost their significance. It is not just the hobby of a few, like squash, or Hornby railways, but an astonishingly large proportion of humankind take part in worship with at least some glimmering awareness of its significance. Man seems to be a worshipper – you could almost define him as such. That is not to say that everyone worships God, but that everyone worships something. 'Whereupon you put the trust of your heart,' said Martin Luther, 'that is in fact your God.' No adequate simple definition of worship is possible. The best description may be the answer to the first question in the Westminster Shorter Catechism (1648): 'Man's chief end is to glorify God and enjoy Him for ever.' This speaks of worship as ascribing to God the glory that is properly his and delighting in encountering him, and also suggests that worship is a central, characteristically human, and virtually universal activity of mankind. Worship, encountering God, is the central and most important thing in human life, that which focuses and enriches the whole of life, above all other activities that which is most appropriate or natural for people, the giving of meaning to existence, the purpose for which mankind was made. Just to make statements like these in modern secular and fragmented society is to invite ridicule; after all, even 'religious people' are not infrequently embarrassed about the fact that they pray and participate in worship. It seems somewhat anomalous, it doesn't seem to 'fit' in the modern world – or only as a quaint museum-piece, a furtive and surreptitious activity indulged in by little, curious cliques of cranks.

But if you look at other contemporary cultures the situation is far different. A few years ago the writer travelled, wedged tightly in a crowded and sweltering third class compartment, from Agra to Kanpur in India. After an hour or so a woman who had been sleeping, squatting under a blanket on the bench opposite, stirred, sat up, elbowed her neighbours until she had cleared about a foot of space on the bench beside her, and opened a tin box. She took from the box a tiny brass image, a religious painting, a little bell, a phial of oil, a lamp, and a string of beads. She laid these objects on a white cloth, poured oil into the lamp and lit it. For half an hour or more she performed her *puja*, her worship, ringing the bell with one hand while with the other she swung the little lamp before the image, singing hauntingly beautiful *bhajans* the while. When she had finished she bundled everything away, and pulled the blanket back over her head, but one could still see the little movements as she went over her prayer beads, and hear her low whispering. Nobody, sitting, standing, or hanging onto that compartment (and there must have been close on fifty people within sight of her – the coach was rather like a swarm of bees) paid any attention to her or her *puja*. It was just part of life, an important part, perhaps, but perfectly natural and not deserving of special attention or comment – save from the Christian opposite, who found his own assumptions and attitudes to worship and its place in life challenged and disturbed.

Or sit in the lounge of a westernized Hindu businessman's house chatting while we wait for breakfast. The conversation flows smoothly and naturally, but to the westerner rather incongruously, from the problems of inflation to the miracles of Sai Baba, who produces coins and watches out of the air; from labour troubles to the forthcoming pilgrimage to Sabarimalai, in which our hosts intend to join after three weeks of ritual purification; from the political situation to the beneficial effects on businessmen of meditation – and all the while incense is drifting into the room, and there is a gentle background of tinkling bells and soft singing from next door, where the womenfolk and children are performing the morning *puja*. The *puja* finished, we all go through to breakfast. The worship is a natural, central and determinative dimension of the life of the home and family.

Or stand outside a busy suburban station in Madras during the evening rush hour, and watch how many of the businessmen, with their suits and rolled umbrellas, and the clerks, and the coolies, as they pour out of the station stop at the little shrine of Ganesh to spend a few minutes in prayer, or circle the shrine three times, or make an offering of flowers, or rice, or money. Once again, worship accepted without embarrassment or self-consciousness as a natural and necessary part of life. How different from the western tendency to fragment everything, and to regard worship as the private hobby of the few, without public relevance, incongruous and curious, in a modern society!

But it is, of course, misleading to exaggerate the contrast between East and West, and romanticize the eastern attitude to worship. Not only do vast numbers of people in the West take part, at least from time to time, in some form of worship, but almost everyone seems to have at least a surrogate for it, if not the 'real thing'. And everyone who takes part in worship has some awareness, however faint, that this is an activity which focuses life, allocates priorities, gives meaning and strength, and is the encounter with what is of ultimate importance. Indeed encountering God is near to the heart of what Christians and most other religious people understand as worship. The best images of worship are drawn from the field of personal relationships. And if one really believes that God is impersonal and incapable of relating to men and women in a personal sort of way, worship becomes meaningless and is quickly abandoned, or allocated a very lowly and insignificant place, as it is in some of the philosophical forms of Hinduism. Certainly if we are to understand worship as 'glorifying and enjoying God' there is the clear presupposition that God is pleased to encounter people in a personal sort of way.

Etymologically the word worship means the recognition and celebration of 'worth', value, goodness, holiness, wherever such qualities are to be found. In England they still retain the archaic usage of referring to 'His Worship the Mayor.' The story is told of a primary school class who visited the City Chambers and were greeted by the Mayor. When they were set to record the event in their newsbooks afterwards, one little girl reported that at a certain point in the proceedings a flunkey appeared, hit the floor with his staff, and cried, 'Worship the Mayor'. 'So,' she wrote, 'we all stood up and worshipped the Mayor.' She didn't get it quite right, of course, but she had got hold of something rather important: in standing up to honour the head of the civic community the schoolchildren were taking part in a ritual in which the worth of the Mayor was recognized and a structure of relationships between people symbolically expressed and celebrated. The archaic language of the 1662 Anglican Prayer Book reminds us of other dimensions of the meaning of worship. In the marriage service the groom says to the bride, 'With my body I thee worship.' He responds, that is, in the most appropriate way to his beloved, he recognizes and celebrates her worth and value to him, her lovableness. And this he does not only in words – the words of lovers are often pretty incoherent! – but also with the body. Love is expressed and strengthened in bodily acts; it is something that involves the whole personality. The kiss, the cuddle, gazing silently into one another's eyes, coitus – these are just some of the bodily ways in which love shows itself. And lovers, like worshippers (indeed the argument is that they are very much the same), use symbols that are charged with rich meaning: the bunch of flowers, the ring, the gift of perfume, and so forth. These are just some of the ways in which a spouse recognizes and celebrates the love and worth of the partner; they communicate with one another in verbal, bodily and symbolic ways, and their communication both shows that love is there and deepens and enlarges and strengthens the love between them.

This image of worship reminds us of various things. First of all, worship is an encounter between God and people, which must be reflected in the quality of relationship between the worshippers and in their attitudes to their neighbours. And, secondly, the relationship involved in worship is, like human love, a *reciprocal relationship*. It is right and proper that we should emphasise that worship is the recognition and celebration of the glory and worth of God and that this should have an absolute priority in our understanding of worship as a human activity. But it is also true that worshippers experience an affirmation of their own worth and value to God. They come to worship aware of their sins; they confess them and experience the forgiving grace and love of God, the divine confirmation that, despite all, they are loved with an infinite love, and are of incalculable value to God.

Worship, then, should be an encounter with God in which we enjoy him. It shows, even in the midst of oppression, poverty, and the bleakest of outward circumstances, the delight of keeping company with God, in whom all true joys are to be found. Of course, this applies to the whole of the Christian life, but worship, even if it percolates through life as it should, is still the time set apart specifically for loving attention to God. In the best of families time needs to be kept for doing things together, for enjoying one another, for talking, for playing together. Of course, those times are not the *whole* of the family relationship, but without them the relationship may wither and die. We need, in other words, to make time for God, jealously guarded time, in which we give loving attention to him, that the whole of our lives may be lived as a loving encounter with God.

Worship is enjoying God. In worship our attention is directed away from ourselves, to God and to our neighbour. We do not 'enjoy ourselves' in worship, indeed the very opposite; at the start we look at ourselves honestly and confess our sins, then as forgiven sinners we can cease to be absorbed by self and open out to God and his glory, and our neighbour and his needs. C. S. Lewis in his autobiography, *Surprised by Joy*, describes how as a young man he was engrossed with his own inner workings. He constantly and morbidly scrutinized his motivation, his attitudes, his feelings as if these were matters of cosmic moment. Conversion drew him out of himself; he became far more open to other people, far more sensitive to their feelings, because he was now open to God. Sin, according to a phrase much used by Augustine and Luther, means being *incurvatus in se*, turned in on oneself. C. S. Lewis found an amazing release from this obsession with self when he was given the capacity of enjoying God and consequently his neighbour. Understanding worship as enjoyment of God should save us from the trap of becoming obsessed with the minutiae of liturgy and the details of worship as if these things were important in themselves. They are simply aids, which should be unobtrusive, to the glorification and enjoyment of God by his people.

Worship is rather like a party. The hundredth psalm is typical of many passages in the Bible which see worship in this way:

All people that on earth do dwell,
Sing to the Lord with cheerful voice.
Him serve with mirth, his praise forth tell,
Come ye before him and rejoice.

A good party demands meticulous preparation and attention to detail on the part of the organizers. They must give careful attention to the choice, preparation, and layout of food and drink; the arrangement of flowers and candles; to lighting and music. They should be careful to invite a good mix of participants; they should ensure that people are introduced to one another; they should arrange the furniture to encourage conversational groupings; and good hosts move people around from time to time and keep an eye open for those who are lonely or don't fit in. Details such as these are all important and contribute to the making of a good party in which people enjoy one another. And it is not only the role of the hosts that matters; guests who wish to enjoy a party will ask themselves questions like these: do I take flowers or a bottle of wine for my hosts? Do I offer to wash up the dishes, or to help hand round food and drink? Do I bother to meet some new people rather than sticking with my old cronies all evening? Parties, well arranged parties, parties that people enjoy, are important. A good party can do much for someone who is disturbed or confused or just plain lonely – but a bad, poorly arranged and cliquish party only makes matters worse! And parties are significant for any group of friends, as a way of expressing and cementing and extending their friendship and enjoyment of one another.

If worship is rather like a party, it is clearly necessary that people who lead worship or participate in it should know what it is about and be meticulous in their planning and arrangements. The mechanics must be unobtrusive; arrangements are no more than vehicles to enable the glorification and enjoyment of God. But when the arrangements are sloppy or inadequate or ill-thought-out they jar and detract from the spirit of worship. This book is intended to help people to reach greater understanding of the principles of Christian worship and the structures within which God's people have found they may best glorify and enjoy their God.

Worship and storytelling are remarkably close to one another. In worship stories are retold, re-enacted, recalled, meditated upon, and the story of the community of faith is grafted together with the personal stories of the worshippers. When the kings of the old Anglo-Saxon kingdoms of England were converted to Christianity, they looked afresh at their personal histories as represented by their genealogies. These traced their descent back many generations to the old Norse gods – Thor, and Wodin and so on. Rather than renounce their stories, deny their history, and assume an entirely new identity, the Anglo-Saxon Kings simply extended their genealogies backwards, so that now, as Christians, they traced their descent through the Norse gods to the patriachs of the Old Testament and back to Adam. They had grafted their stories into salvation-history, and assumed a Christian identity without a total repudiation of the old. Every believer has to relate his personal story to the story of the community of faith. Worship is one of the crucial places where this grafting takes place.

In the Jewish Passover a central part of the ritual is when the youngest child present asks four questions:

> Why does this night differ from all other nights? For on all other nights we eat either leavened or unleavened bread, why on this night only unleavened bread?

> On all other nights we eat all kinds of herbs; why on this night only bitter herbs?

> On all other nights we need not dip our herbs even once, why on this night must we dip them twice?

> On all other nights we eat either sitting or reclining; why on this night do we all recline?

The reply from the elders comes in terms of the story of the first Passover and of God's deliverance of his people from Egypt, the story which they are ritually re-enacting, and the story which tells the child and the whole gathering what it means to be a Jew, who they are, the great story of God's people into which their personal stories dovetail:

> We were Pharaoh's slaves in Egypt, and the Lord our God brought us forth with a mighty hand and an outstretched arm. And if the Holy One, Blessed be He, had not brought our forefathers forth from Egypt, then we, our children, and our children's children, would still be slaves in Egypt.

> So, even though all of us were wise, all of us full of understanding, all of us elders, all of us knowing the Torah, we should still be under the commandment to tell the story of the departure from Egypt. And the more one tells the story of the departure from Egypt, the more praiseworthy he is.[1]

And that is precisely what happens at the Passover feast. They tell again the old story, they sing and pray about it, they discuss it, but above all they re-enact the first Passover, appropriating afresh the story of God's deliverance and making it live in contemporary experience. And so it is also in Christian worship, most notably in the Lord's Supper and the Easter Vigil.

The Passover reminds us of another central characteristic of worship in the historical religions of Judaism, Christianity and Islam: in worship we find our place in time and understand the present moment by looking back and by looking forward. It is a little like a game of chess, where one can only understand the position of the pieces and the state of the game at any moment in the light of the past moves and the strategies and hopes for the rest of the game.

In worship we look back. In order to understand ourselves and our times we must hear again and relate ourselves to the stories of God's dealings with his people. We need constantly to repossess our past as something that is still operative and influential in the present. And in this process we see where we 'fit in'. Just as a child delights to hear the story of his birth and early days, of events of which he has himself no memory, and to hear about his mother's and his father's childhood, so in worship we need to hear the living voice of the past, the Word of God himself showing us who we are and how we came to be here.

But worship would quickly become maudlin, wistful and disabling if it were simply concerned with the past. Worship looks towards the future and encourages hope and expectation, for the God who meets his people in the present and dealt with them graciously in the past is also the God who will be with them in the future, when all worship will find its fulfilment and culmination in the immediate presence of God. Worship points forward with confidence, and nourishes people's hope and expectation. Once again the Passover is an excellent illustration of this. At times when Jews have been oppressed and persecuted, even in the horrors of the concentration camps, they have celebrated the Passover not simply as a remembrance of a past deliverance, or as an affirmation that before God they are beloved and free men and women despite the agonies of their outward condition, but as a way of nourishing their hope for freedom and their expectation that God has some good thing in store for them. In the New Testament period, the Passover season was a time when revolts against foreign rule were particularly likely because messianic expectations were then at their peak. And worship continues to be the parent of hope.

In most of the eastern religious traditions worship is commonly (but not universally) understood as a way of escape from a temporal process, which is itself meaningless, into a timeless realm of spiritual verities. In Judaism, Christianity and Islam, on the other hand, worship is the point at which one can discern the significance of history, of the temporal process, as the place where one meets God and serves him. In worship understood as the encounter with the God who acts in history, the worshipper is enabled to locate himself in time.

A Hindu temple is the abode of a god. The priests and other functionaries are his attendants and courtiers; the worshippers come individually or in small groups to have *darshan* (audience) of the god, to give him offerings and to submit petitions to him. The daily routine and ritual of the temple is closely analogous to that of an old-style royal court. In the early morning the god is woken up with music, washed, dressed and offered food. The temple gates are opened to worshippers when the god is ready to give audience. Then he has his midday meal, and a time of siesta in the heat of the afternoon. Once a year he is borne out of the temple on a great decorated temple car and tours his domains, hauled around the streets by hundreds of devotees. Most temples and shrines of most religions are much like that, although the Jewish temple had no representation of God in its Holy of Holies, and the Jewish faith affirmed that God does not dwell in temples made by hands (e.g., 1 Kings 8:27–53). But, for all that, the temple was central to Jewish devotion until, after its destruction in A.D. 70, the synagogues had perforce to take much of the place once occupied by the temple. In such a context it is easy to understand the surprise and antagonism aroused by the early Christians' claim that they, unlike the Jews and the pagans, had no shrines and altars.[2] Hence the buildings used for worship were meeting places for the community rather than dwelling places for God, and the earliest Christians showed no interest whatsoever in ecclesiastical edifices. They met in houses or large rooms because they were convinced that the Church was people not buildings. The modern children's hymn captures accurately the early Church's understanding of itself:

> The Church is wherever God's people are praising,
> Singing their thanks for joy in this day.
> The Church is wherever disciples of Jesus
> Remember his story and walk in his way.
>
> The Church is wherever God's people are helping,
> Caring for neighbours in sickness and need.
> The Church is wherever God's people are sharing
> The Words of the Bible in gift and in deed.[3]

Worship is, then, the activity of the people of God. It is not something they watch, a kind of stage-show laid on for them as the audience, nor is it something they listen to, like a lecture. Rather is it something they *do*, and do together. It is the central activity of the Christian fellowship which creates as it expresses, friendship with God and with our fellows.

In worship the individual not only appropriates a history and enters into a relationship with God, but he finds his place in the household of faith. The question of identity is resolved in part by the discovery that one belongs within this particular community, stretching beyond the visible worshipping fellowship to encompass the whole Church down the ages and in every land, the Church on earth and the Church in heaven, the whole *communio sanctorum*. Christian worship is the activity of a community which sees itself as living by grace, existing for the sake of others, welcoming to strangers and concerned for the world – a community with a mission.

We have seen that worship is to be understood as the focal moments in our encounter with God and our neighbours. If these two dimensions – the vertical relationship to God and the horizontal relationship to the neighbour – are separated worship degenerates into a parody of itself. The Old Testament prophets never tire of proclaiming that worship separated from the doing of justice, or used as a cover for cheating and mistreating one's neighbour, is offensive to God; indeed the doing of justice is far more important in the eyes of God than the correct performance of the cult. Amos is typical of the prophetic tradition when he writes:

> I hate, I despise your feasts, and I take no delight in your
>   solemn assemblies.
> Even though you offer me your burnt offerings and cereal
>   offerings
> I will not accept them,
> and the peace offerings of your fattest beasts I will not look
>   upon.
> Take away from me the noise of your songs;
> to the melody of your harps I will not listen.
> But let justice roll down like waters,
> and righteousness like an ever-flowing stream.   (Amos 5:21–24)

The same theme is continued in the New Testament: our relationship to God and our relationship to our neighbour are interdependent and cannot be separated without the perversion of worship. The Sermon on the Mount puts it thus: 'So if you are offering your gift at the altar, and there remember that your brother has something against you, leave your gift there before the altar and go; first be reconciled to your brother, and then come to offer your gift.' (Matthew 5:23–24). If Christian worship is isolated from the spheres of politics and economics it loses its authenticity and easily becomes the opium of the people, a cover for injustice and oppression, or an irrelevance. Archbishop Trevor Huddleston reminded us of this when he commented that many Christians are so concerned with the real presence of Christ in the Eucharist that they forget the real presence of Christ in the needy neighbour.

Within the Christian tradition, some people, particularly from the 'catholic' wing, have emphasised elements of continuity between Christian and non-Christian worship. Christian worship is seen as the crown and fulfilment of all worship; there is no fundamental opposition between different ways of approaching God, only some are less adequate than others. 'Christian worship', writes a contemporary Roman Catholic scholar, 'does not deny the values to be found in any more primitive (sic) kinds of worship. It purifies them, puts them into an entirely new context, and enhances them.'[4] A similar attitude was shown in the letter which Pope Gregory sent to Augustine giving him guidance for his mission to the English. Augustine and his companions were counselled to take over druidic temples, purify them, and adapt them to Christian worship and to continue in Christian form as many as possible of the rituals and customs of the people.[5]

But there arises a problem when we turn to the Bible, for we find there a very sharp distinction drawn between true worship and idolatry. Worship which is not accompanied by, and expressed in, the doing of justice is fraudulent; and worship of any other than the one true God is a kind of adultery, a breaking of the convenant relationship between God and his people. Pagan worship is occasionally mentioned as permitted for Gentiles despite its basic defectiveness. For example, Naaman the Syrian, after his healing in the waters of Jordan, says to Elisha: 'Let your servant have two mules' burden of earth; for henceforth your servant will not offer burnt offering or sacrifice to any God but the Lord. In this matter may the Lord pardon your servant; when my master goes into the house of Rimmon to worship there, leaning on my arm, and I bow myself in the house of Rimmon, the Lord pardon your servant in this matter. And he said to him, go in peace.' (2 Kings 5:17–19). In one place God is said to have allocated worship of the sun and moon and stars to the pagans, but Israel is to have nothing to do with such forms. (Deuteronomy 4:19). The statement in Malachi 1:11 that God's name is great among the nations and incense and pure offerings are made to him 'in every place' suggests that Gentile worship may be purer and more acceptable to God than degenerate and fraudulent Jewish worship. But the Old Testament generally affirms that pagan cults are false, immoral, degrading and dehumanising idolatry.

The New Testament sees Christian worship as flowing out of Jewish worship and continuous with it – remember that both Jesus and the earliest Christians continued to worship in temple and synagogue. Christian worship is the fulfilment of Jewish worship (a point elaborated particularly in the Epistle to the Hebrews) but is radically incompatible with civil religion and most other forms of worship in the ancient world. Yet Paul, preaching to the philosophers in Athens, saw their worship as a confused and ignorant response to a barely understood God. This cult was not to be totally rejected for it was a kind of preparation for true worship. 'What you worship as unknown,' said Paul, 'this I proclaim to you' (Acts 17:23). But false worship is generally seen as more harmful than no worship at all; it goes with all kinds of moral decadence and it degrades the human personality. Karl Marx was at his closest to the Old Testament prophetic tradition when he described the worship of village India as 'A brutalising worship of nature, exhibiting its degradation in the fact that man, the sovereign of nature, fell down on his knees in adoration of Hanuman, the monkey, and Sabbala, the cow.'[6] Such attitudes may be arrogant, but they also betray a conviction that worship is of great significance. So important was this matter to the early Christians that they were willing to die rather than burn a pinch of incense to honour the Emperor as divine. They realised that in worship they were doing something of ultimate importance, celebrating the mystery of God's love and grace. Their passion for purity in worship was no nostalgia for the rituals of the past, but arose out of the excitement of encountering the true God, and finding that their thirst for God was both satisfied and stimulated by their worship in Spirit and in truth. They would have agreed with Karl Barth who said that 'Christian worship is the most momentous, the most urgent, the most glorious action that can take place in human life.'

NOTES

1. N. N. Glatzer, ed., *The Passover Haggadah, with English Translation, Introduction and Commentary*, New York 1969, pp. 21–3.

2. Minucius Felix, cited in Jungmann, *The Early Liturgy*, p. 45.
3. Carol Rose Ikeler, *Church Hymnary*, 3rd Edition, No. 427.
4. J. D. Crichton, in Jones, Wainwright & Yarnald eds., *The Study of Liturgy*, London 1978, p. 7.
5. See Bede, *History of the English Church and People*, Harmondsworth 1955, pp. 86–7.
6. 'The British Rule in India', in Marx & Engels, *On Colonialism*, Moscow n.d., p. 37.

FURTHER READING

Ninian Smart, *The Concept of Worship*, London 1972.
J. G. Davies, *New Perspectives on Worship Today*, London 1978.
Michael Perry, *The Paradox of Worship*, London 1977.

FOR DISCUSSION

1. What human needs does worship satisfy?
2. Does idolatry have any significance in the world today?
3. What is distinctive in Christian worship?
4. Why does the Bible stress the need to link worship and the doing of justice?

CHAPTER 2

THE ROOTS OF CHRISTIAN WORSHIP

Louis Bouyer argues that, though one of the most original creations of Christianity, Christian worship did not spring up 'from a sort of spontaneous generation, fatherless and motherless like Melchizedech'; in discussing Christian worship, one must search for its roots; in recounting its genesis and development, one must strive to understand it in its proper context.[1]

In the past, when little was known about worship in the Old Testament, scholars were wont to explain the origins of Christian worship in terms of the rites and ceremonies of Hellenistic mystery religions. No one would be justified in holding such opinions today. The sources of Christian worship must be found mainly, though not exclusively, within Judaism. Progress in biblical studies has shown the artificiality of the dichotomy between the Old and the New Testament. Again in the words of L. Bouyer, to isolate or separate 'the Word of God expressed once and for all and the life in the People of God of the Spirit who inspired this expression' is as impossible today as it would be to 'imagine the relationship of the New Testament with the Old as a relationship that would be connected here only with the inspired texts in the strict sense alone and could or should ignore its contextual surroundings'.[2]

As we pointed out in the first chapter of this book, worship of some kind is a quasi-universal human activity. Its mechanism is basically identical in all human beings. Nevertheless, the fact still remains that searching for the nearest roots of Christian worship outside of Judaism is a dangerous and forlorn enterprise. We shall therefore first of all direct our attention to the concept of worship in the Old Testament.

THE CONCEPT OF WORSHIP IN THE OLD TESTAMENT

Scholars have been known to discern the existence of two distinct theologies of worship in the Old Testament. The first of these theologies would be overwhelmingly based on the liturgy of the Temple in Jerusalem and therefore heavily dependent on the role of the Levitical priesthood. The second of these theologies would be mainly based on the wider platform of everyday life and would therefore appear to be much more people-orientated.

A priesthood-orientated theology of worship

According to some texts,[3] it would appear that the Holy One of Israel could be encountered only in his own Temple in Jerusalem. It was in the Temple's sanctuary that the glory of the Lord was said to reside, rather than in the People of Israel as a whole. In these texts, we are confronted with a sharp distinction and separation of the 'sacred' from the 'profane'. To give but one example, the book of Ezckiel decrees to the last cubit the shape and measurement of the Temple seen by the prophet in his vision. The basic architectural plan of this Temple is that of the Temple of Solomon. Few but significant departures are nevertheless taken from this basic architectural plan. Every time this happens, it is to emphasise the separation of the sacred from the secular and to safeguard from defilement both the holiness of God and the holiness of his dwelling-place.[4] Divine laws are set out concerning those who are to be admitted to the Temple and those who are excluded from the sanctuary. Of all Levitical priests, only the sons of Zadok are allowed to draw near to the Lord and minister to him. The king may come as far as the gateway and the people must remain outside. When they approach the sanctuary, the sons of Zadok are enjoined to wear special linen garments which they are then to remove and leave behind in the holy place 'lest they communicate holiness to the people with their garments' (Ezekiel 44:19).

According to these texts, the highest possible worship can be rendered to the Lord only on his own altar in his own Temple. With or without the limitation to the sons of Zadok which is peculiar to the book of Ezekiel, the priests are the unique 'personae' of this worship by the Lord's own decree. The people can be said to worship only in a secondary and derivative sense, and that only by attending from afar. When 'drawing near' (that is when offering sacrifice), the priests must perform their worship according to absolute, immutable and indispensable rules promulgated by God himself. The objects used in the performance of worship are themselves invested with special holiness: the vestments, the vessels and even the furniture. As a consequence, they must not be touched by unauthorised hands. God's unapproachable transcendence is stretched to the limit and the manner of the Lord's presence in his Temple is understood quite literally in spatial terms. The basic unworthiness of all human beings is clearly stated, access to God being guaranteed only in terms of the sacred rites performed by a hierarchy of mediation. Failing to observe the universal cultic law, even on the part of the Gentiles, would incur the most severe penalties such as drought on the land or even plague.

A people-orientated theology of worship

According to other texts,[5] worship would appear to be a kind of 'spiritual sacrifice' leaving little room for outward ritual observances seen as an end in themselves. It must be stressed that in this context 'spiritual' is not to be taken as synonymous with 'anti-materialistic'. The worship advocated by these texts is not one of withdrawal from the world. On the contrary, it is seen essentially in the faithful discharge of one's duties of brotherhood and solidarity towards one's fellow Israelites. It consists of obedience to the voice of the Lord and of faithfulness to his covenant. It means caring for the hungry, the thirsty, the widow, the orphan, the stranger, the destitute and the oppressed, for the sake of the Lord. The arena of this kind of worship is as wide as that of life itself. According to these texts, worship is not the cult of an unapproachable God, but a celebration of Immanuel, 'God-who-is-with us'. Access to the transcendent God is not brought about by a priestly hierarchy of mediation. On the contrary, the whole of the chosen People understands itself as called to become the place where the glory of the Lord dwells: a holy, royal nation of priests spreading God's Word not by means of sacred ceremonies, but by their lives. The worship advocated by these texts is clearly people-orientated. No hard and fast separation exists between the sacred and the profane. In its original and primary sense, worship refers to the life and belief of a whole nation, a life and a belief that have immediate practical and social consequences. In a secondary and derivative sense, worship may then be said to refer also to outward moments of prayer and encounter reflecting, alongside all the other aspects of ethical and practical behaviour, an indispensable inner ('spiritual') attitude to the God who speaks and acts according to an eschatological plan.

Unity and Diversity in the Old Testament

Since the publication in 1885 of Wellhausen's 'Prolegomena to the History of Israel', biblical scholars have been engaged in a recurrently flaring debate over the precise nature of the prophets' attitude to the worship of the Temple in Jerusalem. As E. Heaton wrote, the controversy 'has generated more heat than light', mainly because of our unreadiness to credit the biblical writers and redactors with the impartiality of which we are not always capable ourselves.[6] Suffice it to say here with J. P. Hyatt that a substantial consensus is being gathered today around the opinion according to which 'the ultimate Biblical and prophetic view is not that cultic worship can be completely dispensed with'.[7] In the first place, prophets appear regularly on both sides of the argument. In the second place, as R. Daly points out, 'the very criticism of the prophets makes sense only on the supposition that they believed not only in the idea of sacrifice but also in its practical efficacy'.[8]

If the two theologies of worship we discerned in the Old Testament are not mutually exclusive, how can they be successfully made to relate to each other? Heavily influenced by the liberal *Religionsgeschichte* school, some scholars thought that the priest-centred theology of worship was the original one and that the 'spiritual sacrifice' theory was a later Hellenistic development.[9] A corrective to this theory was more recently supplied by others who showed how the idea of 'spiritualised cult' went well back into Old Testament times.[10] On the other hand, some scholars argue that the priest-centred conception of worship, faithfully reflected in the vocabulary of the Septuagint, was due more to the corrupt ideal of worship at the times of the post-exilic Temple than to the biblical texts themselves.[11] A similar and more attractive theory is that of T. Chary, who argues that there were indeed initially in the Old Testament not one but two understandings of worship of which Jeremiah and Ezekiel were the forefathers. These two understandings did to a large extent run in opposite directions, Ezekiel and his followers having broken away from the tradition of the earlier prophets to introduce into the history of Israel a new and potentially dangerous factor, as Deutero-Zechariah and the pre-Maccabean section of the book of Daniel show. The concentration of worship in the Temple of Jerusalem and the rise of a distinctly priestly-orientated mentality greatly contributed to the stressing of the Ezekiel-based theology of worship at the expense of that theology of worship which was characteristic of pre-exilic times. The balance had shifted. The emphasis was now on sacrificial worship rather than the imparting of the Torah; but this shift was due more to the practical abuses condemned so totally and effectively by all the prophets than to any real element in the theology of Ezekiel himself. Though heavily outweighed by the priest-centred strand, the Jeremiah-based theology of worship did not die out completely, but continued in the Wisdom literature and the 'psalms of the poor', to merge eventually with the previously more successful Ezekiel-based strand in the uneasy harmony of the Maccabean section of the book of Daniel in the second century B.C. The harmony reached at this point was an uneasy one because it was no more than a vision of hope for the future, a vision of perfect worship in which the ritual element would find complete resonance in the lives of a People embracing all nations, races and tongues. The people would then be truly a People of Saints gathered around the 'Holy of Holies', a term deliberately signifying in the opinion of the ancient rabbis both a Temple and the person of the coming Messiah, the Son of Man.[12]

As anyone in Israel, be he a priest or not, was seen above all as the subject of God's revelation and covenant, it would be misleading to call the People of God a 'democracy'. Since it was principally through an encounter with the living God that correct ethical behaviour was seen to ensue, it would be equally misleading to point exclusively to the moral issue: justification by works was never a truly biblical theme in either Testament. Without falling into either trap, Chary's thesis takes nevertheless into serious account the clash between a strongly priest-orientated theology of worship and what might be called rather misleadingly a more 'democratic' and 'ethically minded' view. It throws new light on W. Eichrodt's masterly account of the distinctive character of the priestly tradition's understanding of God and his dealings with man and the world, of the place of man in creation and of the meaning and purpose of history.[13] In his comparative study of the priesthood across times and cultures, L. Sabourin shows that 'no serious investigations of Old Testament institutions can be conducted unless due attention is also paid to the streams of tradition which led to the texts as we have them'. He warns us that this applies particularly to the study of the evolution of the Old Testament priesthood, 'since the redaction of the texts which are likely to be informative depend largely on the priestly circles being investigated'.

For him 'it is clear, for example, that the varying biblical interpretations of the Levitical status reflect historical ambitions and rivalries', and that 'some texts set forth a program of action, others sanction, justify or explain what has already taken place'.[14] Without incurring such strictures, Chary successfully explains the evolution of the concept of worship in the Old Testament with due care to both texts and traditions. Chary's thesis is no doubt the most satisfactory theory to be advanced so far.

THE CONCEPT OF WORSHIP IN THE NEW TESTAMENT

In approaching the question of what theology of worship – if any – is contained in the New Testament, we are again confronted with the usual, familiar difficulties of exegesis. On the one hand the Gospels in general and the Synoptics in particular are the almost exclusive source of information on the life and teaching of Jesus. On the other hand, the Gospels are not the most ancient of New Testament writings. Moreover, all these writings, including the most ancient such as the Pauline epistles, are dependent upon a stream of preaching and theologising the growth of which predates the writings themselves: as R. Daly points out, although the chronology of the New Testament is by now fairly well established and the lines of theological growth are becoming increasingly recoverable, not enough work has as yet been done to allow even the best exegesis to avoid altogether the circularity of arguments.[15] Happily, the different New Testament sources, though starting from different points, appear so to converge on the subject of worship as to suggest basic agreement. A proper exegetical study would have to take very seriously the complexities of both New Testament chronology and theological growth. No adequate study of the New Testament theology of worship has appeared to date. In these pages, we must therefore be tentative, relying on the apparent unanimity of the primary sources rather more heavily than we would otherwise choose.

The Synoptic Gospels and the Book of Acts
The Gospels of Matthew and Luke portray Jesus' respect for the Temple by putting on his lips traditional expressions of contemporary Jewish piety. In the Gospel of Luke, Jesus is made to refer to the Temple as 'my Father's house' (Luke 2:49). In both the Gospel of Matthew and the Gospel of Luke, Jesus refers to the Temple as the 'house of God' (Matthew 12:4; Luke 6:4). In the Gospel of Matthew, Jesus quotes Psalm 48:2–3 and refers to Jerusalem as the city where God the great King has chosen to dwell (Matthew 5:35). All three Synoptic Gospels portray Jesus as going to the Temple; he is never said to have prayed there or to have offered sacrifices (Matthew 21:14–23; Mark 12:35; Luke 19:47; 21:37). Mark and Luke show us Jesus' preference for praying alone and in secret (Mark 1:35; 6:46; Luke 5:16; 6:12; 11:1), and Matthew makes him enjoin his disciples to do likewise (Matthew 6:5–6). Matthew seems to imply that Jesus felt a stranger to the Temple, and that the Church, based on the confession of

Peter, should also be a stranger to it (Matthew 17:24–27. Cf. also Matthew 16:16–18 in the light of Malachi 3:5).

Jesus' real attitude to the worship of the Temple and his championing of the 'spiritual cult' (foreshadowed in Matthew 9:13), is particularly evident in the account all three Synoptic Gospels give of the episode of the cleansing of the Temple and of the trial of Jesus. It is made perfectly clear that the action of the cleansing of the Temple was directed against the priests and the masters of the Law and not against the merchants and money-changers by making Jesus quote publicly Isaiah 56:7 and Jeremiah 7:11. The clearest and most reliable account of Jesus' trial before the Sanhedrin, paralleled in Matthew and Luke, is to be found in the Gospel of Mark (Mark 14:55–64). After many accusations that could not be made to stand up in court, Mark 14:58 gives us the one accusation on the basis of which Jesus was condemned to death: 'We heard him say, "I will destroy this temple that is made with hands, and in three days I will build another, not made with hands." ' Since the Septuagint had reserved the expression 'made by hands' to refer exclusively to idols, calling the Temple of Jerusalem a temple made by hands was tantamount to denouncing all Temple practices as idolatrous. This was something the ancient prophets had never done. Challenged to reply to these accusations, Jesus remains obstinately silent (Mark 14:61). Directly challenged by the high priest, Jesus not only admits to being the Messiah, but actually quotes Daniel 7:13. In doing so he identifies himself with the Son of Man around whom the new temple-community was to be built and who therefore would spell the end of the old Temple cult (Mark 14:61b–62). No further evidence is needed and Jesus is condemned. His crime, the crime for which he was condemned to die, was not that he had claimed to be the Son of God (in a post-Nicaea sense), but that he had blasphemed against the Temple, the most sacred of Jewish institutions.

This interpretation of the Synoptics is confirmed by the Acts of the Apostles, chapters 5 and 6. Stephen fiercely criticises the worship of the Temple, quotes Exodus 32:4–6, Amos 5:25–27, Isaiah 6:1, and ends by referring to the Temple as an idolatrous artefact; upon which he is immediately put to death as his Master was, and for the same reason.

The Pauline Epistles and Hebrews
The Greek translation of the Old Testament, the Septuagint, uses *leitourgeĩn* and cognate words not less than 173 times to refer to the priestly worship of the Temple. In the New Testament, *leitourgeĩn* and cognate words are used only fifteen times. Apart from one quotation in the Gospel of Luke referring to the cultic role of the Levitical priesthood in Jerusalem (Luke 1:23) and a quotation in the book of Acts which it is practically impossible to interpret correctly without having recourse to other books of the New Testament (Acts 13:2), *leitourgeĩn* and cognate words appear entirely in the Epistles: three times in the Epistle to the Romans, once in 2 Corinthians, twice in Philippians and seven times in the Epistle to the Hebrews. From these we may safely discard for our purposes two passages from the Epistle to the Hebrews referring to the cultic role of the Levitical

priesthood in Jerusalem (Hebrews 9:21 and 10:11), two passages from the same Epistle referring to the angels' ministry to God (Hebrews 1:7–14) and one passage from Romans referring to civil magistrates as 'ministers of God' (Romans 13:6). Of the remaining passages, the two from Romans and the two from Philippians refer respectively to the *leitourgia* of Paul (Romans 15:16; Philippians 2:17) and the *leitourgia* of Christians (Romans 15:27; Philippians 2:30); the one passage from 2 Corinthians refers only to the *leitourgia* of Christians; the three from Hebrews to the *leitourgia* of Christ (Hebrews 8:1–2, 6). In all these passages, *leitourgein* and cognate words are deliberately used in a polemical sense and directed to show, by way of contrast and antithesis, that the *leitourgia* of Christians consists primarily in a life of service to others. On the basis of these texts, we may safely conclude that:

1. Christ is the key-foundation stone of a new Temple not made by hands and composed of living beings;

2. Christ is the high priest of this new kind of worship, the *leitourgòs tōn hagíōn* (where *tōn hagíōn* is deliberately left to signify both the new temple and the people of which the new temple is composed);

3. Christ's *leitourgia* was and is one of obedience to God and service to others;

4. through their obedience to God and service to others, Christians are empowered to be with Christ one priest, one altar and one victim;

5. like Christ's, the *leitourgia* of Christians is indeed a 'liturgy of life'.

The theme of the priestly sacrificial community as the new 'spiritual temple' is particularly strong in the Epistle to the Hebrews. In Hebrews 10:22, the readers of the Epistle are given a last solemn exhortation to 'draw near', that is to participate in Christ's high-priestly sacrificial activity, and verses 23–25 spell out what this sacrificial activity consists of, namely Christian life itself lived in community. Commenting on this passage, R. Daly is in no doubt that 'living the Christian life has taken over the atoning function of the sacrificial cult' and that therefore 'the deliberate sin of Hebrews 10:26 for which "there no longer remains a sacrifice for sins" would seem to be the separating of oneself from the only sacrificial action that now has any validity: Christian life itself'.[16]

The New Temple theology of the Epistle to the Hebrews finds confirmation in the theology of the Pastorals (e.g. 1 Timothy 3:15; 2 Timothy 2:20–22; Titus 2:14), that of the Deutero-Pauline corpus (e.g. Ephesians 2:19–22) and also in those strictly Pauline passages referring to the Christian community as God's dwelling in the Spirit (e.g. 1 Corinthians

3:9–17; 6:15–19; 2 Corinthians 6:16). Further impressive confirmation of this interpretation is to be found in those passages in which Paul expands his ideas on Christian service as 'liturgy of life'[17] and in particular in the pastoral section of the Epistle to the Romans (Romans 12:1–15, 35).

The First Letter of Peter

Quite apart from the question of its authorship, the first letter of Peter deserves here a special mention. Though a very practical letter, it constitutes a valuable summary of Christian theology.

The purpose of the letter is clear and uncontroversial: to give strength and hope to a Church persecuted for its beliefs. From the very beginning of the letter we learn, somewhat obliquely, that God has a provident purpose (1:2) by which the readers were chosen to receive salvation and to be obedient to the Lord Jesus. The salvation the readers received consists of a new birth as children of God through the resurrection of Christ from the dead (1:3–9). In searching and inquiring for this salvation, the prophets foretold the sufferings of Christ and the grace those sufferings would bring (1:10–12), but the fullness of the salvation brought by Christ will not appear until the day of the final judgement (1:13). Christ was destined from the foundation of the world to be the Lamb without blemish (1:19–20). The readers are therefore exhorted to make a habit of obedience (1:14): obedience to God means love and service to the brethren (1:22). The gift of the new birth is not enough. Like babes, the readers need the nourishment of the milk of spiritual integrity: now that they have tasted the goodness of the Lord, that milk will help them to grow up to salvation (2:1–3).

Obedience and spiritual integrity are the secret of the growth to salvation which the readers receive as a gift in Christ Jesus. It is at this point in the letter that Jesus is called the living stone rejected by men but chosen by God to be the foundation-stone of his new temple. The readers are invited to 'draw near' and 'be built' like living stones into a spiritual house, to be a holy priesthood and to offer spiritual sacrifices acceptable to God through Jesus Christ (2:4–5). Others disobeyed the word of God and for this they shall be punished. The readers, on the contrary, since they obeyed the word of God, are a chosen race, a royal priesthood, a holy nation, God's own people: in other words, being united with Jesus in obedience to God's word and purpose, they are with him one temple and one priesthood. The *purpose* of this new priesthood is that the readers might declare the wonderful deeds of him who called them out of darkness into his marvellous light (2:6–10); the *way* in which this new priesthood is to be exercised consists of the discharge of one's duty to others (2:11–3, 12). Christ suffered to lead us to God (3:18). In baptism, the readers have died with Christ (3:21). They must therefore arm themselves with the same resolution as Christ had: to obey the will of God even if this means suffering and death (4:1–2).

The full revelation of Christ, the letter says, is now close (4:7). In the meanwhile, each one of the priestly body, having received his or her gift for a purpose, must use it efficiently: like good stewards responsible for all these different graces of God, they must put themselves at the service of others, that in all this God may receive the glory which, through Jesus Christ, is his due in the world (4:8–11). Christ suffered for all who are prepared to accept the grace of the new priesthood. The sufferings of the readers are a share in the suffering of Christ: a blessing and a privilege (4:12–16). Yet, the letter warns, the judgement which is upon all will begin with the judgement of the household of God (4:17). So even those whom God allows to suffer must trust themselves to the constancy of the creator and go on doing good, that is go on offering to God as his new temple and his new priesthood the worship of a good life in Christ (4:19 and 3:16).

Paul's familiar theme of the new temple is firmly connected with the concept of the new priesthood. Both themes are then clearly expounded in a way which is strongly redolent of the Pauline ideal of Christian service as a liturgy of life: all in all, a striking confirmation of our interpretation of the New Testament theology of worship.

The Johannine Literature
The theology of Christian community as the new temple, greatly developed in Paul and Hebrews and confirmed by 1 Peter, is more clearly articulated in the Johannine literature than in the Synoptics.

For the Synoptics, the Temple was the *hierón*, or the place where God could be met. For the Gospel of John, the Temple was the *naós*, or the place where God dwells. The very first chapter of the Gospel of John states that the Word pitched his tent among us (1:14). Commenting on this verse, R. Brown writes: 'When the Prologue proclaims that the Word made his dwelling among men, we are being told that the flesh of Jesus Christ is the new localisation of God's presence on earth, and that Jesus is the replacement of the ancient Tabernacle'.[18] According to Brown, the theme of 'replacement' is the *leit-motif* of the first ten chapters of the Gospel of John. In chapters 2–4, we have the replacement of Jewish institutions and Jewish religious views: the replacement of the water for Jewish purifications in turning of water into wine at Cana and in the announcement of the new birth in water and the Spirit, the replacement of the Temple in the episode of the purification of the place where God dwells and, finally, the replacement of worship at both Jerusalem and Gerizim in the episode of the Samaritan woman. Chapters 5–10 are dominated by Jesus' action and discourses on the occasion of religious feasts: the replacement of the Passover with the new Manna from heaven, the replacement of the feast of Tabernacles with the new water and the new light coming from Jesus, the new Temple, and the replacement of the festival of Dedication with the consecration of the Messiah Son of God as the new Temple's altar.[19]

The Gospel of John is universally recognised to be more concerned with making theological points than with the details of chronology. In order to make a theological point, it places the episode of the cleansing of the Temple at the very beginning of Jesus' public life and ministry: the cleansing of the Temple and its replacement with the person of Jesus himself may well have happened historically just before Jesus died, but the whole of his life and ministry cannot be understood except in the light of that replacement. The Gospel of John is also the only Gospel to put on Jesus' lips Zechariah 14:21 rather than Jeremiah 7:11 and Isaiah 56:7: in the new Covenant there shall be no trader in the house of the Lord because there shall then be a new Temple, a new altar, a new sacrifice, a new priesthood, new worship, new light and new life-giving water.

In view of the centrality of the Temple theme in John, we should stress with R. Daly the importance of John 19:34–37. He writes: 'John's witness in 19:35 pushes us to a clearer awareness that Jesus is the new temple, that he alone is the source of living water (*i.e.* faith), and that by drinking (believing in Jesus) we also become sources of living water for others.' The whole of that passage – Daly maintains – should be seen in the light of John 10:17 (where Christ's sacrificial self-giving is seen to be both perfectly voluntary and done in loving obedience to God), John 13:1–15 (where the washing of the feet is seen as an act of service for us symbolising Christ's readiness to die for others and impelling us to do the same for the sake of our brethren) and of 1 John 3:16 (where we are exhorted to lay down our lives for the brethren in imitation of Christ's self-giving). In so doing, Daly successfully removes any remaining doubt that 'the same intimate association between the sacrifice of Christ and the sacrifice of Christians which we found in Paul and Hebrews is also richly witnessed to in the Johannine writings'.[20]

The book of Revelation is often dismissed as an unhelpful source for the theology of worship in the New Testament.[21] Since the greater part of the book consists of allegories to which we have long lost the key, this judgement may prove to be too severe. Often, with regard to the last section of the book of Revelation, not enough attention is paid to the parallels with the books of Isaiah, Ezekiel and Zechariah in which the themes of light and water, so characteristic of the Johannine literature, are also highly prominent. To use the familiar language of Hans Küng, in its last two chapters the book of Revelation is aware that 'the Church as it is' is not yet either 'the Church as it should be' or 'the Church as it shall be'. The real, down-to-earth Church is still a place harbouring the cowardly, the faithless, the polluted, murderers, fornicators, sorcerers, idolaters and liars as well as the holy (21:8). The Christian 'ecclesia' is not yet altogether the Temple embracing all people and all nations giving to God the pure worship of their spotless lives. The Lamb who died is indeed the lamp of the new Temple (21:22–24) and the fountain of the water of life, but that life does not as yet flow freely in the midst of a city in which no one practises abomination and falsehood (21:27–22, 2a). Firmly planted in the midst of the city, the tree of life does not yet produce its fruits each month. The leaves of that tree are not yet properly used for the healing of the nations (22:2b). All the familiar themes of the Johannine literature are present in these two last chapters, backed in even greater profusion by references to Isaiah, Ezekiel and Zechariah in which the same themes appear. Since the evil-doer is still doing evil and the filthy is still being filthy here on earth (22:11), true worship will not take place in its entirety until such time as the real, down-to-earth practicalities of the Christian life will be observed, and observed by all (22:3). A clear parallel exists between

Revelation 22:8 and John 19:35. The judgement of Revelation 22:10–15 is extended to the Christian community as well as to the world at large. A more down-to-earth statement of the nature of true worship would be hard to find, and so would a more striking confirmation of the overall teaching of the New Testament on the subject.

WORSHIP, THE FATHERS AND THE EARLY CHRISTIAN WRITERS

No survey of the roots of Christian worship, however brief, should forget to make reference to the ways in which the early Church understood the subject in the light of the teachings of the Bible.

There is no doubt that for the majority of the Church's Fathers and early writers the sacrifice expected of Christians was that of obedience to God. In certain cases, the sacrifice of obedience would take the form of partaking in the cup of Christ by actually laying down one's life in witness to the Gospel.[22] In more ordinary cases and in direct opposition to the sacrificial system of the Old Testament, the only, perfect and well-pleasing sacrifices Christians undertook to offer were those 'of prayer and giving of thanks, when offered by worthy men'.[23] The early Church understood this 'spiritual sacrifice' in the most concrete of terms. So Clement of Alexandria (before A.D. 215) could write that the sacrifice which the Church offers was that of the 'composite incense' of which the ancient Law spoke and which, in the new Covenant, 'is brought together in our songs of praise by purity of heart and righteous and upright living grounded in holy actions and righteous prayer'.[24]

A strongly incarnational theology led the early Church to see the perfect temple of God in the 'spiritual man'.[25] Individual Christians became such a temple when they acted justly throughout their lives and therefore gave God 'uninterrupted worship in His own temple, that is in the body of man'.[26] The community of such individuals, and not a building, was for them, collectively, the true house of prayer and worship.[27] In this sense, the individual Christians were seen as 'the chosen stones well fitted for the divine edifice of the Father'.[28]

For the Church's Fathers and early writers, the 'spiritual sacrifice' of Christians was a bloodless sacrifice,[29] offered on an altar which was both Christ and the company of believers.[30] At the turn of the 5th century Augustine (A.D. 354–430) could therefore write that 'the whole redeemed city, that is to say the congregation or the community of the saints, is offered to God as our sacrifice through the great High Priest, who offered himself in his passion for us, that we might be members of his glorious head, according to the form of a servant'.[31] Augustine argued that, since 'true sacrifices are works of mercy to ourselves or others, done with reference to God', it followed that 'this is the sacrifice of Christians: we, being many, are one body with Christ' and that therefore 'this is also the sacrifice which the Church continually celebrates in the sacrament of the altar, known to the faithful, in which she teaches that she herself is offered in the offering she makes to God'.[32]

Not surprisingly, the early Church was often accused of 'impiety' or religiouslessness.[33] 'Why have they no altars, no temples, no consecrated images?', well-meaning pagans asked themselves.[34] In their answer, the early Church turned these accusations into proud boasts. So Minucius Felix (third century A.D.) could write that 'the victim fit for sacrifice is a good disposition, and a pure mind, and a sincere judgement ... Therefore he who cultivates innocence supplicates God; he who cultivates justice makes offering to God; he who abstains from fraudulent practices propitiates God; he who snatches man from danger slaughters the most acceptable victim. These are our sacrifices, these our rites of God's worship: thus, among us, he who is most just is he who is most religious.'[35] Thus, Origen (A.D. 253–54) could argue against Celsus: 'We regard the spirit of every good man as an altar from which arises an incense which is truly and spiritually sweet-smelling, namely the prayers ascending from a pure conscience ... The statues and gifts which are fit offerings to God are the work of no common mechanics, but are wrought and fashioned in us by the Word of God ... In all those, then, who plant and cultivate within their souls, according to the divine word, temperance, justice, wisdom, piety, and other virtues, these excellences are the statues they raise, in which we are persuaded that it is becoming for us to honour the model and prototype of all statues: the image of the invisible God ... By far the most excellent of all these (statues) throughout the whole of creation is that image of our Saviour who said, "My Father is in me." '[36]

The early Church was often accused also of atheism, that is of the absence of belief in the State gods, and therefore of subversion and civil disobedience. The accusation, the Fathers argued, was deeply unjust: absence of belief in the State gods did not at all involve any such consequences. So Tertullian (after A.D. 220) could firmly state that Christians everywhere did indeed 'invoke on behalf of the safety of the emperors a God who is everlasting, a God who is real, a God who is living ... We already pray for the emperors, that they may have a long life, a safe rule, a family free from danger, courageous armies, a faithful senate, loyal subjects, a peaceful world, all that a man and a Caesar pray for'. Since however, 'these things I cannot pray for from any one else than from him from whom I know I shall get them', I, 'who on account of his teaching am put to death', can only offer to God the best fat victim which God himself commanded: 'prayer arising from a pure body, from an innocent soul, from the Holy Spirit'.[37]

From the already quoted Minucius Felix (third century A.D.) we learn that Christians were thought 'to threaten conflagration to the whole world, and to the universe itself' and to 'meditate its destruction' in the hope of substituting 'a life of want, hard work and hunger' with 'a blessed and perpetual life after death'.[38] In their eagerness to reply to such accusations, the Fathers and the early Christian writers afford us further insights into the kind of 'spiritual worship' they were advocating. They stressed that Christians, like others in the Empire, were dutiful citizens, deeply involved in the complex fabric of their concrete historical, social, cultural and political environment. Their religion was not one of destruction or escape. So in the Epistle to Diognetus we can read (third century) that, 'inhabiting Greek as well as barbarian cities, according as the lot of each of them has determined, and following the customs of the natives in respect to clothing, food and the rest of their ordinary conduct', Christians displayed as their only distinguishing mark 'their wonderful and paradoxical method of life'. They dwelled in their own countries, 'but simply as sojourners'. As faithful citizens, they shared all things with others, yet they endured 'all things as foreigners'. They did good, yet they were 'punished as evil-doers'. To sum up all in one word, 'what the soul is in the body, that are Christians in the world'.[39] Rather less prudently and in a way hardly calculated to reassure the authorities, Tertullian similarly argued that Christians were solid citizens and friends of the Empire. He pleaded that the proof of this was in the fact that 'nearly all the citizens you have in nearly all the cities are Christians ... We are but of yesterday, yet we have filled all that is yours, cities, islands, fortified towns, country towns, centres of meeting, even camps, tribes, classes of public attendants, the palace, the senate, the forum; *we have left you only your temples*'.[40]

Broadly speaking, the theology of worship of the Fathers and early Christian writers contains and reflects all the familiar themes of the New Testament theology of worship: the worship of Christians is both 'spiritual' and 'perfect' not becuase it is free from material, social, this-wordly elements, but precisely because it presupposes an involvement in the affairs of this world for the sake of others as total and unreserved as the involvement of the Incarnate Word. As christology and soteriology developed, they were increasingly brought to bear upon the concept of Christian worship, through Irenaeus (bishop of Lyons from A.D. 177–78) and Hippolytus (A.D. 235), to be fully spelled out in the works of Origen (A.D. 253–54), who most eloquently of all taught that the whole of Christian life was a sacrifice and whose main concern it was therefore to show how the Church and indeed the whole world are called to share in the sacrifice of Christ.[41]

The early Fathers and Christian writers are remarkably consistent in their teachings on the subject of Christian worship. Yet, as so often, the theology of worship of the early Church contained the seed of its own destruction. Writing around A.D. 96, Clement of Rome, who did not hesitate to teach that true sacrifice was a life according to the will of God,[42] was the first solitary voice to uphold strict regulations on the subject of worship and to teach that priestly worship should be offered at the appropriate time, in the appropriate places, by appropriate persons, lay worship being bound by the laws pertaining to lay people.[43] In making this claim, Clement made recourse to the very Old Testament regulations which the other Christian writers were so busy proving to have been superseded, the most notable among these writers being Clement's fellow-countryman from Syria who, also around A.D. 96, wrote the so-called Epistle of Barnabas. Hippolytus himself, whose great merit it was to have been able to connect both christology and soteriology with his theology of worship, was ultimately unable to resist the temptation of following in Clement's archaizing footsteps.

After the establishment of Christianity as the only permitted religion within the Roman Empire under Theodosius I (A.D. 371), the flood-gates of the Church were open to all kinds of barely christianised attitudes. Human nature was soon to do the rest, since attempting to tame the sacred comes more easily to a human being than allowing oneself to be swept up by it. In practical terms, the original freedom of Christian worship soon turned into the ossification of liturgical forms.[44] By the beginning of the 5th century, the private house where the Church met[45] had universally become the *ecclesia* (*Église, Iglesia, Chiesa, Eglwys*) or *kyriakón* (kirk, church): the house of God, a temple filled with sacred objects the most important of which was the stone altar of sacrifice standing in a 'sanctuary' reserved exclusively for the ordained and separated from the rest of the building by the 'tetravela'[46] – a cloth-screen designed to insure, as John Chrysostom himself (A.D. 354–407) explained,[47] that no profane eye would set its gaze on the 'sacred mysteries' (cf. *Exodus* 36:35–36). Within that sanctuary there would be placed seven ceremonial candlesticks as a latter day 'menorah': a perfect outward reconstruction of the Temple whose veil (Matthew 27:51) was torn from top to bottom.[48] Under the onslaught of such practices, the teaching of the earlier Fathers was soon to be overlaid by all kinds of *ex post facto* theologies. Throughout these changing times, the Church continued to teach that Christian worship was worship 'in spirit and in truth': charity should not prevent us from asking ourselves what, if anything, was understood by that.

NOTES

1. Bouyer L., *Eucharist: Theology and Spirituality of the Eucharistic Prayer*, Notre Dame, Indiana 1968, p. 15.
2. *Ibidem*, p. 19.
3. Cf. e.g. Ezekiel 40–46; *Numbers* 1:50–54; 3:5–10; 4:15; *Leviticus* 1–7; *2 Chronicles* 5:5; 13:10–12; *Zechariah* 14:16–20.
4. Chary T., *Les Prophètes et le culte à partir de l'Exil*, Paris-Tournai 1955, pp. 4–16 and 276.
5. Cf. e.g. *Exodus* 19:5–6; *Deuteronomy* 10:12–22; *Psalms* 50:7–23; 51:17–19; *Amos* 2:6–8; 5:12–15, 21–25; *Hosea* 6:4–10; 8:11–14; *Isaiah* 1:10–17; 56:6–8; 60 and 61; *Micah* 6:6–8; *Jeremiah* 7:1–12, 22–23; *Zechariah* 8:14–23 and *1 Samuel* 15:22–23.
6. Heaton E. W., *His Servants the Prophets*, London 1949, pp. 78–79.
7. Hyatt J. P., *The Prophetic Criticism of Israelite Worship*, in: Orlinsky H. M. (ed.), *Interpreting the Prophetic Tradition*, New York 1969, p. 210.

8. Daly R. J., *The Origins of the Christian Doctrine of Sacrifice*, Philadelphia 1978, p. 23.
9. Cf. e.g. Wenschkewitz H., *Die Spiritualisierung der Kultusbegriffe in Alten Testament: Tempel, Priester und Opfer in Neuen Testament*, in: Angelos 4 (1932), pp. 70–281.
10. Cf. Hermisson H.-J., *Sprache und Ritus im alt-israelischen Kult: Zur Spiritualiesierung der Kultbegriffe in Alten Testament*, Wissenschaftlichen Monographien zum Alten und Neuen Testament 19, Neukirchen-Vluyin 1965, pp. 156–60. Cf. *also* Clements R. E., *The Idea of the Divine Presence in Ancient Israel*, Oxford 1965, especially ch. 7.
11. Cf. Marsili S., *La Liturgia, momento storico della salvezza*, in: *Anamnesis* (AA.VV.), vol. 1, Torino 1974, p. 38.
12. Chary T., *op. cit.*, pp. 265–74.
13. Cf. Eichrodt W., *Theology of the Old Testament*, vol. 1, London 1961, pp. 392–436.
14. Sabourin L., *Priesthood: A Comparative Study*, Leiden 1973, p. 102.
15. Daly R. J., *op. cit.*, pp. 53–54.
16. *Ibidem*, p. 73.
17. Cf. Corriveau R., *The Liturgy of Life: A Study of the Ethical Thought of St. Paul in His Letters to the Early Christian Community*, Studia 25, Brussels-Montreal 1970, pp. 155–80.
18. Brown R. E., *The Gospel according to John*, vol. 1, New York 1966, p. 33.
19. *Ibidem*, pp. CXL-CXLI.
20. Daly R. J., *op. cit.*, p. 77.
21. *Ibidem*, p. 82.
22. Cf. e.g. The Martyrdom of Polycarp, ch. 14, in: Roberts A.-Donaldson J. (ed.), *Ante-Nicene Christian Library*, vol. 1, Edinburgh 1967, p. 91.
23. Justin Martyr, *Dialogue with Trypho*, in: Roberts A.-Donaldson J., *op. cit.*, vol. 2, p. 246.
24. Clement of Alexandria, *Stromata*, book VII, ch. 6, para. 34, in: Hort F. J. A.-Mayor J. B. (ed.), *Clement of Alexandria, Miscellanies Book VII*, London 1902, p. 59.
25. The Epistle of Barnabas, ch. 14, in: Roberts A.-Donaldson J. (ed.), *op. cit.*, vol. 1, p. 105.
26. Irenaeus of Lyons, *Evangelical Demonstrations*, n. 96, (our translation). Cf. also Ignatius, *Epistle to the Ephesians*, ch. 15, in: Roberts A.-Donaldson J. (ed.), *op. cit.*, vol. 1, p. 165 and Epistle of Barnabas, ch. 16, *ibidem*, pp. 129–30.
27. Justin Martyr, *Dialogue with Trypho*, in: *op. cit.*, p. 209.
28. Ignatius, *Epistle to the Ephesians*, ch. 9, in: *op. cit.*, p. 156.
29. Athenagoras, *Plea for the Christians*, ch. 13, in: Roberts A.-Donaldson J. (ed.), *op. cit.*, vol. 2, p. 389.
30. Ignatius, *Epistle to the Magnesians*, *ibidem*, vol. 1, p. 179; Polycarpus, *Epistle to the Philippians*, ch. 4, *ibidem*, p. 71; Clement of Alexandria, *op. cit.*, book VII, ch. 6, para. 31, in: *op. cit.*, p. 53.

31. Augustine, *City of God*, book X, ch. 6, in: Dods M., *The Works of Aurelius Augustine*, vol. 1, Edinburgh 1871, p. 391.
32. *Ibidem*, pp. 391–92.
33. Cf. Justin Martyr, *The First Apology*, chapters 5 & 6, n *op. cit.*, pp. 10–11; Athenagoras, *Plea for the Christians*, chapters 4, 10, 12, 13 & 27, *ibidem*, pp. 379, 385, 387, 388 and 410.
34. Minucius Felix, *Octavius*, ch. 10, in: Roberts A.-Donaldson J. (ed.), *op. cit.*, vol. 13/2, Edinburgh 1894, p. 465.
35. *Ibidem*, ch. 32, p. 504.
36. Origen, *Against Celsus*, book VIII, ch. 17, in: Roberts A.-Donaldson J. (ed.), *op. cit.*, vol. 23, Edinburgh 1894, pp. 505–506.
37. Tertullian, *Apologeticus*, ch. 30, in: Mayor J. E. B.-Souter A. (ed.), *Q. Septimi Tertulliani Apologeticus*, Cambridge 1917, p. 97.
38. Minucius Felix, *Octavius*, chapters 10, 11 & 12, in: *op. cit.*, pp. 464–468.
39. The Epistle to Diognetus, chapters 5 & 6, in: Roberts A.-Donaldson J. (ed.), *op. cit.*, vol. 1, Edinburgh 1867, pp. 309–10.
40. Tertullian, *Apologeticus*, ch. 37, in: *op. cit.*, p. 109.
41. Irenaeus, *Against Heresies*, book IV, chapters 30 & 31. For Hippolytus and Origen, see Daly R., *op. cit.*, pp. 98–100 and 122–27.
42. Cf. Clement, *The First Epistle to the Corinthians*, chapters 10 & 31, in: Roberts A.-Donaldson J. (ed.), *op. cit.*, vol. 1, pp. 14 & 28.
43. *Ibidem*, chapters 18, 35, 52, pp. 20, 31 & 36.
44. For this see e.g. Latte K., *Römische Religiongeschichte*, München 1960, p. 62.
45. Cf. e.g. *1 Corinthians*, 16:19.
46. Cf. Duchesne (ed.), *Liber Pontificalis*, vol. 2, p. 120.
47. John Chrysostom, *Homilies on the Epistle to the Ephesians*, hom. 4, in: *Patrologia Graeca*, 62, col. 29.
48. *For this see* Marsili S., *La Liturgia, Momento Storico della Salvezza*, in: *Anamnesis* (AA.VV.), vol. 1, Torino 1974, pp. 53–58.

FURTHER READING

Yerkes R. K., *Sacrifice in Greek and Roman Religions and Early Judaism*, London (A. & C. Black) 1953.
McKelvey R. J., *The New Temple: The Church in the New Testament*, London (OUP) 1969.
Corriveau R., *The Liturgy of Life: A Study of the Ethical Thought of St. Paul in His Letters to the Early Christian Communities*, Studia 25, Brussels-Montreal (Desclée) 1970.
Daly R. J., *The Origins of the Christian Doctrine of Sacrifice*, London (Darton, Longman and Todd) 1978.

FOR DISCUSSION

1. How far does our idea of God influence our worship?
2. Does it make sense today to speak of holy places and holy things?
3. What inferences for a renewed understanding of the Lord's Supper, if any, may be legitimately drawn from the biblical and early patristic understanding of the nature of Christian worship?

CHAPTER 3

IN SPIRIT AND IN TRUTH

The words, actions and gestures we use in our worship are so familiar to us that as a rule we tend not to question either their nature or their effectiveness. The ways of our worship are not by and large the product of our own discoveries as individual worshipping communities, but a precious inheritance from the past handed down to us by tradition. Some sociologists would say that they are part of the common sense world of everyday life, of what everybody knows, and therefore part of a social stock of assumed and unchallenged knowledge. Often enough, when asked why we should act in such ways, our answer would be a vague assertion that the Church has behaved in this way for a long, long time: because of its obvious connection with the sacred, worship is often thought to share in the very unchangeability of God.

All too often we assume that what we do now means to us what it meant to our forefathers. We have no real guarantee that worship as set out in the liturgical books, worship as proposed by the cultic officials, worship as explained by theologians, and worship as lived by the congregations are in fact one and the same thing. The truth is that no form of worship, not even that of the New Testament, mirrors the essence of worship perfectly and for all times. As Hans Küng remarks with regard to the theology of the Church, 'a delicate balance must be struck between the unthinking conservatism of a *dead* past, an attitude which is unconcerned with the demands of the present, and the careless rejection of the *living* past, an attitude which is all too concerned with the transitory novelties of the present'.[1] To remain true to itself, Christian worship must always allow itself to be conditioned anew by history; it must always be both a call and a response within constantly changing historical situations.

The history of the Christian Church in its complex pattern of growth and decay, renewed understanding, forgetfulness and betrayal provides ample material for the construction of a theology of worship. The embarrassment is one of riches. The problem is one of method. The danger is not that we might pervert truth, but that we might forget that all human knowledge, including theology, is provisional by definition. The truth of the God who gives himself to his people should never be confused with statements about it. As Karl Barth wrote, theology will always be 'a thinking, an investigation and an exposition which are relative and liable to error',[2] since all theology can do is 'attempt to understand, expound, see, hear, state, survey, coordinate and present the theoretical meaning and the practical consequences of an encounter-dialogue which must be experienced before it is talked about'.[3]

Some theologians have attempted to solve the methodological impasse by attributing to the worship of their Church an artificial kind of changelessness the better to judge individual historical developments on the basis of their conformity with the supposed archetype of the ancient liturgical books. The certain knowledge that Christian worship is constantly conditioned anew by history should dissuade us from following this path. Other theologians have adopted as their touchstone a system of confessional theology built without much reference to either liturgical documents or historical fact. The perennial quarrels between the Catholics and Protestants of old should be enough to dissuade us from following in these footsteps. Yet other scholars have chosen to engage in a purely phenomenological study of the history of religions in an attempt to find a minimum common denominator. Without wishing to criticise the appropriateness of this method in other fields of study, one can only lament its exclusive application in theological research.

In this chapter, we shall attempt to construct an organic and coherent framework (theology) within which we might understand more deeply a particular phenomenon (worship) from the vantage point of the common faith of the Church and in the light of our commitment and action in the world of today. In pursuing this end we shall proceed in faithfulness to our past and on the understanding that the paramount reality is that God speaks to us in the here-and-now.

A—CHRISTIAN WORSHIP

The Psalms and Prophets of the Old Testament taught us that God takes no delight in the sacrifice of bulls and rams. The New Testament teaches us that God takes no particular delight in our liturgical endeavours. Christian worship is worship in spirit and in truth: not so much a question of time and place and even less a question of orthodox words and suitable ceremonies, but above all a question of the right attitude of openness, surrender and obedience to God in a life consecrated to his purpose.

Yet worship in spirit and in truth is not disembodied; it is not divorced from everyday experience. In spiritual worship, the real God encounters and addresses the real human being, and the real human being is made able to respond in the power of the Spirit. True worship is not escape from the temporal, but communion between the human and the divine. As God encounters us with his Word, we are identified with God's purpose and are made able to consecrate our existences to his will. In themselves, liturgical words and gestures are neither good nor bad. They are not transparent and therefore hide and veil what truly lies behind them. They are unable to carry by themselves a meaning of their own. As such, they are never condemned in the Scriptures: we are so built that, without outward expression, spiritual realities cease to be present and to have meaning for us. Worship can only be conducted in the human tongue, according to human ways. Even before a word is on our lips, the Lord knows it altogether, and since we do not understand the tongue of Angels, God addresses us in the tongue of men.

The word 'tradition' (in the Greek, *parádōsis*) refers to a process whereby something is offered, handed over to us. For the community of faith, what is primarily offered and handed over to us is the reality of God himself as a gift of love ('parádōsis', in the singular). About this fundamental fact, there are a variety of 'traditions' ('paradóseis', in the plural), some of which are expressed in liturgical form and none of which exhausts the meaning of God's self-gift. In giving to us both himself and his power to transform what is still imperfect, God speaks. Our role in worship is that of obedience to God's spoken Word.

In speaking of worship, we often forget that nothing can be added to or taken away from God's purpose. The response of the Church is not a condition for the ultimate coming of the Kingdom. The Kingdom will come whatever we do or fail to do. By grace, we are called to give present embodiment to the Kingdom and to share in God's creative, redeeming and fulfilling activity. If we refuse to cooperate, the loss will be ours and not God's. When we approach God in worship, we do so only too aware of our needs. Our needs are always fulfilled, though not always according to the measure of our immediate expectations. As St. Augustine writes, 'no one will think he did a benefit to a fountain by drinking or to the light by seeing.'[4] God does not need our worship either in terms of what we do in our churches or in terms of what we do with our lives outside of them. It is we who need to worship, so that, as the Epistle to the Ephesians says, we might attain to the unity of the faith, to mature manhood, to the measure of the stature of the fulness of Christ (Ephesians 4:13–14).

According to the same Epistle, the experience of Christians is that 'the God and Father of our Lord Jesus Christ chose us before the foundation of the world to be his children'. God's empowering call is not only to sanctification, but also to mission. The teaching of the Old Testament Prophets, reinforced by the New Testament, is unequivocal on this subject: life must feed our worship as worship must feed our life. What we do when we worship has no value if the Word has no resonance in the quality of our existence. In all kinds of ways, God makes known to us, his Church, 'the mystery of his will, according to the purpose which he set forth in Christ as a plan for the fullness of time, to unite all things in him, things in heaven and things on earth'. It is our belief that, within this will and purpose, 'we who first hoped in Christ have been destined to live for the praise of God's glory' (Ephesians 1:3–14). Worship is therefore both a personal and a corporate encounter with God. The Word of God is spoken and we are renewed for the service of his Kingdom. The initiative is God's, the power is God's: ours is only the response of a life transformed by the Spirit. Our experience shows what the Bible teaches: if in a strict sense the word 'worship' refers primarily to what happens when we gather to pray, in a wider sense it embraces the whole of our lives.

The worship in spirit and in truth which is characteristic of Christians should be governed by several principles which can be numerated as follows:

1. Christian worship and Christian life are indissolubly linked together;

2. a corporate activity needed by man and not by God, Christian worship is both the moment and the consequence of an encounter in which God gives himself to his people as a gift of love, reveals to them his will for the world, demands and empowers a response, and consecrates to his purpose the life of the whole community of faith;

3. therefore, before it is seen as an activity of man towards God, Christian worship should be seen as an activity of God directed towards those whom God has chosen to live and work to his praise and glory.

B—THE WORSHIP OF JESUS THE CHRIST

Among others, S. Marsili teaches that our salvation has a historical dimension and contains three distinct moments. The first moment was one of prophecy and announcement. In it the eternal love of God was progressively disclosed, with which the Father who wishes all men to be saved, chose us as his own children in his dear Son (1 Timothy 2:4; Ephesians 1:4; 2 Timothy 1:9). The second moment was that of the fullness of time. The time of preparation being over, the Word, now Incarnate, was himself the bearer of the good news of the present event of salvation. In this second moment, from 'announcement to men' the Word of salvation becomes 'reality in men', that is 'flesh' (John 1:14). It was the moment in which the grace given to us from eternity was actualised in the appearing of our Saviour (2 Timothy 1:10). In the Word made flesh, the reality of salvation found both its constitutive elements: perfect at-onement with God and the fullness of worship. The third moment, the moment in which we live, is both the result and the perpetuation of the second moment: the 'time of Christ' continues into the 'time of the People of God'. Made one with Christ, his at-onement is our at-onement, his worship is our worship. When God addresses us in worship we can respond because we are one Body with Christ the one high priest. Christ's priesthood makes of him the primary source of our worship. In worship, we respond to God in Christ, with Christ, through Christ, having been made one Body with him. When two or three are gathered together, there is the Church. There is also her Lord, the Incarnate Word. The Word which is announcement, proclamation and call to salvation is made present. The call is heard and the power to respond is given in, with, and through the one high priest.[5] As

E. Brunner remarks, 'an exchange takes place here that is wholly without analogy in the sphere of thinking. The only analogy is the encounter between human beings, the meeting of person with person'.[6] In worship, Christ is our only Mediator. We are with him one priest, one altar, one victim. His self-offering is our self-offering, his obedience our obedience, his priesthood our priesthood. His response is our response. As Scripture says, we are crucified with Christ: since our life is hidden with Christ in God, it is no longer we who live, but Christ who lives in us, and the life we now live in the flesh we live by faith in the Son of God who loved us and gave himself for us (Galatians 2:20).

In the person of Jesus, the people of Palestine met the God who called them. In him, they met the human being who responded to God with the perfect answer. In his life, they saw the perfect example of the response to God required of them. As the Epistle to the Philippians says, 'though he was in the form of God, he did not count equality with God a thing to be grasped, but emptied himself, taking the form of a servant, being born in the likeness of men', and 'being found in human form he humbled himself and became obedient unto death, even death on a cross' (Philippians 2:6–8). Because of his obedience and in fulfilment of the prophecies of Isaiah, Christ is the perfect servant and the perfect worshipper of God (since, in the Hebrew, *'ebed YHWH* means both). In him, we have the perfect high priest. From the Epistle to the Hebrews we learn that 'when he appeared as the high priest of the good things that have come, then through the greater and more perfect tent (which is his Body) he entered once and for all into the Holy Place, taking not the blood of goats and calves, but his own blood, thus securing an eternal redemption'. We learn that 'he entered not a sanctuary made with hands, a copy of the true one, but into heaven itself, now to appear in the presence of God on our behalf', and that, therefore, 'he is truly the mediator of the new covenant' (Hebrews 9:11–24): subjectively, because of his obedience, and objectively because of his very being in whom the fullness of God was pleased to dwell. In him, as the ancient Easter liturgy sings, 'heaven and earth are joined in one, and man is reconciled to God'.[7] He is therefore the 'bridge' as well as the 'bridge-maker' (in the Latin, *pontifex*, that is high priest).

The belief of the Church is that, in Christ the fullness of deity dwells bodily and that from his fullness we have all received, grace upon grace (Colossians 2:9; John 1:16). We therefore believe that through the high priesthood of Jesus the life of God has become our life and that, through the Incarnation of the Son, God has now a human face. Through Christ the high priest, all have now direct access to grace and are made able to 'draw near' and offer their existence as a service of love and a spiritual sacrifice. We are now a new temple, a spiritual house built of living stones to be a holy priesthood (1 Peter 2:5). Hans Küng writes: 'Christians do not stand on the threshold of the temple like impure people begging for grace, in fear and trembling': they are themselves the new temple of which Jesus is the cornerstone, so that 'the decisive factor in their new situation is not the barrier that divides them from God, but the fellowship which links them to God through Christ'.[14]

The fellowship which links us to God through Christ is the fellowship of the Holy Spirit. The mediation of Christ the high priest bears its fruit within us through the mediation of the Holy Spirit. Since we do not know how to pray as we ought, the Spirit himself, who dwells in us, intercedes with us and helps us in our weakness (Romans 8:26–27). We are strengthened with might through the Spirit in the inner man, so that through the power at work within us, God is able to do far more abundantly than all that we ask or think (Ephesians 3:16–20): when we worship, we worship in, with and through Christ the high priest in the unity and power of the Holy Spirit.

The doctrine of the objective mediation of Christ the high priest (common to many of the Greek Fathers) and the doctrine of the mediation of the Spirit (common to all) soon disappeared both from Western theology and Western liturgical formularies, as A. J. Jungmann explained, due to an excessive reaction to the dangers of Arianism in Europe.[9] Europe was saved from Arianism, but the price paid for that rescue was a serious perversion of the understanding of worship. From a joyous encounter with God through Christ and in the fellowship of the Holy Spirit, worship became the action of an impure people begging for grace and offering from afar, in fear and trembling and by means of human mediators, due homage of praise interspersed with repeated entreaties for a forgiveness already offered by God to all who would care to accept it. Neither Catholics nor Protestants are free from this indictment and no truly Christian theology of worship can be constructed until the two forgotten doctrines are reinstated not only in our books, but first and foremost in the consciousness of the People of God.

C—THE WORSHIP OF CHRIST'S BODY

A human being can perceive God only by means of something created. It may be a word, a sentence or a sonnet. It may be a sculpture, a painting or a piece of music. It may be a natural occurrence such as a storm in the mountains, the becalming of the sea, a sunrise or a sunset. It may be, and it often is, another human being.

In this sense, the very person of the Incarnate Word was the highest possible means of God's presence to Man. Since the flesh and blood of Jesus cannot be met in this fashion today, the Church which is Christ's Body is called into being as a living temple of God's presence. As E. Schillebeeckx teaches, this is what we mean when we say that the Church is called to be the earthly sacrament of the Primordial Sacrament which is Jesus the Christ.[10] We may choose not to respond to God's call. Even when we respond, our answer is never complete. To be faithful to God's Word, the Church has to be renewed day by day. Apart from being Christ's Body on earth, the Church has no reason to exist.

In the last chapter we said that where two or three are gathered together, there is the Church and there is her Lord: to be the Body of Christ on earth, the Church needs to meet for both prayer and action. When the Church meets for prayer, the meeting must be so ordered as to facilitate both the encounter between God and his People and the empowering that ensues from it. The words, the sounds, the actions and the gestures that compose our worship must be directed to this end without a trace of self-indulgence or complacency. To achieve this end, the leader in worship must pay equal attention to the Word of God and to the laws of human nature.

The God of our faith took humanity seriously enough to become flesh and to pitch his tent among the pilgrim people. No truly viable theology of worship can be constructed without a more extensive theological anthropology than we possess to date: anyone who takes the human less seriously than the divine can do so only at his or her risk and peril. The work needed in this direction is of staggering proportions. In this chapter, we will offer a small contribution in the shape of a theory on the function of symbols in the perception of invisible realities.

(i) *A theory of symbols*

From the moment of the quickening in our mother's womb, awareness of self and awareness of our surroundings are inseparable, correlative and dependent upon a stream of sensory experience which is at the basis of all conscious life.

The stream of sensory experience on which our conscious life depends is made up of separate and diverse sense impressions which, coming to us in no particular logical order, nevertheless require our attention. We are rational beings: to make sense both of ourselves and the world around us, the data of sensory perception become the subject of a process of reflection. As a result of this process, as G. Horton of M.I.T. writes, 'the chaotic diversity of "facts" is mastered by erecting a structure of thought on it that points to structure and order.'[11] At the origin of all conscious life, the stream of sensory experience and the stream of reflection upon its data give rise to a stream of subjective apperceptions of the real. Whatever we know is the result of the application of reflection upon the data of sensory experience: from the data of the senses, via reflection, we establish the 'meaning' of things and, at the same time, the meaning of 'self' in relation to what is other than ourselves. From the data of sensory perception, via reflection, we go back to the original data having gained a certain degree of understanding of the phenomenon reflected upon. Whatever knowledge we gain, we gain by means of a 'hermeneutical circle': from the data, via reflection, to the interpretation ('hermeneia') of the data themselves.

Our knowledge, however partial, is nevertheless organic. It can be compared not only, as Pascal claimed, to a chain of logical thought suspended between two infinites, but even more so to a living and growing organism in which all parts are constantly related to each other. Moreover, since our knowledge is neither the creation of the thinking subject nor the mirror representation of objective reality but a subjective apperception of the real, the subjective and the objective, the qualitative and the quantitative, the relative and the absolute are aspects of our knowledge which cannot be distinguished except by means of a 'reduction' or 'suspension' consisting of excluding or 'putting in brackets' other aspects of the real. Meaning can only be meaning-for-Man.

In our attempt to interpret the stream of sensory perception and its chaotic diversity, we divide our experience into different sections or compartments and explore the different sectors in partial isolation the one from the other. We realise that the world of dreams is not the same as the world of wakefulness, that the world of play is not the same as the world of work, that the world of the natural sciences is not the same as the world of art or the world of religion. We realise that in the different sectors of our experience there are different sets of rules and that the conclusions we reach in each one of these sectors have a different kind of validity. It is not, as some followers of Wittgenstein think, that in the different sectors of our experience there are merely different kinds of 'language games', but rather that there are different 'provinces of meaning'. The unity of the hermeneutical process is safeguarded by the unity of the thinking subject, the unity of the stream of sensory perception, and by the unity-in-diversity of the language we use to cover the whole span of our knowledge and experience.

After the application of reflection on the data of experience, the result of our investigations is gathered into a number of well-tried routines of thought and behaviour and stored into a personal stock of knowledge. Eventually, through social interaction, what-I-know merges partially with what-we-know and finally with what-everybody-knows: different personal stocks of knowledge partially merge into the stock of knowledge of families and groups and finally into the stock of knowledge of a whole society. The common knowledge is then handed over by tradition as goods from a store to others who by the very nature of things have not necessarily had the opportunity by means of their personal thought or experience to win through to the information they receive and absorb. Once out of our immediate reflection, and even more so in the case of material received from tradition, whole areas of knowledge undergo a process of 'sedimentation'. They become unproblematic until a new set of facts or circumstances challenges them. Individual items of accepted knowledge on which we base the living organic whole of our self-understanding and the understanding of our surroundings become then absolutised, or as one would say today 'reified'.[12] Since our own self-understanding is involved in an organic way with our understanding of the world around us, when 'sedimented' or 'reified' experiences are challenged the natural reaction is often one of disorientation and fear, giving rise as often as not to anger and aggression against all innovators and proposers of new-fangled ideas.

According to Berger and Luckmann, in normal circumstances the transition from one province of meaning to another required a shift of attention the intensity of which is directly proportional to the similarity or dissimilarity between the province of meaning we leave and the one into which we enter.[13] So for instance the shift of attention needed to move from work to play or *vice versa* is presumably less than the shift of attention needed to move from the consideration of a work of art to a problem in nuclear physics. We are particularly interested here in three provinces of meaning which are contiguous the one to the other: the world of interpersonal relationships, the world of art and the world of religion.

Our discourse is of course based on an assumption that not all are ready to make: there is more to reality than what our senses can directly perceive. Realities such as the intersubjective, the artistic and the religious cannot be perceived unless they are mediated by means other than themselves. Love, for instance, cannot be separated from the words, actions or gestures which, though in themselves they are not love, express and convey it. Apart from the material means which convey the intuition of the artist, art does not exist. In the same way, faith is neither words nor actions. Yet, apart from the words and actions that put it into effect, faith is not. According to A. Vergote, without concrete expression nothing is communicated in these areas: all we have is 'an emotion, a kind of inner commotion, a vague and as yet unsubstantiated perception of the qualities of the world and others',[14] but certainly not love, art or faith.

The patterns of thought involved in these three different provinces of meaning are similar. Some would claim they are identical. In the province of mathematics and in the provinces of the so-called 'exact sciences', we deliberately concentrate on the objectively quantifiable. The reverse happens in the three provinces of meaning in which we are here particularly interested: we deliberately concentrate on the qualitative and the subjective. The conclusions reached in either area are no less 'true' than the conclusions reached in the other: they just happen to be 'true' in a different sense.

In the sphere of religion, as in intersubjective life or a work of art, meaning cannot be dissociated from symbol.[24] A clear distinction needs to be drawn between sign and symbol. The distinction is useful as long as we do not see it as a hard and fast separation between the two: there are as many symbols in mathematics as there are signs in theology or art. In his work entitled *The Symbolic Language of Religion*, T. Fawcett distinguishes between signs and symbols along these lines:

1. Signs operate at the level of object-thinking. Symbols operate at the level of subject-thinking: they push us beyond empirical objectivity towards a subjective appreciation of the transcendent.
2. Signs have only one meaning and are in a one-to-one relationship to what is signified. Symbols often have polyvalence, multiplicity of signification, and are in a one-to-many relationship to what is signified. Above all, symbols possess always a surplus-meaning which signs do not possess.
3. Signs are invented and established by convention. Symbols are not created, imagined or invented, but born out of life, 'given'. Their signifying power cannot be established by convention. They need no explanation to convey their meaning and to mediate a reality which transcends them.
4. Signs are a social phenomenon in so far as their meaning is explained and accepted (traffic signs, pub signs, etcetera).

Symbols are a social phenomenon in so far as they arise out of the common experience of the social group and out of the common way of responding to experience.

5. A sign-language may become universal when the conventions underlying it become socially accepted. A symbolic language may become universal when the common experience and the common way of responding to that experience are universally shared.

6. Signs operate only in so far as they remain in a relationship to what is signified: if x, y and z, from meaning an unknown quantity in an equation were suddenly to mean at once one or two more things, they would cease to be useful. Symbols operate only in so far as they continue to bear a multiple relation to what is signified. Though 'open', symbols are never unlimited. Moreover, symbols live and die: when they exchange their original power to transcend for a one-to-one relation to what is signified, symbols become signs.

7. Signs 'denote' (that is 'fully refer to') what is already completely understood or taken for such. Symbols 'connote' (that is 'point to') what is recognised to be still beyond our full understanding: they open up new horizons without ever circumscribing them.

8. Signs do not direct our thinking and orientation towards life. Symbols do. The symbols a person or a group experience determine the limits within which that person or group can understand reality. Receptiveness to symbols determines a person's or group's outlook on life.

9. A change of signs means no more than a change of conventions. A change of symbols means a change of one's view of both self and universe. Conversely, a change of the view of oneself and the universe demands a change of symbols.

10. Signs do not ask for commitment to what is signified. On the contrary, symbols are born in and for an encounter. The encounter in which and for which symbols exist influences our lives by demanding commitment to the reality the symbols disclose and to which they point. But, as symbols live and die, commitment to a symbol rather than commitment to what is signified is only another form of idolatry.[15]

Symbolic communication may take place only when three conditions apply at once:

1. We use material means possessing a literal meaning which is both known to and shared by the group we are addressing;
2. We use material means which may be used metaphorically to refer to experiences in the field of the intersubjective, artistic

or religious which are equally known to and shared by the
same group;
3. The literal and symbolic meanings of the means we use are
related in a way that comes naturally to that group.

In the areas of the intersubjective, the artistic and the religious, we have
no other language apart from the language of symbols. The similarity
between these three provinces of meaning may be clearly seen in the fact
that, through the symbols we experience, transcendent reality reveals itself
to us, announces its 'kerygma', demands and empowers a response of
commitment and shows us the kind of answer it requires within a
'sacramental' moment of encounter. And yet we may still mistake a kiss for
love, a painted canvas for art, or a Prayerbook for worship.

(ii) *Gestures and rites*

A symbol may be verbal as in poetry, non-verbal as in music, dance,
architecture and the representational arts, or a combination of both as in
worship, a play or song. Among non-verbal symbols, we are particularly
interested here in actions, gestures and postures, or gestures for short.
According to A. Vergote, symbolic gestures unite a bodily attitude with
an intended meaning. The entire symbolising power of the body is put at
their disposal: for this reason, purely verbal symbolism is not likely to
attain the richness of their communication. Words without gestures may
easily ring hollow and unreal and lose the power to assume our existence.
On the other hand, since gestures do not possess the autonomy of verbal
language, gestures without words may lose altogether their significance
and power to communicate. A distinction is generally made between
gestures that are purely symbolic and gestures that express something
while achieving it, namely the intention of the action. According to
Vergote, the liturgical gesture unifies sentiment and action. It expresses
and achieves: in other words, the liturgical gesture is 'faith in action'. It
makes no break between the order of senses and the order of ideas. Far
from transporting the worshipper into the realm of the sacred as into a
realm distinct from the space of the body as lived, the efficacious liturgical
gesture unites the worshipper with the space-world in which he or she
operates. It does not separate expression, communication and action. It is
a concrete relationship established with God and others, and in this
relationship it gives meaning to the visible world.
The term 'rite' refers to a combination of liturgical words and gestures.
Vergote teaches that human gestures may be broadly divided into two
categories – technical and symbolic – and that the efficacious liturgical
gesture must always belong to the latter. He makes the following four
points:

1. Technical gestures are performative and follow a
predetermined end: driving a car so as to get somewhere,
eating and drinking so as to satisfy a bodily need, turning a
switch so as to have light. Symbolic gestures on the contrary

express an intention and, while expressing it, achieve it at the same time: giving a present, embracing, bowing one's head in submission.

2. Technical gestures consist in the manipulation of tools. Symbolic gestures do not involve manipulation, though they employ material means.

3. Technical gestures do not express, but perform. Symbolic gestures express. They do not perform, but nevertheless achieve what they signify.

4. Technical gestures do not communicate at the level of the personal: they do not perform in and for an encounter. Symbolic gestures communicate creatively at the level of the personal. They exist in and for an encounter, expressing and requesting engagement and commitment to the 'other'.[16]

Nevertheless, we must not be led to believe that liturgical gestures may be used to produce what they signify simply because they are connected with the sacred. In attempting to do so, we would only transform a symbolic gesture into a technical one. As A. Greeley warns us in an important article on symbols and community, symbols do not *create* a sharing, but *flow from* a sharing whilst giving it concrete expression.[17] In the language of A. Vergote, only what is already there at least as an as yet unsubstantiated feeling or emotion can be expressed, given concrete form and therefore achieved and reinforced. Moreover, what a rite symbolises cannot be sought as an end in itself apart from the encounter in which and for which the rite operates.

We should not forget the practical consequences for the structuring and conducting of public worship of the diversity of present day cultural forms. On the one hand, Vergote maintains, the sciences of man have demonstrated that the human community is such that shared symbols enable people of different cultures to meet in the same basic gestures such as the exchanging of gifts, the sharing of one's food, embracing, bowing one's head and so on. On the other hand, Christian belief transforms and informs life and perception. Nevertheless, our perception of things is also considerably modified by the evolution of civilisation. For Vergote, liturgical words and gestures should take place within the space-time of a determined cultural environment. Beyond nodal and basic gestures, our rites should make use of a direct and native symbolism. Therefore, Vergote concludes, 'it is not only by reassessing the ethical demands of the Christian faith that we overcome the dreaded rift between worship and life, but by assuming into the rite all that is human in civilisation.' In his opinion, the liturgy of today should be imaginative and daring. It should open up new ways of understanding our place and mission in the world. It should be at once challenging, comforting and disturbing. The liturgy of today should answer to the diverse needs of contemporary man and speak to him with utter simplicity in his own native tongue.[18]

(iii) *Worship, Theology and Anthropology*

Are we centring our discussion on Man rather than on God? We believe that such an accusation would in fact be unfair. 'Man' may be studied from many different points of view. We believe that a theological anthropology is necessary to the life and mission of the Church. In any culture the model of God and the model of Man are intimately correlated. In Christianity the phenomenon of 'Man' can only be interpreted christologically. We believe that in order to know Man one must know God and that in order to know God one must know Man.

By theological anthropology we mean the attempt to reach, through reflection, an understanding of the human phenomenon by means of the Christian revelation. The purpose would therefore be the knowledge of the human phenomenon in its actual and concrete situation. According to M. Flick and Z. Alszeghy, within the context of theological anthropology the human phenomenon must be approached both from a dynamic-functional and a static-ontic point of view. From the dynamic-functional point of view, the human phenomenon must be considered in the light of Man's four basic functions:

1. *The 'theologal' function.* Though long fallen into desuetude, the word 'theologal' still best expresses the meaning to be conveyed here: the first and most fundamental function of Man is that of entering by grace into a living dialogue with the Encountering God.
2. *The social function.* After one's relationship with God, comes, in order of importance, a person's relationship to other human beings. Man is a social animal that cannot fully 'be' except in relationship with others.
3. *The cosmic function.* The role of Man in the cosmos is one of great responsibility, since the whole of creation is waiting with eager longing for the revealing of the sons of God, when it will be set free from its bondage to decay and obtain the glorious liberty of the children of God (Romans 8:18–22).
4. *The historical function.* Living by grace in freedom, a person is called to realise himself or herself in time and to bring his or her contribution to the history of the world in terms of God's eschatological plan of salvation. Key concepts in this respect are those of *vocation* and *mission*.

From the static-ontic point of view, the human phenomenon must be considered under two fundamental aspects:

1. *The 'oneness' of a human being.* Against the body-soul dichotomy of Plato and his followers, and against the understanding of Man as body-soul-spirit, modern theological anthropology has recovered the biblical sense of Man as a psycho-physical unity.
2. *The 'bodiliness' of a human being.* Since Man is a psycho-

physical unit, the 'spiritual' and the 'bodily' are equally important: modern theological anthropology rehabilitates the 'bodily' and sees Man as a 'person incarnate'.[19]

In the light of all this, we come with A. Cuva to the formulation of one of the fundamental principles of Christian worship: *Worship is for Man*. It must reach a human being in the concreteness of his or her existence. It must respect all genuine human values and promote them by engendering commitment to God's plan for creation. Deprived of these anthropological components, worship is both dehumanising and dehumanised. It ceases to be an instrument of fulfilment and becomes an instrument of alienation.[20]

D—CONCLUSION

The uniqueness of Christian worship stems from the uniquely Christian understanding that worship in spirit and in truth cannot be achieved by our efforts alone: it can only take place when the ontological unity existing between Man and God in the person of Jesus Christ is communicated not ontologically and statically, but historically and dynamically to the person who is united with Christ by faith within the priestly Body which exists for the express purpose of rendering to God the perfect cult of one's life and action as willing tools of God's coming kingdom.

The term *worship* assumes therefore two distinct, correlated meanings. In the wider sense, it means the *leitourgía* of one's life as expressed in Romans 12. In the narrower sense, it means the moment (in the Greek, *kairós*) in which, through Christ and in the power of the Spirit, God ENCOUNTERS his People, transforms them with his power, and sets them free to be Christ's Body in the world. In this second, narrower sense, the worship of the gathered community is the moment (that is, the *kairós*) in which God re-announces and actualises the *mystery of Christ* (that is his eternal plan of salvation) in and through the *mystery of the Church* (that is the earthly reality of the Body of those who are called to become the instruments of God's kingdom). Hans Küng puts it most beautifully in these words:

> The Church does not derive its life only from the work which Christ did and finished in the past, nor only from the expected future consummation of his work, but from the living and efficacious presence of Christ in the present. Christ is present in the entire life of the Church. But Christ is above all present and active in the *worship of the congregation* to which he called us in his Gospel, and into which we were taken up in baptism, in which we celebrate the Lord's Supper and from which we are sent again to our work of service in the world. In this congregation there occurs in a special way God's service to the Church and the Church's service before God. Here God speaks

to the Church through his word, and the Church speaks to God by replying in its prayers and its songs of praise. Here the crucified and risen Lord becomes present through his word and his sacrament, and here we commit ourselves to his service: by hearing the Gospel in faith, by confessing our sins, by praising God's mercy and by petitioning the Father in Jesus' name, by taking part in the meal of the Lord who is present among us and by providing the basis for our service of one another by our public confession of faith and by praying for one another. *This is fundamentally where the Church is, where the Church, the community, the congregation, happens.*[21]

In both its wider and its narrower sense, worship is the one response required by God. In its narrower sense, it is the moment in which the Church *happens*.

In our worship, God encounters us through a system of visible, physical, material means. The need for such means stems from our nature as whole persons. Such means are used in worship *because we need them*, and not because God is supposed to delight in them in any way. They must be vehicles *both* of God's call to us *and* of our answer to God. In other words, they must be *realised human salvation*, that is means of pardon and grace. They must be the visible, historical and concrete actualisation of the Word. They must be *eikónes tōn pragmátōn* (Hebrews 10:15): earthly signs charged with the power of a reality that totally transcends them. These signs charged with power (i.e. *symbols*) are *not* in themselves worship, yet without them worship is impossible. Neither are the symbols which we use in worship in any way unique. They are only one of the *many* ways in which God concretely reaches ordinary men and women, grafts them into the Mystery of Christ, and transforms them into a chosen race, a royal priesthood (1 Peter 2:9), that is in the Body of those who offer to the consuming fire of God, with reverence and awe, the acceptable worship of brotherly love (Hebrews 12:28; 13:1), *having themselves become* a sacrifice of praise continually offered to God (Hebrews 13:15).

NOTES

1. Küng H., *The Church*, London 1971, pp. 4–6 and 13–14.
2. Barth K., *Dogmatics in Outline*, London 1966, p. 11.
3. *Ibidem*, p. 9.
4. Augustine, *City of God*, book 10, ch. 6, in: Dods M., *The Works of Aurelius Augustine*, vol. 1, Edinburgh 1871, p. 388.
5. Cf. Marsili S., *La Liturgia, momento storico della salvezza*, in: *Anamnesis* (AA.VV.), vol. 1, Torino 1974, pp. 88–92.
6. Brunner E., *Truth as Encounter*, London 1964, p. 114.

7. These words survive even in the abbreviated rites of today: cf. e.g. *The New Sunday Missal*, London 1981, p. 163.
8. Küng H., *op. cit.*, p. 373.
9. Jungmann A. J., *Pastoral Liturgy*.
10. For this see Schillebeeckx E., *Christ the Sacrament of the Encounter with God*, London 1971.
11. Horton G., *Einstein's Model for Constructing a Scientific Theory*, in: Aichelburg P. C.-Sexl R.U., *Albert Einstein: His Influence on Physics, Philosophy and Politics*, Braunschwieg-Wiesbaden, p. 113.
12. Cf. Berger P.-Luckmann T., *The Social Construction of Reality: A Treatise on the Sociology of Knowledge*, London 1973, pp. 85–89.
13. *Ibidem*, pp. 35.
14. Vergote A., *Symbolic Gestures and Actions in the Liturgy*: Concilium, vol. 2, no. 7, February 1971, pp. 40–52.
15. Cf. Fawcett T., *The Symbolic Language of Religion: An Introductory Study*, London 1970, pp. 13–37.
16. Cf. Vergote A., *op. cit.*
17. Cf. Greeley A., *Religious Symbolism, Liturgy and Community*, in: Concilium, vol. 2, no. 7, February 1971, p. 59–69.
18. Cf. Vergote A., *op. cit.*
19. Cf. Flick M.–Alszeghy Z., *L'uomo nella teologia*, Modena 1971, pp. 49–81 and 105–112.
20. Cf. Cuva A., *Linee di antropologia liturgica*, in: Salesianum XXXVI (1974), n. 1, pp. 1–31.
21. Küng H., *op. cit.*, pp. 234–35.

FURTHER READING

Wiebe Vos, ed., 'Worship and Secularisation' *Studia Liturgica* 7 nos. 2–3, 1970.
Report of the Theological Commission on Worship, Faith and Order Paper No. 39, World Council of Churches, Geneva 1963.
Vatican II, *Constitution on the Sacred Liturgy*, Cirencester 1963.
World Council of Churches Fourth Assembly, Uppsala, *Drafts for Sections*, Geneva 1968.

FOR DISCUSSION

1. Discuss the consequences for Christian worship of the fact that symbols 'live and die'.
2. How helpful is the distinction between technical and symbolic gestures for the understanding of the Christian sacraments?
3. In what sense may the Church be called the earthly sacrament of Jesus Christ, the Primordial Sacrament?

CHAPTER 4

WORD AND SACRAMENT

We understand worship as being an encounter with God, which can be illumined by analogies with encounters among human beings. An encounter takes place between people; it is intersubjective. In the strict sense we cannot encounter things, or even animals, but only personal beings or (to use C. S. Lewis's term) a God who is 'beyond personality'. The whole Christian understanding of God and his dealings with people rules out an understanding of worship which is less than a personal meeting. Christian worship is not awe in face of an irresistible and unresponsive Power, nor is it the attempt to manipulate by magic or placate by offerings remote deities or the forces of nature.

Christian worship is an 'I-Thou' not an 'I-It' relationship. But immediately we must qualify these words. As they stand they effectively express the personal nature of Christian worship, but they would allow one to understand worship as 'the flight of the alone to the Alone'. In fact Christian worship is always a communal affair, and that in two senses. First, as we argue elsewhere in this book, all prayer and all worship is the worship of the Church. The individual worshipping is never alone but always joining at least spiritually with the whole Church on earth and with 'angels and archangels and all the company of heaven'. We come to God as '*our* Father' even when we worship alone – a good reminder that we bring our neighbours and our fellows with us when we come before God. At the heart of Christian worship is the worship of the congregation, the fellowship of those who encounter God together, God in one another and one another in God. Prayerful believers who abstract themselves from the worship of the congregation, like the U.N. Secretary General Dag Hammerskjöld, are distinctly anomolous, as W. H. Auden noted in his introduction to Hammerskjöld's remarkable book of thoughts, *Markings*.[1] The norm must be participation in congregational worship 'both as a discipline and as a refreshment', as well as an awareness of participation in the fellowship of the saints. In the second place, Christian worship is communal because it is participation in the life of the Holy Trinity. God himself, in trinitarian theology, must be understood on the model of a fellowship rather than an isolated individual person. In worship we encounter the Father, our Father, through Jesus Christ. In other words, he offers our worship; he is, as it were, our spokesman; he gives access to the Father; we share in his encounter as Son with his Father. That is why prayer is normally addressed to the Father 'through Jesus Christ our Lord'. And our capacity to worship and our inclination to worship are the work of the Spirit, moving us towards and encouraging us in the *mysterium tremendum* of an encounter with the living God.

At the human level an encounter is not a superficial or momentary meeting but an engagement at depth in which each becomes aware of the mystery of the other. Real encounter always involves an element of mystery: not a contrived and artificial mystery but the authentic mystery that is integral to personality and only reveals itself to love: above all, the tender, reliable covenant-love of which the Bible speaks. And encounter is not a partial matter, but a meeting with whole people. The disembodied voice we hear on the radio may thrill, delight, infuriate or instruct us; we become aware of the speaker's thoughts and style of speaking; but we do not encounter the person. To watch an athlete breaking a record or a great orator speaking on television may be a fuller experience, but it is still far short of an encounter. Even to see an actor or a musician perform – while it may be an enriching, or infuriating, or depressing experience, while it may deepen our understanding of the human condition or delight our senses and may even enrich our capacity for understanding and sensitive relationships – it is not an encounter with the actor or musician as a person. For people are complex as well as mysterious – the two are not unconnected – and there is more to the actor than his acting, and to the musician than his playing. Of course, human meeting is often very partial, with people shielding much of themselves from others, or acting a part rather than opening themselves to an encounter at depth with the other. But real encounter is lasting and deep, and involves the whole person, not just some qualities, aspects or dimensions.

The encounter with God in Jesus Christ, which is Christian worship, is not the hearing of a disembodied voice but a meeting with the incarnate Word, with the one who expresses in his being and his works the very heart of God, who is God's complete and adequate communication to humanity. Nor is Christian worship a matter of 'naked signs', of sacramental acts and symbols which magically ensure a meeting with transcendent powers, in isolation from words, the Word, or speech. No, Christian worship is rather the encounter with the living, speaking Lord who is himself both the living Word and the primordial sacrament. If worship is understood as encounter, word and sacrament belong together. They are complementary; both are necessary, for they interpret and illumine one another and neither in itself is complete or adequate. God has chosen Word and Sacrament as the two-dimensional locus of his encounter with his people, and to separate them, or neglect one in favour of the other, is to invite an incomplete encounter and an inadequate understanding of God and how he relates to people.

Almost all the churches are today rediscovering the vital unity of Word and Sacrament and seeking to express it more adequately in their worship. But it still remains true that many in the Reformed and Lutheran churches regard worship as essentially preaching, with the rest of the service seen as no more than the preliminaries to the sermon. And there are still seminaries and faculties of theology where detailed attention is given to training in homiletics but very little time is devoted to the principles of liturgy, so that clergy who have almost complete freedom in the construction and content of public worship have a very sketchy preparation for this vital part of their role. In Roman Catholic and some Anglican seminaries, on the other hand, the ministry of the word has sometimes been treated as a rather unimportant postscript to liturgy. Students have been given detailed instruction in the history and practice of the church's liturgy (but seldom much theology of worship), while the training in homiletics has been rudimentary. Even some current textbooks reflect and perpetuate this unfortunate split between the Word and the Sacrament, so that one can go through books such as *The Study of Liturgy*[2] and gain the impression that the ministry of the word, and preaching in particular, played no part in the worship of Christendom down the ages. And many books on homiletics proceed with sublime disregard of the fact that preaching is an integral part of Christian worship and cannot properly be considered in isolation from this context. The present book regards the unity of Word and Sacrament as a fundamental principle of Christian worship, which has been rediscovered by modern theology of all traditions but still has to penetrate fully into the practice of the churches' worship and the education of clergy and all who lead the worship of God's people. The recovery, in practice as well as in theology, of the complementarity of Word and Sacrament involves cross-fertilization and mutual enrichment between the two great traditions, the one emphasizing the place of the Word, and the other the centrality of the sacraments, and must be a major contribution to the ecumenical renewal of worship, which is surely at the heart of the revitalization of the Church and the Christian Faith.

A—THE WORD

Christianity understands worship as the encounter with God's Word; speech and hearing are indispensable to the authenticity of this meeting; God becomes really present with his people in his Word. And according to Augustine, in a phrase beloved of the Calvinist Reformers, a sacrament itself is a *verbum visibile*, a visible word. In worship we hear the Word of God addressed to us, calling us, encouraging us, challenging us, forgiving us, nourishing us, uplifting us, strengthening us. All this implies that we must have, as it were, a sacramental understanding of the Word in worship, just as we must understand the sacraments as encounters with the God who addresses us in his Word.

As Karl Barth has observed, the Word meets us in a threefold form: in preaching (which is discussed in chapter five), in scripture and as the Word incarnate, Jesus Christ, to whom the scriptures bear witness.[3] Clearly, scripture is an important element, and one which requires careful handling. Scripture always points beyond itself: 'We do the Bible a poor honour,' writes Karl Barth, 'and one unwelcome to itself, when we directly identify it with this something else, with revelation itself.'[4] To avoid such verbal idolatry is important, but it is also necessary to have a clear idea of how scripture functions in the believing community and how it speaks as Word. A historical perspective allows us a useful point of entry.

(i) *Scripture and worship in ancient Israel and Judaism*
The practice of worship is strongly reflected in the O.T. scriptures as we know them. Indeed, the recital of sacred tradition at Israel's religious festivals was an important part of the process whereby the traditions of Israel were shaped and developed. One function of scripture is to give authoritative guidance for worship, cult and ritual; another is to narrate the story of salvation in the context of worship. It has therefore an important interpretative function for the worshippers:

> Give ear, O my people, to my teaching;
> incline your ears to the words of my mouth!
> I will open my mouth in a parable;
> I will utter dark sayings from of old,
> things that we have heard and known,
> that our fathers have told us.
> We will not hide them from their children,
> but tell to the coming generation
> the glorious deeds of the Lord, and his might,
> and the wonders which he has wrought.   (Psalms 78:1–4)

Ritual, story, interpretation, revelation ...: these important elements in the worship of Israel are not only the direct concern of scripture; they also serve, in conjunction with scripture, to involve the worshippers in the divine mystery and in the inner, contemporary meaning of worship. Psalm 116, for example, is the liturgy used by the person who has come to the temple to pay his vow and make a thank-offering to Yahweh. It is particularly appropriate to one who has been very ill and who promised in his distress to fulfil just such a vow on his recovery. Notice the loving response of one who finds his prayers answered, the recollection of his distress, the celebration of God's mercy, and the paying of the vow itself. The liturgy makes personal to the worshipper the relationship between Yahweh and Israel (cf. Deuteronomy 26:5–10).

Diversity is particularly noticeable in post-exilic Judaism, not least in the place given to scripture. To the priests in the temple tradition (cf. the Sadducees in Jesus' day), the Books of Moses formed the Torah, the essential and only scripture. For them, scripture prescribed and interpreted the cult, and directed the way of the worshippers. In these terms, the priest was the teacher of Israel. The destruction of the Temple by the Babylonians, however, led to new religious developments. The absence of temple worship in Babylon gave an impetus to the editing, study and standardising of the Torah as scripture, and called into being a new or at least greatly enlarged class of scribal experts in the Torah and written tradition. The rise of the synagogues in post-exilic Judaism provided centres for the discussion and study of the Torah as a continuing duty, allied to the saying of prayers. The scribal teachers (later, rabbis) regarded scripture as essentially the Torah, but admitted the Prophets and later the Writings as authoritative commentary on the Torah, interpreting and applying it to the daily lives of the people. That, too, was the function of the rabbis' sayings, the 'tradition of the elders' on which the Pharisees of Jesus' day placed so much emphasis. Indeed, so important was the interpretation and application of scripture to the rabbis that it could even be said that the modern commentary which related directly to the contemporary situation was more important than the ancient text considered in isolation. A third broad grouping might be characterised as sectarian, the Essenes of Qumran being the most accessible example. Here, the worship took place within monastic communities, which had their own distinctive cultic practices (especially washings or baptisms); and scripture, not confined to the Books of Moses, was copied, studied and interpreted in relation to the community which believed that it had a special role to play in the Last Days. Such eschatological beliefs governed all aspects of their life. Their scriptural interpretation was designed to reveal the hidden meaning which the text held for them, standing as they believed at or near the completion of God's mighty works in Israel. They wrote commentaries on the scriptures with this purpose in mind. A characteristic procedure was to cite the O.T. text (sometimes with modifications) and add an exposition, usually introduced by 'interpreted, this concerns ...' or some similar formula.[5]

It must not be thought that such radically creative procedures were found only in sectarian Judaism. Because the traditions of Israel were constantly interpreted and applied in the living context of community worship and practice, new meaning was constantly being found in them. It was said that every word of scripture had seventy aspects,[6] so there was plenty of new meaning to be discovered by each generation! Hence, the literature expanded. Deuteronomy is just such a recasting of the ancient laws; the Priestly Code is a further example. The book we call Isaiah encapsulates a lengthy tradition of prophetic exposition. Chronicles recasts the historical tradition; apocalyptists and sectarians were similarly expansive, and so on. Finally, the rabbis closed the canon, the list of books recognised as scripture and hence regulative of faith and life. (The precise date when they did so is unknown – certainly later than Jamnia, c. A.D. 95: the priestly tradition had closed its canon many centuries previously.) But the expansion of meaning necessary to a living community was not halted or 'put on ice' by such action. The rabbinic tradition of authoritative exposition continued and was itself encoded in Mishnah and Talmud.

How can we sum up scripture and its relation to worship in ancient Israel and Judaism? Emerging from and operating within worshipping communities, scripture reflects and is shaped by their worship in many respects. It also regulates and informs continuing worship. It relates and interprets the story of God's wonders in the history of the people, and enjoins recital of them in worship. It enshrines and encapsulates the truth given to Moses but rediscovered in new ways from generation to generation. It helps Israel to walk in God's ways and to trust for the future. Hence, while it prescribes ritual and liturgical action, it can also attack Temple and cult when they do not truly reflect God's will and purpose for his people. Designed to speak a contemporary Word to the believing community, it continues to do so through commentary and renewed application. Of course the dangers were immense: such as legalism, pedantry, and openness to external influence (e.g., hellenising). But such dangers were not exclusive to Judaism. The resilience of the Jewish biblical tradition is well attested by its history since biblical times.

(ii) *Scripture and worship in the early Christian tradition*

Christian worship has always had a scriptural dimension: the O.T. was there from the beginning; both in Hebrew and in Greek translation (the Septuagint, second century B.C.). Although the O.T. canon was open-ended in the first century, all inspired writing was recognised as useful for teaching the truth and refuting error ... (2 Timothy 3:16). So where did Christian use of scripture in worship differ from the Jewish?

In the Jewish Christianity of the early days, the difference was not too marked. The brethren worshipped in the temple and were to be found in the synagogues until such times as they were declared *personae non gratae*. Why? The root cause is found at the core of the Christian position: belief in Jesus as Messiah and Lord. If this was understood in a limited way, the Christians might have remained a sect within Judaism – albeit an extremely heterodox one. But as soon as Jesus' Lordship was interpreted in a radical way, so that the foundations of Judaism were shaken at their most vital points – Law, Temple, nationhood – then the possibility of compromise was ruled out. After initial hesitation, the salvation that Christ offered was made open to all believers, without distinction of race, sex or status. In Christ, the New Age had been established; the Old was swept away. The End-time had come into the midst of history. Here was a new 'eschatological community', and it was wholly Christo-centric, centred on the Word.

Such a position was of immense consequence for scriptural interpretation. It is true that the O.T. has an expectation of the future: whether the coming forth of a 'shoot from the stump of Jesse', or 'the Day of the Lord', or Elijah the Prophet, or 'one like a son of man', or the servant of the Lord ... But the early Christians did not limit their interest in the O.T. to the exposition of such passages. Because they regarded Jesus, the crucified and risen Christ, as the fulfilment of all God's work through Israel, they believed that all the scriptures testified to him. As the Jesus of the Fourth Gospel says to his fellow Jews, 'You search the scriptures because you think that in them you have eternal life; and it is they that bear witness to me; yet you refuse to come to me that you may have life.' (John 5:35f.). Jesus as the Christ was therefore the starting point of their scriptural interpretation. They read the O.T. in the light of their Christian faith and found it responding in innumerable ways to their interrogation. It was as if the motifs which coalesced in Christ were prefigured in varied and fragmentary ways in the story of God's previous dealings with Israel.

Hence Paul can take the notion of Moses' veil and use it to suggest that the splendour of the old covenant was a fading splendour (2 Corinthians 3:13) – not because there is anything in the Mosaic tradition to suggest this, but because Paul *knows* that 'what once had splendour' (i.e., the religion of the old covenant) 'has come to have no splendour at all, because of the splendour that surpasses it' (2 Corinthians 3:10). For Paul, this was not a tortuous or far-fetched argument: it was nothing other than 'the open statement of the truth' (2 Corinthians 4:2), as the truth was revealed in Christ. The cycle of interpretation began with Christ, read the O.T. in the light of Christian faith, and then found the scriptures witnessing to the finality and completion that Christ represented. Such interpretation was integral to Christian worship and essential to evangelism among the Jews. Not for nothing did Paul spend three sabbaths in the synagogue at Thessalonica, arguing from the scriptures and 'explaining and proving that it was necessary for the Christ to suffer and to rise from the dead, and saying, "This Jesus, whom I proclaim to you, is the Christ." ' (Acts 17:3).

This Christo-centrism was not a merely intellectual stance, a kind of hermeneutical game played on the chequer-board of Judaistic biblical usage. It permeated the whole Christian community, which resonated to the crucified-and-risen Christ. The relational aspect came to the fore in community life and worship: 'where two or three are gathered together in my name, there am I in the midst of them'. The new community was nothing less than 'the temple of the living God' (2 Corinthians 6:16), separated alike from the old community with its faded glory and from the paganism of the nations, but above all enjoying the welcome of God who was a Father to them, his sons and daughters.

In fact, scripture and worship inter-relate in several ways here. The worship and community life are informed by scripture. Because Christ came 'not to destroy the Torah but to fulfil it', the Christians could use and adapt Jewish psalms and liturgies; hence the 'psalms and hymns and spiritual songs' (Colossians 3:16, Ephesians 5:19), the great hymnic utterances in Revelation, and the Odes of Solomon, 'the earliest Christian Hymn-book'.[7] Hence too the doxologies, the use of 'Amen', and the great confessions: Cullmann has observed, 'All these old confession formulae have this in common, that they are Christocentric and that they stress the *present Lordship of Christ*'.[8]. Christian prophets too would inject scriptural lessons and interpretations into the service of worship, as the Spirit moved them: a criterion of genuine prophecy was again Christo-centrism.[9]

This Christo-centrism was only possible by reason of a strong deposit of tradition about Jesus the Christ; both his teaching and the apostolic witness to his life, death and resurrection. One can see it in operation when Paul explicitly cites a 'word of the Lord' to correct error in his churches. Paul's use of the tradition of the last supper (1 Corinthians 11:23–6) is particularly informative. He stresses the chain of tradition, records the action at the meal and its purpose in a concise and careful way, and enlarges freely on the points he wants the Corinthians to understand in particular. However, from our point of view, the most significant fact is that Paul cites dominical tradition as the complete model for Christian practice, to be imitated and applied in the contemporary situation. Here we have Christian tradition already possessing a prescriptive function. And the apostle himself was consciously contributing to a deposit of apostolic letters, designed to be read in churches and even to circulate among them (though possibly conceived by the writer as having immediate rather than long-term significance).

From the earliest days of the Christian movement, therefore, the 'searching of the scripture' in the context of 'the apostles' teaching and fellowship' was a creative movement which led to a definitive understanding of the scriptures in Christo-centric perspective. Like the Ethiopian in Acts 8:26–40, Christians and enquirers need guidance in order to 'understand'; and like Philip, apostles and community leaders ('prophets and teachers') had to begin with the scripture and relate the good news of Jesus (cf. Acts 8:35). Hence, the logic of the situation suggests that the O.T. scriptures were accompanied in Christian worship by Christian commentary; that this commentary would comprise 'the things concerning Jesus'; and that the commentator would attempt to bring scriptures and Christian tradition alike into dynamic relationship with the contemporary situation of the hearers. It is therefore not surprising that impressive evidence is now being put forward to suggest that Matthew, for example, 'wrote his Gospel to be read in church round the year; he took the Jewish Festal Year, and the pattern of lections prescribed therefor, as his base; and it is possible for us to descry from MS. evidence for which feast, and for which Sabbath/Sunday, and even on occasion for which service, any particular verses were intended'.[10] Whatever may be the final verdict of scholarship on this detailed case, it certainly fits the general pattern that has emerged in our discussion. It was inevitable that in course of time, the traditions concerning Jesus, 'handed down to us by the original eyewitnesses and servants of the Gospel' (Luke 1:2), would cease to be simply 'the utterances of a living and abiding voice'[11] and acquire written form. In the case of Paul's (and other) letters, written to specific churches as part of his care of the churches, the question was one of collection and perhaps even editing. Certainly, 1 Clement (96–7 A.D.) is familiar with Pauline writings as well as being 'saturated' in the O.T.[12] Justin (c. A.D. 155) completes the picture:

> ... on the day called Sunday there is a meeting in one place of those who live in cities or the country, and the memoirs of the apostles or the writings of the prophets are read as long as time permits. When the reader has finished, the president in a discourse urges and invites (us) to the imitation of these noble things. Then we all stand up together and offer prayers ...[13]

The prayers are followed by the eucharist. It is noteworthy that the service *begins* with scripture lessons; then comes the homiletic application; then the sacrament. There is no specific suggestion of lectionary here: the readings seem 'open ended'; but there is a decided move towards a Christian canon of scripture. Although this matter would not be finally settled until much later, it is interesting that Eusebius conducted his research into the issue by noting which books were actually in use in the churches.

(iii) *Scripture and worship*

How may we express briefly the relations between scripture and worship?

(a) *Scripture permeates worship.* Old and New Testaments proceed from living communities of faith. They include compelling examples of these communities at worship. In the O.T. we have the prayers of Solomon at the dedication of the temple, the Book of Psalms with its wide range of spirituality and worship, and the worship practices of Israel in festival. In the N.T. we have the instructions given by Jesus to the disciples on the matter of prayer; and in the apostolic letters a variety of prayers is exemplified: thanksgiving, supplication, intercession, and at least by implication confession. The same sources give abundant evidence of the praises that are inherent in all worship. An interesting aspect of all this is the extent to which the O.T. prayers and praise were taken over and 'christianised' in the churches. The hymns which we find in the Gospels (cf. first two chapters of Luke) are directly derived from the worship of Israel, yet they refer specifically to the coming of Christ. The early Christians apparently made the transposition without difficulty. For them, Jesus was Lord. It is not without significance that the first outside view we have of Christian worship speaks of them 'singing hymns to Christ as to a god'.[14] The language needed for such hymns was readily available through the scriptures and worship of Israel and Judaism. The intensity of Christian devotion, fired by prophet and charismatic, sparked the gap and made the transposition possible.

By its very nature, worship is offered by worshippers in their particular situation in life. In the Christian tradition above all worship must not become so formalised as to be thoughtless and automatic. The teaching of Jesus expressly forbids it. There must always be a *contemporary* aspect to worship, otherwise it is not truly the offering of the worshipper. That is not to say that Christians cannot use the words of others in the worship they offer. As we have seen they have traditionally done so in using scriptural language, and not least the Lord's Prayer itself. But they must identify with the scriptural meaning so that it speaks for them.

The most famous example of scriptural worship is the use of the Psalms, prose and metrical, in Christian worship. *Literally*, their points of reference are outwith the Christian tradition: the place of Zion is a case in point. However, Christian worship itself provided the context which informed and reinterpreted the psalmist's imagery. Thus, Zion became the symbol for the church or the New Jerusalem, while the spiritual life of the psalmist was reinterpreted in Christian terms. Christian worship supplies its own hermeneutic, which is similar to that applied from the beginning to the Old Testament. Sometimes this is made explicit by appending to a psalm, for example, an ascription of praise in Christian terms. While we can make no objection to this practice, it would be unfortunate to say the

least if this appendage were regarded as legitimising or 'christianising' the
O.T. material for use in Christian worship.

Generally speaking, the scriptures have immensely enriched Christian
worship throughout the ages. They have given a wealth of symbolism
which has helped the worshipper to understand his own position in
relation to God and the *koinonia*, and also to express this in prayer. In
short, Christian prayer must be contemporary, but not *merely*
contemporary, with the worshippers. In their devotions, they are united
with the devotions of the faithful of all the ages; and nothing is better
equipped to give expression to this facet of their experience than the
language and symbolism of scripture, their common heritage.

(b) *Scripture is itself a major element in worship.* The church service that
Justin describes began with an unspecified number of scripture readings.
Probably a certain informality characterised the proceedings: possibly
interpretations and discussions of meaning interspersed the readings.
Certainly, exposition followed. One thing is clear: scripture itself was the
first major element in the service. It represents and conveys the revelation
of God to man, supremely in Jesus Christ. Without this, there can be no
Christian worship. In time, it was thought fitting to begin worship on a
note of praise and prayer, before introducing the Word. The focus has not
changed. One simply approaches it in a wider liturgical context than
Justin's order provides.

Thus, worshippers today approach the place of revelation through
praise and prayer. The reading of the scriptures takes them beyond the
vestibule, so to speak, into the holy place where God reveals himself
through the scriptures. Hence there is an obligation on the part of those
leading the worship to ensure that the lessons are as appropriate and
meaningful as possible. There is, however, no automatic relationship
between reading the scriptures and hearing the Word of God. To identify
the Word with the words of scripture in a literal and positive way is a major
error which obscures the moving of the Spirit in the hearts and minds of the
worshipping community. Hence one might say that the words of the Bible
are heard as the Word of God only in the context of worship and devotion
where the human spirit is made open to God's spirit. A pre-condition is the
attentive hearing of the words; participation by the congregation in
reading – orally or silently – helps towards this end. A full appreciation of
the liturgical movement of the service – hearing the Word, responding to
the Word, exposition of the Word, response to the exposition – alerts
worshippers to the demand which the service is placing upon them. There
is therefore an element of mystery at the heart of the liturgy here: a mystery
which consists of nothing short of the encounter of God and his people.
Truly, when this encounter takes place, it is as the gift of God and as an act
of his grace. Yet the liturgy itself also helps worshippers in their search for
God and for the divine revelation through the scriptures. 'Seek and ye shall
find ...' is appropriate to them, 'for it is in seeking that we are found ...'

Finally, the impression may have been given that Christian worship as
described here is rather academic and cognitive. This has not been the
intention, although one would wish to suggest that in the position in which

the churches find themselves today it is important that all worshippers who have the capacity should understand what is involved in Christian worship and interpretation, and be able to 'give a reason for the faith that is in them'. But the Christian response to the divine approach is a response of 'the whole person': it involves both the cognitive and affective domains, and is concerned with knowledge, feeling, relationships and action.

(c) *Scripture gives specific warrant for certain practices in worship.*

> Go therefore and make disciples of all nations, baptizing them in the name of the Father and of the Son and of the Holy Spirit ...

> For I received from the Lord what I also delivered to you, that the Lord Jesus on the night when he was betrayed took bread, and when he had given thanks, he broke it, and said, 'This is my body which is for you. Do this in remembrance of me' ...

Whatever else may be said about these passages, two liturgical acts are expressly warranted by them: baptism and the Lord's Supper.

This is not the place to follow out the baptismal controversies of many centuries. The dominical warrant sanctions baptism in the context of evangelism and teaching. Matthew sees 'all nations' (i.e., the Gentiles) as potential catechumens, to be baptized by water and so received into the true Israel. It must be admitted that the Evangelist's concern is far removed from later controversies. He does not specify whether adults alone should be baptized and children excluded, any more than he specifies at what age one becomes adult! He does not specify *how* the rite of baptism is to be carried out, although some hints may perhaps be derived from other N.T. writings. The basic point is that baptism, in Christian understanding, is carried out by Christ's warrant. When the rite is administered, appropriate scriptural passages are read, both as warrant for and interpretation of the meaning of baptism. Thus in the case of infant baptism, the reading of the 'child pericopae' interprets what the church is doing in terms of Jesus' attitude to children while instructing the adults present on important aspects of discipleship. As always, the church's teaching function is important. The whole rite, being Christo-centric, is properly interpreted further in terms of Christian doctrine; but care should be taken not to overload the liturgy with too much didactic material, for this will lessen the impact of the liturgical action rather than enhance it.

The Lord's Supper is the climax of Christian worship. Its place in the liturgy is discussed below. One notes, however, that when Paul was writing to the Corinthians, a eucharistic tradition – whether as 'the breaking of bread' or the *Agape* or fellowship meal – was already in existence: Paul was not introducing the sacrament for the first time. Equally, Paul had to assert his apostolic authority in order to correct the excesses which church tradition by itself was unable to handle. Hence the significance of incorporating the narrative of 1 Corinthians 11:23ff. in the communion service as warrant and model for the liturgical practice. One notes also the kerygmatic emphasis in Paul: 'for as often as you eat this bread and drink this cup, you proclaim the Lord's death until he comes'. The Lord's Supper is a powerful proclamation of the Cross and Resurrection, and this proclamation must be made and heard. The ministry of Word and Sacrament is a unity. Indeed, in the full service of Christian worship, the people of God are helped by the liturgy to approach God through the vestibule of praise and prayer to the holy place where the Word is heard and understood and response made; and finally to the most holy place where the bread of life is offered in word and action: a holy mystery interpreted by scripture and therefore properly the object of study in the continuing teaching ministry of the church.

B—SACRAMENT

The term 'sacrament' is not found in the Bible, and was not used in the earliest Church, although what we now know as sacramental worship was a central focus of the encounter with God. The equivalent term to sacrament in the New Testament is *mysterion*, 'mystery'. In the synoptic Gospels we read of the 'mystery of the Kingdom of God'. In Paul the mystery is God's plan for the salvation of all which has been realized in history as well as revealed in Christ's death and resurrection – the 'paschal mystery' which is implanted again and again in history through the proclamation of the Word. The 'mystery of God' (1 Corinthians 2:1 in some MSS.) is identical with the mystery of the crucified Jesus (1 Corinthians 1:23; 2:2), and with the proclamation of the Gospel. The good news, God's secret plan, is now revealed and realized in the events of passion and resurrection. The mystery which had been hidden in God is now revealed through the Spirit (1 Corinthians 2:7–16). In Colossians and Ephesians it is explained that the mystery once secret and now made manifest is that in Christ God was reconciling the whole cosmos to himself, and all things are involved in a process which might be called 'christification' (Colossians 1:15–29; 2:8–12; Ephesians 1:8–10; 2:4–10; 3:1–13). To sum up the N.T. understanding of the term *mysterion*: it is used in three related senses. (a) God's secret purpose for the salvation of all, now revealed in Christ (e.g., Romans 2:25; 8:19–21). (b) An earthly reality expressing in a hidden way a meaning related to God's secret plan (e.g., Ephesians 5:32; Revelation 1:20; 17:5–7). (c) An historical happening with a special significance related to God's plan (e.g., 1 Corinthians 15:51; 2 Thessalonians 2:7).

In secular usage *mysterion* meant, in a general way, a secret, while the plural form, *mysteria* referred to the cults of the pagan 'mystery religions'. The question of the relation of early Christianity to these mystery religions is a very complex matter into which we cannot go here, except to say that most modern scholarship rejects the view, enthusiastically propounded in a former generation, that early Christianity (and particuarly its cult) was shaped very largely on the model of a mystery religion. The Fathers are on the whole very cautious about any use of the term mystery to refer specifically to Christian worship, presumably because they fear confusion

with the pagan rites of the mystery religions. But Clement of Alexandria –
notable among the Fathers for his eagerness to relate the Faith to its
cultural context – speaks of three Christian mysteries, or categories of
mysteries: first, the 'lesser mysteries' which were received as preparation or
preliminary to greater ones, for example, initiation by baptism; secondly,
the 'greater mysteries', the central truths of the Faith, which were to be
lived and contemplated so that gradually more of their meaning became
plain and could be appropriated by believers; and thirdly, the 'great
mystery' which the other mysteries reflect or point towards, Jesus Christ
himself. The Latin Fathers seem to have had a certain suspicion of the
Greek term *mysterion* and tended to borrow a current term *sacramentum*
as an alternative. *Sacramentum* had a plurality of meanings, but the one
which made it most suitable for Christian usage was the *sacramentum
militiae,* the ritual of entry of recruits into the Roman army, which
included the taking of a solemn oath of loyalty and was often accompanied
by the 'brand of fidelity' *(fidei signaculum).* Tertullian was the first to use
sacramentum in a Christian context. In the case of baptism, he understood
it on the model of the military recruit's *sacramentum,* as indicating a
binding faith and commitment of one's self and the start of a new life. His
talk of marriage as a sacrament suggests that he saw *sacramentum* as a
direct translation of the *mysterion* of Ephesians 5, where the analogy
between the love of Christ for his church and a husband and wife is
declared 'a great mystery'. Cyprian interprets *sacramentum* in a less legal
(or military) way than Tertullian; a sacrament is a matter of symbols,
figures, and signs representing spiritual realities. Accordingly he speaks of
the eucharist as a sacrament in addition to baptism and marriage. Hilary of
Poitiers knows of three *sacramenta*: initiation, eucharist and the
incarnation. But the three are clearly not 'on a level', as it were: the
Incarnation is the foundation and basis for the other two; they draw their
meaning and significance from the Word made flesh.

Augustine, the first great systematizer of Latin theology, understood a
sacrament as the 'sign' of a sacred reality, the visible form of an invisible
grace. He distinguished four components: (a) the *signum,* the outward,
visible and material element, such as bread, wine, or water; (b) the *virtus
sacramenti,* the 'virtue' or inward, invisible grace conveyed in the
sacrament; (c) the *verbum,* the spoken formula pronounced by the minister
which provided the link between the sign and its 'virtue'. The *verbum* is in
fact the Word of God, not a magic spell, and the sacrament must never be
separated from the Word or it ceases to be a sacrament. As Augustine
wrote in relation to baptism: 'Take away the Word and the water is
nothing but water. But when the Word is joined to the element the result is
a sacrament ... Where does the water get its lofty power to bathe the body
and cleanse the soul if it is not through the action of the Word? And not
because it is spoken, but because it is believed.'[15] (d) *The 'agent' of the
sacrament is Christ himself, who is the Word.* One cannot but notice that in
the transition from the N.T. understanding of *mysterion* to the developed
theology of *sacramentum* in Augustine something has been lost and the
concept has been significantly narrowed. What had originally denoted

God's secret plan for all creation now revealed and realized in Christ, and only derivatively the cult in which the Church re-presents the mystery of Christ, now suggests mere rites rather than on-going realities. The primordial 'sacramentality' of Christ is all but forgotten, and the understanding of the cult consequently impoverished and opened to all sorts of distortions. Sacraments considered as rites are viewed in isolation from their proper context and accorded a significance on their own which differs substantially from the primitive view. Now new questions of a quite different order arise, such as the number of sacraments that exist (Peter Lombard taught that there were seven; the Reformation recognized only two) or whether explicit institution by Christ is required to make a sacrament (Hugo of St. Victor – twelfth century – emphasized the need for dominical institution, as did the Reformers, but there was disagreement as to how explicit such institution need be). Consequently, Thomas Aquinas taught that the sacraments work *ex opere operato*, which came to be interpreted as a way of affirming the objectivity of the sacraments and their independence of the spiritual, moral or emotional state of the minister or of the recipients.[16]. Sacraments, he taught, are the work of God and not of man, and the minister (representing the Church) and the Church itself (in whose name the rite is administered) are only instrumental causes of Christ's own saving activity. A sacrament is an objectively valid offer of grace made by God himself. Sacraments confer the grace they signify, not for any superstitious reason or in a magical way, but because in them Christ the High Priest is acting through his Body, represented by the minister, whose worthiness, while desirable, is not essential to the efficacy of the sacrament. After Thomas the prevalent legal and juridical thinking resulted in the validity of the sacrament being seen as depending upon the correct performance of the rite in the prescribed form, with the proper words, by the legally authorised minister. This legalistic understanding of the sacraments became very widespread in the later middle ages so that sometimes a juridical view almost totally obscured a theological understanding of their meaning and significance.

The Reformation attempted to recover a biblical understanding of the sacraments but was only partially successful in escaping from the legacy of the later middle ages. The Reformers' views covered a wide spectrum, from the Zwinglian extreme where they were understood as little more than visual aids for the commemoration of past events, to strong affirmations of the Real Presence of Christ with his people in their celebration. For an act of worship to be a sacrament it had to have been specifically instituted by the Lord, with a promise of divine grace attached; accordingly only two sacraments, rather than the medieval seven, were recognized. This narrowing of the category of sacrament was not really a recovery of the N.T. view – as we have seen the early Church was perfectly familiar with baptism and the Lord's Supper but understood them as elements in the vast *mysterion* of God's dealings with mankind in Christ rather than the two members of a particular class of rites. The strong affirmation that Word and Sacrament belonged together protected the two sacraments from an unhealthy isolation, but fell short of a rediscovery of the primitive comprehensiveness. Because sacramental quality was believed to inhere only in baptism and the eucharist, the theological understanding of other forms of worship was inhibited and the reformed churches were even reluctant to speak of preaching as sacramental although their practice seemed to suggest such an interpretation. In principle the assertion of the complementarity of Word and Sacrament and the understanding of a sacrament as a *verbum visibile*, or as a seal and confirmation of God's Word of promise, should have opened up the recovery of the proper integration of Christian worship into the economy of salvation; in practice medieval problems about the number and validity of the sacraments and opposition to late medieval sacramentalism ensured that a narrow view of sacramentality was maintained while baptism and the eucharist were separated sharply from all other forms of worship (which were thereby deprived of any sacramental significance) and theologically relegated to little more than an appendix rather than relating to the heart of the Christian mystery.

The eastern churches followed a very different path. They continued to use the term 'mystery' in their liturgies in the biblical sense: for them the Incarnation, the Eucharist, Marriage, Baptism, the Veiling of a Virgin, the setting apart of oil for liturgical use and numerous other events, acts, rites, and doctrines are all 'mysteries', in the sense that they are earthly realities fundamentally related to Christ, the mystery of our salvation. There was no question of identifying two, three, seven, or more *rites* as sacraments or mysteries to the exclusion of all else. Rather, they were concerned with identifying the whole of revelation and salvation with a series of historical, temporal focuses of encounter fundamentally related to the primordial mystery of Christ. These views were partially abandoned only where the influence of Latin thought led to the adopting of western post-Aquinas sacramental theology.

At the heart of the modern movement for liturgical renewal is a recovery of the understanding of sacrament as mystery, never totally lost in the East. Going back to scripture and the Fathers, pioneers such as Odo Casel in Germany understood sacraments as rites in which participants encountered the living Christ, and his saving activity was re-presented to them. Worship was seen as participation in the mysteries of the Christian Faith, and the rite itself had a significance which was simply instrumental. Building on such foundations a number of recent theologians, most notably Edward Schillebeeckx, have developed a sacramental theology which faithfully reflects neglected emphases in Scripture and the Fathers and transcends many ancient controversies, suggesting possibilities of ecumenical consensus in this field so long devastated by warring armies. Sacraments are understood as loving encounters between the believer and God which, like loving encounters between two human beings, reveal truths which are not apparent on the surface or accessible to the detached, 'objective' observer.

Disciples of today, just as the disciples of long ago, in encountering Jesus come into touch with a mystery which they know to be the mystery of God's being and acts, the secret of the universe and the meaning of life. In the primary sense, then, we should speak of Jesus Christ as being the Sacrament.[17] In Christ, the Incarnate Son, through his physical, historical and material humanity we encounter the mystery, and the reality of God himself. In a secondary sense, the Church which is the Body of Christ should be regarded as a sacrament. It is the community in time and space, the visible fellowship, in which the God and Father of our Lord Jesus Christ is encountered, and as his Body, it represents Christ sacramentally to the world. Thus the Church is also to be understood as the sacrament of the unity of all mankind: it shows in sacramental form the saving purpose of God for all humanity, it is a sign of hope for all, a working model (to use a rather crude image) of what God wills for everyone: loving fellowship with God and with one another. And the Church is a sacrament because the visible, empirical reality of the fellowship points beyond itself to its Lord, to Christ the sacrament of the encounter with God. Thirdly, there are sacraments of the Church which are sacraments, Schillebeeckx argues, precisely because they are also acts of Christ himself. 'A sacrament', he writes, 'is primarily and fundamentally a personal act of Christ himself which reaches and involves us in the form of an institutional act performed by a person in the Church who ... is empowered to do so by Christ himself.'[18] And since the sacraments are acts of Christ, Schillebeeckx insists that 'he must in some way have instituted them himself'.[19] Indeed, without conceding the extreme Protestant position that there are two and only two sacraments, baptism and the eucharist, an emerging ecumenical consensus concurs in according a very real primacy to these two rites while affirming that they cannot be properly understood except as special focuses of a more broadly conceived sacramentality. God is not confined to encountering his people only in baptism and the eucharist, but he has trysted to meet them there, and these two meeting places encourage and help believers to discern the presence of God elsewhere and encounter him in Christ in all sorts of times and places, which thereby become sacramental. For wherever God is encountered believers may say, with Jacob, 'This is none other than the house of God, and this is the gate of heaven.' (Genesis 28:17).

Finally, to understand sacraments as ways of introducing and intensifying the experience of encounter with God in Christ involves the necessity of holding together the Word and the Sacrament. Apart from the Word, the symbols and actions of a sacrament would mystify rather than reveal the mystery of God's purpose in Christ; the Word integrates these acts and symbols into the mystery of salvation; Word, symbol and action mutually clarify one another and cannot be held apart without danger of radical distortion.

NOTES

1. London 1964.
2. SPCK, 1978.

3. *Church Dogmatics* 1/1, Edinburgh 1936, pp. 98-140.
4. *Op. cit.*, p. 126.
5. 'Midrash' (commentary) could be both explicit and implicit: see G. Vermes, *The Dead Sea Scrolls in English*, Harmondsworth 1962.
6. See I. Epstein, *Midrash Rabbah I* (Genesis), edd. Freedman and Simon, London 1939, p. xi.
7. J. H. Charlesworth, *The Odes of Solomon*, Oxford 1973, p. vii (Preface).
8. *Early Christian Worship*, Eng. tr., London 1953, p.23.
9. Cf. 1 Corinthians 12:3; and see in particular James Moffatt's comments *in loc.* in his volume on *1 Corinthians* in the Moffatt N.T. Commentaries.
10. M. D. Goulder, *Midrash and Lection in Matthew*, London 1974, p. 172.
11. Papias (early 2nd century), cited in Eusebius H.E. III.39.
12. Cf. C. C. Richardson, *Early Christian Fathers*, London 1953, p. 37.
13. Justin, *Apology* 1,67; see Richardson, *op. cit.*, p. 287.
14. Pliny, Epistles X (to Trajan), xcvi.
15. *On the Gospel of John* 80.3, cited in Martos, *Doors to the Sacred*, 1981, p. 191f.
16. The original meaning was the completed work of Christ, but Aquinas has been interpreted the opposite way.
17. Cf. the title of Schillebeeckx's book, *Christ the Sacrament of the Encounter with God*, London 1963.
18. *Op. cit.*, p. 62.
19. *Op. cit.*, p. 137.

FURTHER READING

H. H. Rowley, *Worship in Ancient Israel*, London 1967.
O. Cullmann, *Early Christian Worship*, Eng. tr., London 1953.
C. F. D. Moule, *Worship in the New Testament*, London 1961.
E. Schillebeeckx, *Christ the Sacrament of the Encounter with God*, London 1971.

FOR DISCUSSION

1. How far is scripture itself dependent on the tradition of the faith community, and how far is church tradition guided and corrected by scripture?
2. What is the proper relation between Word and Sacrament?
3. Is a 'non-sacramental' service of worship a defective or incomplete form of Christian worship?

CHAPTER 5

THE WORD AND THE WORDS IN WORSHIP

A—INTRODUCTION

The ability to use language, at least in a developed form, is one of the distinguishing marks of human beings. Language has many purposes; it is an essential part of human self-expression and human relationships. Above all, it is used to convey information and meaning to another party. The 'language game' involves coding a message in such a way that the recipients can decode it satisfactorily and so interpret the meaning of the message as we intend that they should.

Fundamental to this process is the recognition that, in communication of this type, both the sender (or 'source') and the recipient (or 'receptor') are active participants. The message is not simply a parcel put together by the sender, which the recipient simply unwraps. The receptor must interpret or decipher the message so that there is an effective meeting of minds and sharing of understanding. The process must take place, therefore, within a common cultural context, so that the sender, moving in a similar thought-world to that of the receptor, knows the kind of language and concepts that is likely to be meaningful to the receptor. Thus missionaries, coming from an alien culture, must give priority to understanding not only the language but the cultural framework of the people to whom they wish to communicate their message, and they must be prepared to transpose that message into the language and thought-world of their hearers: a task which involves a high degree of sensitivity to and respect for the cultural setting in which they are now working as well as a judicious selection and development of those aspects of the message that are likely to be culturally relevant.[1]

The importance of cultural setting, however, is by no means limited to the missionary situation. Confronted with the problem of mission to its own parish, a Church must be aware of the fact that there is a certain heterogeneous quality within a given society, arising not only from explicitly multi-cultural elements in it but also from class, occupation, status, education, upbringing and even temperament. Hence the kind of encoding which the minister must do in the course of conducting worship and, not least, in preaching, can only be done effectively if there is a full understanding on his/her part of the cultural setting or thought-world of the receptors and a sympathetic engagement with it throughout the service or sermon. To be effective, preaching must establish, if not common ground, at least points of contact with the hearers.[2] In this respect, the pastoral ministry is the essential complement of preaching and liturgy.

The communication of the Christian message is, of course, even more complex than surmounting cultural barriers in contemporary society, formidable though these are. The message comes to us from the wholly different cultural setting of the Graeco-Roman world, two thousand years ago (or the equally strange world of ancient Israel). Rudolf Bultmann underlined the 'three-decker universe' of the ancient world, a world-view alien to the age of modern science and technology; but Bultmann was very concerned for the task of biblical interpretation today.[3] Dennis Nineham suggested that cultures were virtually self-contained structures, so that communication across culture was extremely difficult and perhaps always imperfect.[4] Yet one can make little sense of history if there is not the possibility of communication from one culture and epoch to another.

To be sure, the New Testament writings not only move in the thought-world of demons, 'principalities and powers' and angelic appearances; they also deal with explosive issues such as 'eating meat offered to idols', 'Korban' and table-fellowship at Antioch.[5] In all such issues there is an attempt to apply, in the relevant cultural setting, the Christian message or 'good news' as the basic principle and motive of Christian existence. *This* is what is translatable into other cultures and ages. And its translatability is enhanced in that there is, down the ages, a chain of Christian worship and witness, each link of which denotes the attempt, in different cultural milieux, to express the gospel in contemporary terms. To stand in this tradition and recognise oneself to be part of this chain is to acknowledge that the gospel *can* be translated meaningfully into the language and culture of today. It does no more, however, than provide an initial impetus to the process. The actual translation has to be undertaken afresh in each generation, if not in every sermon or act of worship.

Yet the most important dimension of all remains. The 'source' of the message is two-fold: in the immediate perspective, it is the encoder (i.e., the preacher, teacher, liturgist or communicator); but ultimately, it transcends the human dimension. The words of the encoder are designed to convey the Word from Beyond, a Word that can never be fully comprehended by the human agent. It is always an Address to someone in a particular historical and cultural milieu, a Disclosure in history and human experience. Hence, the articulation of the Disclosure or Revelation in human language, the existence of a believing community and its witness to the Disclosure-event or event of salvation, the relaying of the 'good news' in mission, the formation and adoption of a scriptural canon, the translation of the witness into other languages and in other cultural situations – all these are essential elements in the birth and development of the historical Christian tradition.

The Church is the extension and the expression of the believing community in every age. Hence it is at once the receptor of the divine Address and the source of the human words that convey the divine Word to mankind. To be the receptor is, as we have seen, both to receive and to respond to the message and the source of the message. Hence the liturgy, prayers and life of the Church express awareness of the Word that speaks and has spoken from Beyond and the response of the believing community to that Address. In other words, there is genuine dialogue, made possible by the manner of the divine Address. For the Word from Beyond has been made manifest within the human dimension in the person of Jesus, the Christ. Therefore, he is the means by which the Address is most fully conveyed, the Mediator through whom the dialogue with God is most effectively established, the embodied Word through whom the divine Disclosure is most concretely expressed.

In consequence, the prayers and liturgy of the Church are both christocentric and contemporary with the worshippers; for it is they who are brought into dialogue with the Word in contemporary worship and devotion. The divine Address comes to them *now*. That this fact has immediate consequences for the language of prayer is obvious. Yet this prayer is offered also as an integral part of that dialogue with God which has characterised the saints of all ages: it is offered in the context of the *communio sanctorum*. This means that the prayers of the past give help, guidance and inspiration to those who pray today. The chain of prayer across the ages is a reality for latter-day worshippers and influences the language and structures they use. But their prayers are inescapably prayers of today.

An important part of the liturgy is the ministry of the Word. As in Justin's time, the witness of the early faith-communities – Israel, the evangelists, the apostles – is read and heard as the Address of God. Preaching is an integral part of this ministry. The words of scripture are expounded and proclamation made in human language, so that the Word may be heard and appropriate response made. The language must be contemporary; it must be appropriate to the liturgical context and well adapted for its kerygmatic purpose. It must, in short, communicate to the hearers and bring them into active participation in the message.

B—PREACHING

(i) *Origins*
Preaching is sometimes assumed to be a peculiarly Christian phenomenon and to characterise particularly the Reformed Christian tradition. In fact, it characterises many religious traditions. After his enlightenment, Siddhartha Gautama, the Buddha, committed himself to a preaching ministry. The Benares sermon, with its kernel of *dhamma*, translated his spiritual experience into intelligible doctrine; the 'sermon on burning' sets forth the Buddhist view of human existence as fevered by passions and thus enslaved to the world.[6] In Christianity, the catholic tradition of East and West enshrined a great preaching tradition: Origen, John

Chrysostom, Gregory of Nazianza, Augustine, Ambrose and Savonarola are names to conjure with in this regard.

The prophets of Israel were essentially messengers of Yahweh. The formula 'Thus says the Lord ...' appears to be derived from the sending of royal messages: 'Thus says my Lord the King ...' It is a proclamation, to be delivered with sovereign authority. The apprehension of the message falls within the realm of religious mystery and is not fully open to our scrutiny. Often, we deduce, it occurred in the course of intense religious experience; it was accompanied by a commission to convey the message, whatever the consequences, sometimes with more than a sense of urgency, almost a compulsion to utter the divine communication.

Amos at Bethel and Jeremiah at the gate of the Temple are examples of prophecy which assumes the form of proclamatory sermon. Deuteronomy provides further examples of sermons as the instruments of prophetic leadership. A characteristic of true prophecy is that it uses intelligible language (cf. Paul in 1 Corinthians 14) and that it reinforces and applies the tradition of Moses, the *magnalia* or mighty works of salvation which God wrought in Israel in the event of the Exodus and at Sinai. Preaching in the prophetic tradition basically consists of two related forms: the message of salvation and the message of judgment. In addition, it can convey eschatological urgency ('the day of the Lord is near ...'). These characteristics are carried over into early Christianity. Here, the message of salvation (*euangelion*: good news) predominates; but its obverse is the warning against rejecting God's grace and incurring his judgment, and the eschatological emphasis, though modified by the fact that the Christ has already come in the midst of history, nevertheless remains strong in New Testament proclamation.[7]

One of the distinguishing marks of post-exilic Judaism is the emergence of written scripture, the Torah, as focal in the life and worship of the faith-community. With it there came the synagogue, the scribes, rabbinic exegesis – and synagogue preaching. At what point the homily or sermon became a regular part of synagogue worship is unclear, but Luke 4 implies it was not uncommon in Jesus' time, while in Alexandria Philo was a philosophical preacher with apologetic objectives. However, the rabbinic tradition of preaching was fundamentally exegetical. There were two forms of homily which merit particular note. One was the *proem* homily, in which the preacher selected a text which would enable him to bring the second lesson (from 'the Prophets') into new life and relevance for the hearers and move on from there to elucidate the primary lesson (from the Torah). As with the Pharisaic tradition generally, the emphasis was on the claim of divine obligation on the lives of the hearers. Hence parable, analogy and illustration formed a prominent part of the homily. The second major form was known as the *yelammedenu* homily. Here the starting point was a question put by the leaders of the congregation: 'Let our teacher instruct us ...' In the ministry of Jesus, the address in the synagogue at Nazareth and the discourse on the bread of life in the fourth Gospel appear to be of the former type, while questions such as 'Is it lawful to heal on the sabbath?' (Matthew 12:10) appear to be of the latter variety.[8]

That the synagogue homily was at least influenced in its development by external models, especially hellenistic preaching, is very likely, for Greek rhetoric and education had a lasting impact on Jewish practice, even when Greek culture as a whole was rejected as inimical to the Jewish faith.[9] Popular preaching emerged in the Greek world with the Stoic-Cynic diatribe, which deliberately adapted philosophy to the popular market. The homily was therefore a homely, conversational presentation of a philosophical position: the word itself implies 'familiar dialogue'. Vivid illustrations and analogies abounded. Questions – sometimes rhetorical, sometimes direct – brought the hearers into active engagement with the subject-matter. Humour, repartee, stories and a variety of rhetorical devices heightened the effect. In a later phase however, the homily became much more of a formal discourse or lecture. There can be little doubt that early Christian preaching was considerably influenced by this Graeco-Roman homiletic tradition and that the synagogue homily also mediated rhetorical form and art.[10]

Examples of early Christian preaching in the New Testament suggest that the various strands were well represented in it. The prophetic strand is reflected in the kerygmatic sermons of Peter and Paul in Acts: they proclaim the Christian *magnalia* or 'mighty acts of God'; they call for repentence, with urgency born of an eschatological faith. Indeed, such prophetic models pinpoint the basic Christian stance from which the scriptures of the Old Testament are 'peshered' or given their distinctive Christian interpretation.[11] On the other hand, Paul's address to the synagogue congregation at Antioch in Pisidia (Acts 13:15–41) bears some resemblance to a *proem* homily, though it has been thoroughly Christianised. Another good example of a Christianised synagogue sermon is the speech of Stephen (Acts 7:2–53), while a more hellenistic example is the Areopagus speech in Acts 17:22–31. Paul's preaching is echoed in many of his letters, and homiletic influence is strong in letters such as Hebrews and 1 Clement. The words *dialegesthai* (Acts 20:7, 9) and *homilein* (20:11) both suggest that Paul's preaching invited participation in dialogue and argument.

The main factor which separates Justin's description of early Christian worship from that of the New Testament is that Christian writings have taken their place alongside the Old Testament scriptures, and Christian preaching is basically exegetical. In Origen, the homily expounds a pericope or selected passage verse by verse. Even such unpromising material as the Song of Songs is expounded in this way in two homilies. In Origen, careful commentary or textual study lays the foundation of homiletics, though of course he had his own assumptions about how scripture should be interpreted.[12]

The homily, however, was not the only preaching form Origen knew. He used *logos* to describe a more systematic discourse on a selected theme. Augustine too distinguished between homily and sermon, the former being used as in Origen and the latter (the *sermo*) referring to a discourse in a great basilica. The *sermo* had a more systematic structure, building up an argument by logical steps and reaching a conclusion which combined the completed argument with an appeal to the hearers. Increasingly, it reproduced the procedures and devices of classical rhetoric, and was a form that was to have much influence on the Christian tradition of preaching.

(ii) *Theology*

The notion that the Gospels, and much other material in the Bible, are essentially kerygmatic, i.e., designed to proclaim God's message of salvation, was given proper prominence by Martin Kähler in 1892. He wrote, 'The real Christ is the preached Christ, and the preached Christ is the Christ of faith.'[13] Thereafter, for the best part of a century, Reformed theology has been 'dialectical', 'kerygmatic', 'the theology of the Word'. Hence it is integrally related to the preaching ministry. Through the work of Karl Rahner and others, this emphasis has also come to the fore in Roman Catholic thinking.

Karl Barth was one of the most outstanding proponents of kerygmatic theology. Particularly in his earlier writings – e.g., in *the Word of God and the Word of man*[14] – he gave prominence to the perspective of the preacher, concerned to relate simultaneously to the word of scripture and the world of his hearers. Even in the *Church Dogmatics*, the emphasis he placed on preaching is evident in the way he pinpointed the three forms of the Word of God: (i) the proclaimed Word; (ii) the written Word; and (iii) the revealed Word.[15] The proclamation which the preacher makes Sunday by Sunday nourishes the faith of the Church. It is not *simply* a human process; for where the Word is truly proclaimed, the Holy Spirit is at work in the proclamation leading the hearers into truth (cf. John 16:13). Indeed, it has been suggested that we can apply the full Trinitarian analogy and develop – but with suitable caution – the relation between the written Word and God the Son, and the relation between the revealed Word and God the Father.

> The New Testament seems to require these analogies. They are not artificial dogmatic constructions, but reflect truly the fact that it is the Father who creates and commands with His Word, that it is the Son who is the expectation of the Old and the witness of the New Testament, and that it is the Holy Spirit who leads us into the full truth after the Ascension.[16]

On the other hand, one could claim that all three 'persons' or 'modes of being' are present at each stage, and that the christological dimension is particularly relevant to the understanding of preaching.

Rudolf Bultmann combined three main elements in his kerygmatic model. (a) It is dialectical: God is proclaimed through the Word he utters, particularly on the Cross. Bultmann has a strong affinity with Pauline theology: 'We preach Christ crucified ...'. (b) It draws freely from Heidegger's existentialist analysis of human existence. How does the Word of preaching relate to those who hear it? It summons them to decision. It calls upon them to adopt a new understanding of their own existence: to effect the transition, by the grace of God through his Word, from the 'inauthentic' life of unbelief to the 'authentic' life of faith. Hence, according to Bultmann, biblical language and imagery ('myth'), which derived from an ancient world-view wholly alien to modern man, has to be interpreted existentially. Heidegger's descriptive analysis of human existence, Bultmann believed, was of great assistance in setting out the meaning of the 'new life in Christ' for his hearers. (c) It makes full use of biblical criticism to enable us to understand the purport of the text in its ancient context and so identify its essential message for today. Thus, when the biblical text is preached and heard as the Word of God, *something happens*: in Bultmann's terms, preaching is an event that effects change or transformation in the life of the hearer. In some sense, he or she becomes a new being.[17]

This relational aspect of preaching is beautifully developed by Paul Tillich in a justly celebrated sermon:

> Sometimes at that moment a wave of light breaks into our darkness, and it is as though a voice were saying: 'You are accepted. *You are accepted*, accepted by that which is greater than you, and the name of which you do not know. Do not ask for the name now; perhaps you will find it later. Do not try to do anything now; perhaps later you will do much. Do not seek for anything; do not perform anything; do not intend anything. *Simply accept the fact that you are accepted!*' If that happens to us, we experience grace. After such an experience we may not be better than before, and we may not believe more than before. But everything is transformed ...[18]

Preaching is therefore a *personal* transaction in the fullest sense: a person-to-person encounter, permeated by grace. The proclamation must be made lovingly, for it is an expression of and a vehicle for the love of God. It is – now and forever – *good news* (gospel), even though it carries the pain of revelation of the truth about oneself, or the sting of judgment or rebuke (and the preacher can never exclude himself: he too is a receptor). It is gospel because, if it is authentic Word, it conveys with the judgment the assurance that God accepts us *now*: that this gracious moment of truth is the effecting of the transformation, the *now* of salvation.

Nevertheless, we do well to heed the protest of J. B. Metz and others against the 'privatizing' of the gospel, which occurs when preaching is related too exclusively to the individual.[19] Preaching, like worship, is a community action; and, like worship, it sends us out into the world in Christ's name. 'God so loved *the world* ...' The ministry of Jesus was a public event, as political as it was spiritual. It is all too easy for preacher and congregation to retreat into the comfortable shelter of some form of neo-orthodoxy. The essential complement of 'orthodoxy' (right belief) is 'orthopraxis': right expression of faith in action. Love to God is inseparable from love to neighbour, and the latter involves action in the world. If Christians are to share in Christ's ministry of reconciliation, then preaching must provide some of the training for this front-line engagement.

(iii) *Exegesis*

Important as it is for the preacher to have a theological understanding of his preaching, the acid test comes when he sits down at his desk to prepare the sermon for next Sunday. If he is to be faithful to the ministry of the Word, a central concern must be with sound exegesis. Allied to this is the necessity to communicate with his hearers. He must steer a course, as Karl Barth put it, 'between the problem of human life on the one hand and the content of the Bible on the other'.[20] There are no easy answers to this predicament, nor should anything offered below be interpreted in that way. At most, certain guidelines can be indicated.

(a) The preacher owes it to his hearers, if not to himself and his vocation, to have a knowledge and appreciation of the full range of the Biblical literature that comprises the canon of scripture, to be aware of the findings of Biblical scholarship and to be able to apply its insights to the interpretation of scripture. All this represents, as it were, the primary elements of his science.

The preacher will only reach a defensible and productive resolution of the problem of scripture through an intelligent study of all the evidence. That there is considerable danger in divorcing the academic and the practical (*theoria* and *praxis*) is illustrated from time to time by solecisms perpetrated by churchmen: e.g., the appeal in time of war or conflict to the warlike Yahweh, leader of Israel's hosts in the destruction of her enemies; the appeal to the Mosaic Law to justify capital punishment or opposition to (say) blood transfusion or spiritualism, or the appeal to the first century codes cited in the New Testament to justify opposition to all forms of abortion or to the relaxing of the law on homosexuality; or the pathetic spectacle of the 'creationist' *versus* 'evolutionist' debate in some circles today. Such 'direct transference' or 'instant exegesis' takes no account of the importance of the context or the difficulty of extrapolating texts in this way.

(b) The use of a lectionary assists exegesis. It is helpful to have a carefully arranged selection of passages – usually Old Testament, Epistle and Gospel – related to the Christian Year; for the liturgical season itself is a help to interpretation, and the lectionary provides a discipline for the preacher. One cannot simply repeat one's favourite passages or themes; and the discipline imposed by the lectionary affords greater objectivity to his use of scripture and makes for better coverage of the whole range of Biblical texts. Above all, it requires the preacher to clarify his understanding of the relationship of Old Testament, Epistle and Gospel.

Whatever part of the Bible it comes from, a biblical passage attempts some kind of crystallization: of faith, tradition, message, understanding of life, or gospel. It is a crystallization that includes the original receptors in the faith-perspective in question. Later generations (including ourselves) are partly excluded from immediate appreciation of this perspective because the original communication presupposed a wholly different cultural setting from our own.[21] Hence the need, in the Church as in Judaism, for interpretation, midrash, exposition – in short, for the work of exegesis that 'gives the sense', translates and applies the meaning in modern terms. Christian exegesis is christo-centric, since Jesus the Christ represents the full expression of God's saving work: hence the interplay of Old and New Testaments, and the Christian *pesher* standpoint. Every exegetical sermon, therefore, is a new crystallization of the Gospel of Christ: a new statement of God's acceptance of us in Christ. And this new statement involves the receptors, the congregation. Preaching is an event which changes and reshapes their lives, their community and their world. E. Best concludes his study of exegetical preaching in this way:

> The purpose of all understanding of Scripture is to make Christ appear in his church so that he shapes that church to be like himself. The purpose of preaching is the formation of the church to be the true body of Christ. The purpose of the devotional study of Scripture is the harmonizing of the individual into the whole which is the church. But the preacher needs to remember that there are more factors at work than his preaching in the shaping of the church to be the true body of Christ. Certainly this takes place through worship and in the sacraments, but it also takes place as the individual members come to their own understanding, form in themselves a new crystallization, and so contribute to the upbuilding of the whole body. The movement is then from Christ through the crystallizations which are Scripture and the history of the church into the crystallization of the sermon and out again to be the life of the Church, which is the life of the risen Lord, and the only crystallization that really counts.[22]

(c) The methods of exegesis are governed by our overall understanding of exegetical interpretation. Careful study of the text, with commentaries, is a pre-requisite; but the material from the commentary is not the substance of the sermon. If it were so, the sermon would, almost certainly, be academically overcharged and conceptually inappropriate to the congregation, and it would in consequence lose impact. Commentaries enrich our understanding of the passage and enable us to bring about a more worthy crystallization of the Gospel for the congregation.

'Every sermon should be ruthlessly unitary in its theme,' writes Ian Pitt-Watson. 'This is the first and great commandment!'[23] It is important, therefore, to determine what the central thrust or theme of the passage is. Provided the selected theme is inherent in the passage and not extraneously imposed, it is of much help in establishing a consistent line of approach in the interpretation and exposition, for it establishes the kerygmatic unity – the crystallization of truth – that brings the hearers into active exploration of the meaning for themselves. H. Thielicke commends this textual-thematic kind of preaching.

First, in this way one remains within the text and allows it to be an end in itself. One discovers in it a centre and periphery and one illuminates it on the basis of its main ideas.

Second, this way of determining the theme not only helps to keep the sermon true to the text but also helps the preacher to achieve order and clarity ...

Third, this method is also helpful to the hearer. He retains it better and can more readily pass it on to others ...

But the thematic sermon is helpful most of all to hearers who are interested in a question and perhaps have no desire to listen to any biblical exposition whatsoever.

This will be true especially of those who are on the fringes or outside of the church. They may sit up and take notice when they find that the theme announced is 'The Meaning of Life' and perhaps they will be much surprised to hear a sermon on the Rich Young Ruler subsumed under this theme. They may also recognize that some unexpected problems are dealt with in the Bible.[24]

(iv) *Forms*

Thielicke's exegetical procedure aptly illustrates the relationship between the substance of the sermon (i.e., exegetical concern) and the form which the sermon assumes. Biblical material in fact prompts more than one form, as we shall see. Thielicke seems most at home with the thematic (or textual thematic) discourse.

(a) *The thematic discourse.* A descendant or heir of the tradition of classical rhetoric, the thematic discourse represents the systematic development of a selected theme, which may be based on a verse, a passage or even a book of scripture. It has an introduction, designed to capture the attention of the listeners and to lead them to interested engagement with the substance of the discourse. It develops its argument by means of a series of reasoned steps: not only systematically expounding and commending the theme or thesis, but also refuting objections or counter-theses. The whole armoury of rhetorical devices – questions, illustrations, anecdotes, quotations, repetitions, similes and other figures – is at the disposal of the speaker. The impact which the preacher hopes to achieve does not operate at the intellectual level alone (even if the argumentative nature of the procedure might suggest otherwise): it is concerned with the emotions and the will, the affective and volitional as well as the cognitive. It seeks a response from the hearers as whole beings. The conclusion, therefore, is not only the goal of the argument: it is the crowning appeal to the listeners, summoning them to respond in faith and obedience to the Word which has been mediated to them through the exploration of the theme.

The above sketch is possibly enough to convince readers that most of the sermons they hear in Church are indeed thematic discourses. They will doubtless have their own views of the efficacy or otherwise of this form.

When appropriately related to the context in which it is delivered, it can undoubtedly have impact, be persuasive as well as informative, and assist or challenge the hearers in matters of faith and life. This is to recognise, of course, that there is more to preaching than *simply* questions of form or structure. If the preacher does not identify with his exposition and speak with conviction, his well-structured utterance will lack authenticity. Again, if the discourse does not connect with the world of the hearers, the impact will be negligible. On the other hand, a disconnected, wandering sort of discourse will lose impact. The question of good structure, though only one of the requirements of effective preaching, is too important to be lightly dismissed.

Reservations may be expressed about the apparent dominance of this particular form of discourse. One of its ancestors is the *sermo* delivered in the large basilica, with an overtone, perhaps, of the lecture hall or large auditorium. But many of the liturgical settings in which the thematic discourse is used today are not of this type. One thinks of the sparsely attended evening service, or the morning service in a rural area or depopulated city centre; and one reflects also on the T.V. age, the effect of the mass media on communication, and a whole range of social changes which mark off our age from its predecessors, not to speak of the age of Augustine. Is the declamatory form of oration really suitable, when the setting might suggest a more informal, perhaps conversational, type of talk? It highlights the authority of the preacher, but may also suggest that he/she stands 'six feet above contradiction', beyond challenge or questioning, despite the fact that some sermon content may be open to question or positively invite discussion. In considering the most appropriate form for the sermon, the preacher must reflect on its relation to the congregation and the liturgical setting. Again, does the thematic discourse lend itself to the exposition of *every* type of scripture, whether prose or verse, narrative or parable, epistle or apocalyptic book? One might take 'race relations' or 'prejudice' as the theme of the parable of the Good Samaritan, but this hardly does justice to the parabolic *story* which Jesus told, which seems to require a different form of discourse, namely one much more directly related to narrative or story-telling. There is therefore a direct relation between sermon form and the nature of the scriptural material.

(b) *The homily*. In its early Christian setting, this is essentially the exposition and discussion of a passage of scripture (or 'pericope'). The application of the passage to the lives of the participants is kept in view throughout and is sometimes made explicit at the end. As H. J. C. Pieterse has put it, 'We can say ... that a homily is linked to a pericope, which it expounds verse by verse in a largely analytical way; that it is characterized by an intimate atmosphere and is geared to dialogue with listeners.'[25] Pieterse points out that it is particularly suited to 'factual' texts: by which we take him to mean texts which only come to life for readers or hearers when they are made aware of the background or setting-in-life. For example, to understand what Paul was saying about 'meat sacrificed to idols', one has to learn something of the social and historical situation of the early Christians at Corinth and also of the groups and tendencies already forming in their community. It is the preacher's task to elucidate this 'background', so that the whole congregation can read and explore the passage and come to an understanding of Paul's meaning and aim in writing. Thus preacher and congregation are brought into dialogue not only with each other but with the biblical writer. Their minds meet with his mind, and their lives are open to the challenge of his message.

The advantages of this method are considerable. It invests authority not in the preacher (who is seen as a facilitator of interpretation) but in the text. It can be applied to a variety of types of texts: to poems and psalms as well as letters or other prose passages. Taken to its logical conclusion, it would provide opportunity for putting questions to the expositor, and for sharing ideas and insights, and it would thus obviate the inherent weakness of the monologue as a mode of communication.

The method as described above lends itself to the smaller, more intimate group: the evening or mid-week service, or the bible study group. The discussion or 'feed-back' may be relatively informal or it may be structured (e.g., dividing into smaller groups). Many may feel that the lack of such opportunities in many Churches is an evident weakness, but that preachers and congregations need time to adjust to a new situation which puts the preacher in a much more vulnerable position and the congregation in a more active role, which may not be to everyone's liking. But if we genuinely believe that preaching has to do with communicating meaning, both adjustments are essential. One reflects on the need for much more effective adult education in our Churches. It is a gap which the expository homily can go some way to fill.

Some may suggest that it is artificial to make such a sharp distinction between the homily and the thematic discourse, even if it can be shown that they are historically distinct. Their argument would be in favour of a mixed form, like Thielicke's 'textual-thematic' procedure: an expository but thematic and unitary discourse which illuminates the text but does not interrupt the liturgical movement of the service by interposing a period of discussion. Feed-back and discussion could be encouraged at an informal session after the service. Some gifted preachers have effected this fusion admirably (in Scotland, William Barclay was a good example). But in some instances, the result can be a reversion to monologue, with its dangers of authoritarian preaching, poor communication and congregational passivity and frustration. Whether the form is a thematic discourse, an exegetical homily or a mixture of both, the congregation must be brought into active dialogue (whether verbally or silently), for a passive congregation defeats the sermon as a means of communication.

(c) *The story sermon.* The Gospels consist largely of stories. The story-teller clearly had an important place in the communication of the early Christian message, and especially the tradition about Jesus. The Old Testament relates the story of Israel, and Jesus himself was a skilled story-teller. It is surprising, therefore, that modern preachers tend to make relatively little use of the art of story-telling, except when talking to children or for the purpose of illustrating a thematic discourse. In other words, the modern preacher seems to be much less *dependent* on the story than his biblical predecessors. Yet it is doubtful if narrative texts can be properly expounded without making substantial use of narrative. The story is more than the means of conveying the message. It is not dispensable. In a real sense, it *is* the message. In the interaction of the characters in a given situation and in the drama that is generated in the telling, the hearers are drawn into dialogue with the picture of reality that is created in the narrative. In this way, they are brought to question their own understanding of life in a new and radical way.

To make proper use of the narrative form, preachers must do their homework on the biblical narrative. They must observe carefully how the biblical story-teller structured his narrative, what his aims were and what devices he used to effect them. The story of Jonah may serve as an example. First, we note what God required the prophet to do (preach the message of salvation to Nineveh, the enemies of Israel): we note the prophet's rejection of the divine vocation and his determined attempt to frustrate God's purpose by sailing off in the opposite direction. Clearly, this is a coherent narrative in itself and can be retold dramatically today. It culminates, however, in the demonstration of the truth that it is impossible to escape from God. We note the author's use of the human impossibility of the great fish episode in order to make his point. Here the preacher may interrupt the narrative to dwell briefly on the lesson set out in the first part of the story (cf. Israel's disobedience and God's constant renewing of her vocation as his people). The narrative is then resumed: the reluctant prophet fulfils his vocation, but his desire to see Nineveh destroyed is not fulfilled. How could God not be concerned for a city where so many people lived – to say nothing of the cattle (which also matter)? A second point of reflection occurs here: love for enemies as opposed to narrow nationalistic prejudice and the desire for vengeance. Then comes the final challenge to the preacher: to devise a narrative in contemporary terms that conveys this message to the hearers. Jonah's alienation – the offence that God's vocation caused him – must in some measure be shared by us today. That is how the Word from Beyond impinges upon our present experience. The alienation, however, can lead to a new formulation of our understanding of ourselves and our world, an amendment of our living, thinking and acting, prompted by the scriptural message as Word of God.

The power of the message resides in the narrative and the reflection it prompts. Extraneous reflection is at best a distraction: e.g., whether or not Jonah was a historical character and – even worse – whether it is possible for a man to survive three days and nights in the belly of a great fish. A fictional story may be no less true – not only in terms of being 'true to life' but in terms of conveying the Word of God – than a story about a historical person. Jesus himself frequently used this very method.

(v) *Impact*

Every sermon is stretched like a bow string between the text of the Bible on the one hand and the problems of contemporary human life on the other. If the string is insecurely tethered to either end, the bow is useless. It is a wise precaution for every preacher to pay special attention to the end of the string which for him is the less securely tethered. The other end will look after itself, meantime at least.[26]

It is possible, I believe, to exaggerate this tension (of which Barth also speaks). The preacher does not necessarily have to 'do the splits' between responsibility to the text and responsibility to the congregation. If our remarks on exegetical preaching were in any way valid, good exegesis includes *both* attention to the meaning in its original context (cf. the writer's intention) *and* its meaning for today. Both poles are included in what we have called the new crystallization that every sermon represents.

In short, preaching and hearing the Word are inseparable: not only because the preacher must first be a hearer, but also because preaching does not take place as the action of one person only, however devout. It is a community action. It takes place as part of the liturgy: part of the movement from God to man and man to God in which the worshipping congregation participates. It is therefore inescapably an act of communication, of proclamation and response, of encoding and decoding; and, as we have seen, a point of contact, a common language and a community of experience are essential to such communication.

Indeed, in the case of preaching we might well go further. A sermon has impact not only as the words of the text command the attention and response of the hearers so that they understand in a new way what the writer is saying; it has also impact when the preacher, through his sensitive handling of the biblical material, enables them to find God in their own life, relationships and world.

The implications of such an observation are manifold. A few only are briefly indicated here.

(a) *Language.* Preaching, like the rest of the liturgy, involves the use of words: more dangerously, the use of rhetoric. The advice given by Fowler and Fowler to writers is even more applicable to preachers: in their use of words, they should try to be 'direct, simple, brief, vigorous and lucid'.

This general principle may be translated into practical rules in the domain of vocabulary as follows:

Prefer the familiar word to the far-fetched.
Prefer the concrete word to the abstract.
Prefer the single word to the circumlocution.
Prefer the short word to the long.
Prefer the Saxon word to the Romance.[27]

Such counsel, however, must not be taken as suggesting that the language of preaching can only be plain and dull. Far from it! Preachers require a double sensitivity: they must use language that is well adapted to their hearers and appropriate to the subject-matter. And the subject-matter is thrilling. The language of preaching should reflect the wonder and splendour of the message. Much religious language is metaphorical: it moves at the deeper level of reality. It uses symbol and imagery, parable and allegory as a key to the disclosure of truth. And as the preacher's imagination is fired by the richness of biblical language, so he or she can lift the hearers above the trite and superficial to share in the disclosure of the divine, 'full of grace and truth'.

The danger is that, facing the demand to produce a hundred or so sermons a year, the preacher becomes a word-spinner. A quantitative rather than a qualitative criterion comes into operation, and familiar repetitions, cliches and other apparatus of pulpiteering replace meaningful discourse. 'The hungry sheep look up and are not fed ...' It may be because the shepherd is run off his feet, but if so activism has replaced proper reflection and preparation for one of the minister's priority roles, the proclamation of the Word.

(b) *Empathy*. If the preacher's message is to be well adapted to the hearers, then the minister must be in close contact with the life of the people to whom the sermon is addressed. The separation of preaching from pastoral work is damaging. The minister must 'know his flock' in order to serve them. An awareness of their home life and problems, of their working life, of how they face redundancy or early retirement or enforced leisure, as well as illness and suffering – in short, an empathy with their whole involvement with life – is a duty and necessity for the preacher of the Word. Only if there is dialogue with them in their every-day setting can the preacher hope to have dialogue with them from the pulpit and so crystallize for them the gospel of Christ.

(c) *Relevance*. Realism, in the sense of truth-to-life, must be the keynote of preaching. It is all too easy to create an artificial world that exists nowhere but in the imagination of the preacher: a sermonic world, fuelled by sermonic illustrations but not impinging dynamically on the world the people know. Even if some members appear to 'enjoy' such sermons, the only long-term effect will be to move the Church even more decisively to the margins of life, and to encourage yet another form of the 'two-world' view among those who persevere: the world of the Church and the real world outside. This is not to deny that an apposite illustration, perferably involving people in a recognisably authentic situation, can have impact and convey gospel meaning. A dramatic illustration, like Wesley's celebrated story of the rescue of a boy from a burning house ('a brand snatched from the burning': it was autobiographical), can rivet the attention.[29] On the other hand, 'pulpit illustrations' (collections of them have actually been published) are the shadow of the real thing, emaciated through over-use. In general, the sermon itself should proceed in such a way that the attention of the hearers is engaged throughout. When a proper degree of concreteness, lucidity and truth-to-life is achieved, there is no necessity to punctuate the discourse with illustrations unless they have a particular point to add to the totality of meaning. Again, overloading the sermon with too much material or underestimating the capacity of the congregation detracts from the relevance of the discourse and undermines effective communication.

In short, when we speak of impact we are concerned with encounter: encounter with the Word, and so with divine truth. While it is true that a preacher sometimes communicates *in spite of* his preaching (e.g., through his personal qualities, infectious faith or pastoral gifts), sermons are not designed with this in mind! Rather, they relate to an important part of the liturgy: they are integral to the ministry of the Word. The sermon that has impact moves the hearers to say with Jacob: 'Truly the Lord is in *this* place, and I did not realise it as I do now. This is the house of God, the gateway to heaven.'

C—PRAYER

(i) *Prayer as Dialogue*
Prayer is like a dialogue between God and his people; a kind of conversation which sustains and deepens a relationship and is indeed virtually indispensable to that relationship. The relationship is continuous; prayer in the sense of time set aside for this particular dialogue, is not, although prayerfulness, a prayerful attitude, should inform the whole of life.

In suggesting that prayer is to be understood on the analogy of dialogue or conversation – an image which must not be pushed too far – we are explicitly excluding the idea of prayer as magic, a matter of spells and incantations. Christian prayer has indeed been understood as magic – witness the English term for jugglery or deceit, 'hocus pocus', very possibly derived in the seventeenth century from the Latin of the Mass, *hoc est corpus meum.* Malinowski and other anthropologists make a clear (perhaps too clear) distinction between magical and social language in prayer. Magic is concerned with the control and manipulation of supernatural forces, it is an impersonal and rather mechanical way of achieving one's ends. Social use of language (in prayer or otherwise) is concerned with the establishing and nurture of relationships, with 'bonding', with the establishment of fellowship through communication. The distinction between the social and the magical use of language is helpful, but should not be pressed too far; many actual instances of prayer language have an intrusive magical element. But Christian theology has a well grounded tendency to be suspicious of magical language in worship, and prefers to understand prayer socially, or as a dialogue. It also follows from this that Christians do not understand prayer as primarily self-exploration. It is rather an encounter with God which inevitably issues in self-examination and a deepening of self-understanding. Similarly, prayer should not be understood simply as a form of psychological hygiene, although prayer may well be cathartic or result in an improved sense of well-being and peace.

The shape, tone and content of any dialogue are always determined by the participants. The Boston newspaper which in reporting the visit of a famous preacher said, 'Never before had so eloquent a prayer been addressed to a Boston congregation', was confused about the parties to the prayer-dialogue, but perhaps pardonably since some public prayer does give the appearance of being addressed to the congregation rather than to God. But if we assume that Christian prayer is addressed to God, tha⁺ God is a participant in the prayer-dialogue, particular understandings of God must deeply affect the understanding and practice of prayer.

Jesus shocked the people of his time by teaching that we should approach God confidently, joyfully, simply as children coming to Daddy, *Abba* in Aramaic. The use of the term *Abba* was so striking that it survives in its Aramaic form in the New Testament (Mark 14:36; Galatians 4:6; Romans 8:15) and lies behind the slightly more formal 'Our Father' with which the Lord's Prayer begins. The use of this term in prayer, as James Mackey writes, 'at once gives expression to the lived conviction and appeals for its continuance, the lived conviction, namely, that God cherishes all things great and small, and all people, good bad and indifferent, as a father cherishes his children. Like so much taught by Jesus, it is disappointingly simple to say, and all but impossible to live.'[29] The Church down the ages has spent much energy trying to escape from the simplicity and directness of Jesus' teaching on prayer. His 'model prayer', The Lord's Prayer (Matthew 6:9–13; Luke 11:2–4), his own practice of prayer and the things he taught all suggest the availability of God to listen to the prayers of his people, his readiness to respond, and the similarity of prayer to conversation within a loving family. It is this basic conviction about the nature of God, his approachability and loving responsiveness, which gives Christian prayer its distinctive shape and mood and content and calls for language, words, appropriate to the encounter with this loving *Abba*, Father, Daddy, who draws his people to participate in the outworking of his purposes and the life of his Kingdom.

(ii) *The Place of Formulae*
In everyday language we constantly use formulae – forms of words which sometimes do not have a very easily specifiable meaning, or are used with scant regard to the meaning of the words (which may not even be known) because it is the social function of the formulae which is important. We say 'hello', or 'hi', 'goodbye' or 'cheerio' simply as formulae of greeting or farewell. We send letters with 'yours sincerely', or 'yours faithfully', and it certainly does not guarantee the honesty or integrity of the writer. 'How do you do?', seems well on the way to ceasing to be a question expecting any answer. And in Britain at least, many conversations start with a highly formulized little exchange of comments about the weather.

Such formulae are a necessary part of social interaction. We teach our children to say 'please' and 'thank you' even when the words bear little relation to what they are in fact feeling. These are not only signs of good manners, but tutors of feeling and not an unimportant part of the socializing process, the induction into a particular community and set of relationships. Much conversation never gets beyond the level of formulae – polite, cocktail-party chit-chat, what is often labelled 'small talk'. Indeed, formulae may be used as a way of avoiding real conversation, real dialogue, real encounter. We may even convert them into magical spells, or allow over-familiarity to deprive them of meaning. But there is also a sense in which formulae may be the preliminary to real conversation, the prelude to frank and fresh interaction. We can use formulae as a way of defending ourselves against real meeting, or as a kind of testing the water before we plunge into significant conversation.

Prayer, and particularly public prayer, is full of such formulae and set forms. Most of them are familiar and much loved, with all sorts of associations gathered around them. But if you asked the members of an average congregation what 'Kyrie eleison', 'Amen' and 'Halleluia' mean, you would get a bewildering diversity of replies and, if people were honest, a large proportion of 'don't knows'. It would be interesting to know what worshippers today make of the phrase 'world without end' with which so many prayers are concluded. A long obsolete translation of the Latin *in saecula saeculorum*, meaning 'For ever and ever', or 'throughout all ages', the old phrase continues vigorously in use, although it either conveys no meaning at all, or a most misleading one. Much of the language of public prayer is constantly repeated. This is a characteristic of most extempore prayer as it is of more formal liturgical prayer. Phrases, sentences, and whole prayers such as the Magnificat, Nunc Dimittis, and the Lord's Prayer are used so frequently in worship that reformers of a puritan inclination dismiss them as 'vain repetitions'. It is, however, a mistake based on a wrong translation of Matthew 6:7 to suggest that Jesus rejected the repetition of familiar forms in prayer. The Greek term *battalogein* translated in the Authorized Version as 'use vain repetitions', is better rendered as 'to heap up empty phrases' (R.S.V.) or 'to go babbling on' (N.E.B.). The clear intent of the verse as a whole is to discourage pointless verbosity in prayer rather than repetition. It would appear that Jesus himself used repetition in prayer (Matthew 26:44), as any pious Jew would be accustomed to doing, and did not see the new intimacy in prayer into which he introduced his disciples as excluding the use of set forms or in any way incompatible with participation in the formal prayers of the temple and synagogue.

Like the formulae of everyday conversation, prayer formulae can be the preliminary to, and a training for, a more profound, spontaneous, and direct dialogue. And the movement from the formalities to more authentic and revealing communication is often a penetration into the depths of meaning and imagery contained in the formulae rather than a passing beyond the formulae in such a way that they are made dispensable.

(iii) *The Shape of Prayer*
All dialogue has a shape, a flow, a movement, a structure. Otherwise it would be nothing but meaningless jumbles of words, phrases and sounds, very much the 'babbling on' that Jesus warned his disciples against in their prayers. All public prayer must have shape; but some prayers in shape and sequence are more spiritually and aesthetically satisfactory than others.

The various kinds of prayer may be classified in terms of their purpose and content. Not all are indispensable in every act of worship, but an awareness of the various types of prayer helps us to maintain a proper balance in worship. There is also a sequence, a development from one kind of prayer to another, which has been found in the experience of the church to be psychologically and spiritually helpful and to fit naturally into the movement of Christian worship. The various forms are not wholly distinct from one another and tend to flow together. Perhaps we should regard them as ways of focusing the content of prayer. A list of the main types is as follows: the order in which they occur is variable. Here we follow roughly the sequence of an act of worship which reflects the shape of the eucharist:

(a) *Adoration.* Here, at the start of worship, the worshippers remind themselves of the presence of God, turn their attention to him, and enjoy his company, giving him the glory and the love that is his due. It thus sets the tone for the whole of worship: the focus is on God and not on ourselves, on his wonderful love and power and faithfulness, rather than on our own feelings.

(b) *Invocation.* This is a prayer asking for God's presence and help in our worship, so that it may be worship 'in Spirit and in truth', acceptable to God and enlightening his people.

(c) *Penitence.* Briefly, and early in the service, we think of ourselves in the light of the glory of God. Shame, penitence, sorrow are expressed for all the ways in which we have fallen short of God's glory and failed in his service. We have broken our relationship with him; now we seek his forgiveness to restore that relationship, a forgiveness which is declared at the end of the prayer.

(d) *Supplication.* Still focusing on ourselves, and before we turn back to God and the needs of the world, the prayers of penitence and confession are naturally followed by a prayer for some special graces and for God's help in living as disciples.

(e) *Illumination.* In the context of the Ministry of the Word, and usually before the sermon, or sometimes before the scripture readings, comes a prayer that our minds may be illuminated so that we can hear and understand what God is saying to us, and respond with alacrity and joy.

(f) *Intercession.* At the beginning of the response to the Word of God, in the prayers of intercession the needs of the church and the world are offered to God, often in very specific terms, with people in need being prayed for by name and the issues of the day and the concerns of the congregation being remembered in some orderly sequence.

(g) *Commemoration* of the Blessed Departed. In churches of the Roman Catholic and Orthodox traditions it is customary to pray for the dead, and to ask the saints and the Virgin Mary to pray for us. The Reformation rejected prayers for the dead as superstitious and too closely tied to the belief in Purgatory, and prayers for the intercession of the saints as impinging the sole mediatorship of Christ. Most Protestant churches now encourage a prayer which is a kind of extension of the prayer of thanksgiving (and may come at the end of that prayer rather than after the intercessions), giving thanks for the life of all the faithful departed, and asking that we may be strengthened to follow their example. It is desirable, however, that even those who feel continuing theological difficulties involved in prayers for the dead should be reminded that their prayers are joined with the prayers of all the saints in earth and heaven, and in that sense we pray with the saints in heaven and they presumably pray for us even if we feel it inappropriate to pray for them!

(h) *Thanksgiving.* This is, of course, the heart of the Great Prayer of the Lord's Supper, and in a very real sense thanksgiving, the praise and glorification of God, is the heart of all prayer. Thanksgiving is accordingly most properly one of the climaxes of a service, whether or not that service be a celebration of the Lord's Supper. It is placed at this point in the service because thanksgiving is the dominant note in the response to the declaration of God's truth and love in the Ministry of the Word. We give thanks for what God has done and will do – leading naturally to a commitment to his service.

(i) *Oblation.* In this prayer the whole Church, each individual Christian in fellowship with one another, with the Body of Christ in every land and every age, and with the Risen Lord, offers herself to the Father to be used for the work of the Kingdom. In the Lord's Supper this prayer commonly comes at the end of the Great Thanksgiving; in other services it may appropriately be allied to the dedication of the offerings of the people.[30]

Prayers may also be classified in terms of their structure, or form.

1. *Collect.* This highly developed and much loved form of prayer has a simple and clear structure, encourages succinctness, and is often of great beauty. Collects usually consist of five parts: (a) an address to God; (b) a relative clause indicating the activity or attribute of God on the basis of which we approach him; (c) the petition; (d) the purpose of the petition; (e) a doxology, and (f) the conclusion declaring the sole mediatorship of Christ. For example:

(a) Almighty and everlasting God,
(b) by whose Spirit the whole body of the Church is governed and sanctified;
(c) hear our prayer which we offer for all your faithful people;
(d) that each in his vocation and ministry may serve you in holiness and truth
(e) to the glory of your name;
(f) through our Lord and Saviour Jesus Christ.
(ASB collect for Good Friday)

Some of the parts may be omitted, but a collect is always terse and follows strict rules of rhythm and development. But all short prayers are not collects, and the collect is only one of the forms of prayer available. Collects have a significant place in worship, particularly at the start of worship (when people are collected), or as a summing up of prayers or of the theme of the Ministry of the Word. But public prayer should never be allowed to become great strings of collects, and nothing else.

2. *General Prayer.* This is a prayer the contents of which is general rather than specific. It is usually longer and more loosely constructed than a collect, but classic prayers of this sort such as the General Confession and

General Thanksgiving of the Book of Common Prayer, the Prayer for the Whole Estate of Christ's Church in the Church of Scotland *Book of Common Order*, 1940 (itself derived from a similar prayer in the *Book of Common Order* of 1564) and indeed the Lord's Prayer itself are splendid instances of English prose, dignified, lucid and musical. The danger with general prayers is that they tend to become verbose and lacking in unity unless very skilfully composed.

3. *Bidding Prayer*. In this form of prayer a list of subjects for prayers of thanksgiving or intercession is given out, either interspersed with versicles and responses or followed by a period of silence and a brief prayer summing up the prayers offered. Most modern liturgies suggest this form for the prayers of intercession. It has the virtues of being highly adaptable and combining extempore elements – or even spontaneous prayer from members of the congregation – and set forms within a clear and simple structure.

4. *Litany*. This is a responsive prayer, rather like a bidding prayer, but usually excluding any extempore or spontaneous elements. Many of the older litanies, such as that in the English *Book of Common Prayer* or those in the *Scottish Book of Common Prayer* (1929) are comprehensive and lengthy prayers, really amounting to a special office in their own right. Modern litanies, such as the two litanies of intercession in the Church of South India *Book of Common Worship*, are far shorter and almost indistinguishable from bidding prayers. The traditional Western litany was a long chain of very short phrases, going through Invocations, Deprecations, Obsecrations and Suffrages, with a concluding collect and often Kyries, the Lord's Prayer and other elements added. Many of the traditional litanies can still appropriately be used in whole or part on special occasions, but are too long and often too archaic to be used frequently.

5. *Acclamations*. Many modern liturgies have restored this ancient form of prayer said, sung or shouted out, by the people. In the eucharistic prayer of the Roman Mass the people say immediately after the words of institution:

> Christ has died,
> Christ is risen,
> Christ will come again.

or another brief acclamation.

Most other modern forms of worship also have acclamations for the people. In addition, the *Sanctus* and *Benedictus* are more properly classified as acclamations than as responses.

6. *Versicles and Responses*. These are short responsive prayers, sometimes used as an introduction to a prayer, sometimes forming a shorter litany in an office such as the *Book of Common Prayer* Matins, or the Office of Compline.

7. *Free Prayer*. For long, charismatic sects were the only groups that allowed members of the congregation to have a 'speaking role' in public

prayer, apart from set responses and prayers said together. It has recently, however, become common in most of the mainline denominations for opportunities to be given to members of the congregation to pray aloud, particularly in the prayers of intercession, confession and thanksgiving. The re-introduction of this primitive practice is often met with some initial but short-lived embarrassment, yet quickly it is accepted as a privilege which adds reality to prayer and greatly improves the sense of participation as well as blending surprisingly well with the more formal prayers.

All prayer has a shape, which may be more or less adequate. 'If in transacting business', wrote Calvin, 'some form must always be observed, which public decency and therefore humanity itself require us not to disregard, this ought specially to be observed in churches.'[31] This applies whether the prayers in question are an ancient or modern set form, composed for the occasion (or 'conceived' prayers, to use Isaac Watts's phrase), extempore (not prepared word for word before the service), or free, when members of the congregation may lead in prayer as they wish and the Spirit moves. The single most important reason why shape or form is important in public worship is that it is far easier for the members of the congregation to appropriate and make their own clear, well-structured prayer than to enter into a disjointed and loosely structured prayer of a kind which may be perfectly appropriate in private or small group prayers, but does not 'work well' in the necessarily rather more formal setting of public worship.

There is an emerging ecumenical consensus that there is a proper place in public worship for all these kinds of prayer, that they blend well together, and that this provides a more balanced experience of prayer for the congregation than the use of one kind alone. The great classical prayers, together with the best modern prayers, remind worshippers of the great heritage of Christian devotion, broaden and deepen their spiritual horizons, remind us that we pray in solidarity with the whole Church, and are so rich that they can be used again and again without exhausting their meaning. Extempore, composed or free prayer allows for the freedom of the Spirit, and recognizes that it is a particular congregation in a particular place at a particular time which is praying, and has specific matters to bring before the Lord. A sensible combination of these kinds of prayer in public worship shows that they complement and fertilize one another, and together enrich and enliven the congregation's experience.

(iv) *The Word beyond Words*
In ordinary conversation we often find it hard to pass beyond polite formalities to a real encounter with other people and significant conversation. Most people have the experience of coming away from a party feeling that everything has been at a superficial level; people have kept one another at a distance and never got beyond small-talk to matters of importance. We have already argued that conversational small-talk and polite formalities have important functions in social relations, as do their equivalents in prayer. Polite but superficial exchanges come alive if we

suddenly realise that the person who is asking 'How do you do?' is really interested in us, really cares for us, and wants an answer which is honest and detailed, not just a verbal push-off. And besides, such conversational formulae can be the preliminaries to a real encounter even when they themselves are not invested with much significance.

Set forms of prayer are not prayer-wheels or magic, earning merit by their repeated incantation. Rather, they prepare us for, and open us to, the possibility of a more profound, authentic, and disturbing encounter with God. This encounter, like all encounters, involves communication. But no language can be really adequate for communication between God and his people. Nevertheless, real communication in prayer can take place through set formulae, now 'come alive' and used with a fuller awareness of the richness of meaning, in coherent, balanced and rhythmic sentences, or in the 'inarticulate groans' in which the Spirit himself pleads for us, because we do not know how to pray as we ought (Romans 8:25 N.E.B.). True prayer is spontaneous, honest, personal, and from the heart; it is a kind of lovers' discourse. And lovers' conversation is not always very polished or grammatical or coherent. What matters is that it comes from the heart.

Lovers often communicate in silence, gazing into one another's eyes, or sitting quietly side by side, holding hands and simply enjoying each other's company with a quiet confidence and joy. In worship, too, there is an important place for silence, the quiet in which the congregation together can enjoy the company of God. Most people need some training in the use of silence in prayer, and some preparation for it, or the time of silence has an atmosphere of tenseness, the uneasy quiet of those who expect every moment to be filled with words, the children of a culture that is saturated with words, tired of words, and distrusts words. The silence in prayer should be the silence of lovers, enjoying one another; the silence in which one appropriates and adds to the spoken prayers; and, above all, the silence in which the worshipper stops chattering and listens to the Word, to the other party in the dialogue of prayer.

(v) *The Language of Prayer*
Christian prayer is properly in the common tongue, in ordinary speech. In this Christianity differs from many other religions which make an emphatic distinction between the sacred language used in worship, and often not understood by the people, and the profane language of everyday discourse. For Muslims, nothing can take the place of the Arabic Qu'ran. The tendency to use a special language for worship is widespread, and it is often felt that it is proper if the language of prayer is not understood. The obscurity and specialness of the language safeguards and emphasizes the mystery. At the time of Jesus a large number of Jews did not understand the Hebrew of the scriptures and the synagogue prayers. The Scriptures were read, first in Hebrew, and then a *Targum*, or paraphrase in Aramaic, the *lingua franca* of the Levant, so that the people got the gist of what had been read in the unknown sacred tongue.

It would appear that from the beginning Christians believed that prayer should not be in a strange and sacred language; ordinary language was the appropriate vehicle for the new and intimate kind of communication between God and man which had been made possible by Jesus. Early Christian prayer may have been commonly in Aramaic – so the survival of words such as *Abba* and *Maranatha* in the New Testament would suggest. And from early times it is clear that Christians used the Septuagint, the Greek translation of the Jewish scriptures, in preference to the Hebrew. The earliest Christian documents to have survived, including many prayers, are in *koine* Greek, the common, ordinary language of most of the Mediterranean basin. Time and again in the early centuries of the Church there is evidence to suggest that there were no doubts or hesitations about the need to translate the Bible and the liturgy into the language actually spoken by the people.

But there appears to be an inherent tendency towards archaism and contrived mystery in the language of prayer, and gradually this infected the Christian Church. By the ninth century some theologians were arguing that only the three languages of the superscription on the cross – Hebrew, Latin, and Greek – were legitimate for Christian worship. These three were recognized as 'sacred tongues'; the emerging vernaculars were profane and undignified. This argument was used against Cyril and Methodius, who translated the liturgy into Slavonic. Ironically their translation continued in use unchanged for many centuries after it, in its turn, had ceased any longer to be intelligible to the ordinary people; such is the conservatism of worship that the ordinary language of many centuries before becomes in course of time a sacred tongue, shrouding rather than communicating the mysteries of the faith.

The most obvious example of the perpetuation in worship and church usage of an archaic language which only a small and declining minority understand is the use of Latin in the West. Originally adopted as the language of the people (rather than Greek, which had become the language only of the scholarly elite), Latin spread throughout the Western Church, eclipsing almost all vernacular forms of worship, eventually becoming for most worshippers a mysterious and unintelligible sacred tongue. This, of course, drastically affected the kind of quality of participation possible for the laity in worship. A strange tongue excluded the people from meaningful participation in worship, as this letter from Bishop Stephen Gardiner to Cranmer in 1547 makes clear:

> For in times past ... the people in the church took small heed what the priests and the clerks did in the chancel, but only to stand up at the Gospel and kneel at the Sacring, or else every man was occupied himself severally in several prayer ... It was never meant that the people should indeed hear the Matins or hear the Mass, but be present there and pray themselves in silence.[32]

In 1661 Pope Alexander VII denounced those who 'in contempt of the regulations and practices of the Church have reached such pitch of madness as to have translated into French the Roman Missal'. Such an 'attempt to degrade the most sacred of rites by both debasing the majesty which the Latin tongue gives to the sacred rites and by exposing them to the eyes of the common people' was condemned in the strongest terms.[33]

As late as 1947 Pius XII argued for the retention of Latin: 'The use of the Latin language prevailing in a great part of the Church affords at once an imposing sign of unity and an effective safeguard against the corruption of true doctrine.'[34] But there are other, and better, ways in which worship may express the unity of the church; and even if the Latin liturgy expresses orthodox doctrine verbally it certainly does not effectively communicate this doctrine, and opens the way to all sorts of strange distortions and eccentric misunderstandings of the faith on the part of ordinary people. In addition the use of a special 'church language' such as Latin emphasizes the difference between clergy and laity, the elite who know and use the cultic language, and the majority who are mystified by it.

The Reformers, with rare unanimity, affirmed that the vernacular, the language of the people, should be the language of prayer, just as they stressed the central importance of putting the Bible, carefully translated, into the hands of the people. 'In the church', said Luther, 'we ought to speak as we use to do at home, the plain mother tongue, which every one is acquainted with.'[35] In this as in so much else, the Reformation strove to recover the emphases and practices of the early Church: the whole People of God should participate fully in worship and this is impossible without understanding. The unnecessary and artificial mystery of an unknown tongue must be removed if the true mystery of faith is to become accessible. The use of a dead language in worship is far more questionable than the ecstatic 'tongues' that St. Paul sought to control by insisting upon interpretation or translation. Cranmer was typical of the Reformers in believing that the move to the vernacular in worship was clearly in accordance with the will of God:

> ... God's will and commandment is, that when the people be
> gathered together ministers should use such language as the
> people may understand and take profit thereby, or else hold their
> peace. For as a harp or lute, if it give no certain sound, that men
> may know what is stricken, who can dance after it? For all the
> sound is in vain: so it is vain and profiteth nothing, saith
> Almighty God by St. Paul, if the priest speak to the people in a
> language which they know not ... For (St. Paul) speaketh by
> name expressly of praying, singing, lauding, and thanking of
> God, and of all other things which the priests say in the
> churches ... ; that whether the priests rehearse the wonderful
> works of God, or the great benefits of God unto mankind above
> all other creatures, or give thanks to God or make open
> confession of their faith, or humble confession of their sins, with
> earnest request of mercy and forgiveness, or make suit unto God
> for anything; then all the people, understanding what the priests
> say, might give their minds and voices with them, and say,
> *Amen* ... [35]

The move to the 'plain mother tongue' did not, of course, mean that the languages of liturgy and of Bible translation became conversational or marketplace vernacular. The Reformers believed in the use of clear, simple and dignified language, and their most notable productions such as the Anglican *Book of Common Prayer*, Luther's Bible, and the Authorized Version did much to shape and encourage the development of the vernacular.

But the norms of liturgical English laid down between 1550 and 1662 tended to ossify, while the 'plain mother tongue' developed vastly. This is as true of extempore prayer as of the authorized forms, for the language of the former was dominated by the Authorized Version and increasingly demonstrated the inbuilt conservatism of liturgical language. As a consequence a good deal of the language of prayer has become opaque and obscure to many worshippers, and sometimes conveys a very different message from that originally intended. Not many worshippers today realize that 'Prevent us, O Lord' in the familiar collect means 'Go before us, O Lord, to enable us' rather than 'Stop us from doing'. The schoolboy who, being asked what 'divers temptations' might be, thought for a moment and then replied, 'Might have been mermaids', was simply demonstrating an extreme case of the misunderstandings generated by the continued use of a cultic language which is now so different from the 'plain mother tongue' of everyday usage. Another complication is that some archaic English has acquired in the passage of time sexist overtones which are understood as excluding a goodly part of the congregation. Even some recent liturgies are replete with gratuitous sexism – 'fellow men' instead of 'fellows', 'all men' instead of 'everyone', and 'men' where 'people' is really meant. A rather different, but no less serious, problem arises from the continued use of the pronouns 'thee' and 'thou' in addressing God. In the sixteenth and seventeenth centuries these were in English, as their equivalents are still in French and German, the intimate terms used in family life or between close friends. 'You' was the more deferential form, used in addressing someone of great status and power. As late as the reign of Charles II a Quaker woman caused a public outcry by addressing the king as 'thou' – it was considered an impertinence. The Reformers' choice of 'thou' language for the address to God was indeed a daring affirmation of what one might call the '*Abba* principle' – that God is above all our Father, and we approach him as children coming to their Daddy. But since the seventeenth century 'thou' language, with all its complicated impedimenta of verbal inflections, has fallen out of common usage. Except in prayer, no one addresses anyone else as 'thou' and all the associated forms – thy and thine, and wilt and shalt and didst and so forth – have so fallen into disuse that those who lead in prayer frequently land themselves in comic and unnecessary confusions. But the real problem is this: the development of the English language and the entropy of liturgical English have led to an exact reversal of the original theologically well-grounded reason for choosing to address God as 'Thou'. Today some people argue that this preserves a sense of the glory and the otherness of God, of his transcendence, and discourages too easy familiarity with him. But it was precisely intimacy and familiarity which Jesus offered in teaching us to come to God as Abba, and the Reformers tried to safeguard by addressing God as 'thou'. Today sound theology and the Reformation insistence on the use in worship of the 'plain mother tongue' both demand that 'thou' with all its quaint linguistic accompaniments be set aside in Christian prayer.

It has to be admitted, however, that there is still a vast, intractable problem in finding an appropriate and satisfactory English style and idiom for public worship – always remembering that no language can possibly be adequate for speaking with God, or for speaking of God. Cranmer, the translators of the Authorized Version and the others who established the norms of 'church English' which were to last for centuries, were primarily translators who put faithfulness to the text, accuracy and clarity above all other considerations. But, like all educated people of the time, they had been immensely carefully trained in language and the art of writing. Their studies in classical literature and in rhetoric gave them a remarkable sense of rhythm, emphasis and style. They did not use the language of the market place, or conversational English or even slang, but a dignified, slightly formal, but above all clear language. They realized that there is a difference between the language of private prayer and that of public prayer; and that the language of prayer and the language of Bible translation are not the same. Nonetheless, the language of Christian prayer must be soaked in the language of the Bible so that the Bible provides a kind of grid on which worshippers locate the images, concepts, symbols and allusions in prayer.

The language of prayer is the language of a community, the Church, which cannot be understood without reference to the community's book, the Bible. The philosopher Wittgenstein is certainly right in saying that meaning depends on the context in which words are embedded, and in the case of the words of prayer, this means the household of faith and its book above all else.[37] The language is not esoteric to the community; it 'is not a special sort of language, but just ordinary language put to a particular use'.[38]

Prayer is not a self-contained language-game without impingement on ordinary language or the ability to communicate beyond the bounds of the church, although it can degenerate to this. But the language of prayer should help people to break out of the banal literalism of so much modern language and demonstrate the ability of language to penetrate to the depths and lift to the heights, to show the riches and the possibilities so often neglected in the modern world.

The language of prayer is replete with images, metaphors, symbols, and narrative, much, but not all of it, borrowed from Scripture. Some of this material is vibrant and living. Other images, metaphors and symbols seem dormant, or dead and incapable of resuscitation. It would seem that one of the functions of liturgy is to preserve a treasury of images and symbols from which each generation finds some that are meaningful. Sometimes an image that had seemed long dead is suddenly reborn and discovered to be relevant to a new situation. Other symbols seem inaccessible and unrecoverable, imbedded totally in ancient contexts alien to the modern experience. And to find fresh imagery which can act as a vehicle for Christian prayer and communicate at the depth of the old is no easy task. A good deal of modern liturgical work has been stripped of so much imagery, symbol and allusiveness that it seems bald, reflecting the banal literalism of so much modern language. Other attempts at a modern imagery do not wear well (for instance, the hymn 'God of concrete, God of steel, God of piston and of wheel', with its rather crude sanctification of modern industry) or are just plain ludicrous:

> Oh ye thirsty of every tribe
> Get your ticket for an aeroplane ride,
> Jesus our Savior is a-coming to reign
> And take you up to glory in His aeroplane.[39]

For really fine modern imagery we should turn, as D. L. Frost suggests, to the poets. He instances T. S. Eliot's fine section on the suffering, healing love of God, the wounded surgeon in *Four Quartets*. To that one might add R. S. Thomas's very different, but equally evocative and moving poem, 'The Musician'; the poems of Edwin Muir, and many others.

'What language shall I borrow, to praise thee, heavenly friend?' No language, ancient or modern, is really adequate for prayer, for converse with God. The finest of words 'the tongues of men and angels', we are reminded by St. Paul, are merely noisy gongs and clanging symbols if separated from love, for the language of prayer is the language of love, which is often simple and fragmentary, but comes from the heart and speaks to the heart. And because prayer language is words offered to God, we should strive to ensure that they are as fresh and authentic and lively and beautiful as may be.

NOTES

1. Cf. E. A. Nida, *Message and Mission*, New York 1960, pp. 48–61.
2. Cf. H. Kraemer, *The Christian Message in a non-Christian World*, London 1938, pp. 130–41, 299–307.
3. Cf. his famous essay, 'New Testament and Mythology' in *Kerygma and Myth*, ed. H. W. Bartsch, Eng. tr., London 1954, pp. 1–44. His hermeneutical concern is found throughout his writings and is discussed further in p. 66 and n. 17 below.
4. *The Use and Abuse of the Bible*, London 1976.
5. For meat offered to idols, see 1 Corinthians 8; 'korban' occurs in Mark 7:11 and for the issue of table fellowship at Antioch, see Galatians 2.
6. Cf. *Man's Religious Quest*, ed. Whitfield Foy, London 1978, pp. 176–80.
7. See J. I. H. McDonald, *Kerygma and Didache*, Cambridge 1980, pp.

12–16; cf. C. Westermann, *Basic Forms of Prophetic Speech*, Eng. tr., London 1967.

8. See McDonald, *op. cit.*, pp. 48ff.

9. Cf. M. Hengel, *Judaism and Hellenism* I, Eng. tr., London 1974, pp. 65–83.

10. See McDonald, *op. cit.*, ch. 2, esp. pp. 39–43.

11. *Ibid.*, p. 43 f. There has been much recent discussion of this matter.

12. Origen had a three-fold hermeneutical method: the literal or direct sense (e.g., Song of Songs is a love song or lyric); the deeper or indirect sense (the Song is an allegory of Christ and the Church); and the spiritual (the Song offers an image of heaven: the marriage of the Logos with the human soul). Cf. R. P. Lawson, *Origen: the Song of Songs, Commentary and Homilies*, London 1957, p. 8ff.; R. A. Greer, *Origen*, London 1979, p. 23f.

13. *Der sogenannte historische Jesus und der geschichtliche biblische Christus*, Leipzig 1892, p. 63; *The so-called Historical Jesus and the historic Christ*, Eng. tr., Philadelphia 1966.

14. Eng. tr., 1928.

15. Cf. *Church Dogmatics*, vol. 1, Part 1, Eng. tr., Edinburgh 1936, pp. 98–140.

16. D. Ritschl, *A Theology of Proclamation*, Richmond, Va. 1963, p. 29.

17. For an introduction to Bultmann's thinking and its relationship to Heidegger, cf. J. Macquarrie, *An Existentialist Theology*, London 1954.

18. *The Shaking of the Foundations*, London 1949, p. 161f.

19. Cf. *Theology of the World*, London 1969, pp. 107–15.

20. *The Word of God and the Word of Man*, London 1935, p. 100.

21. Cf. E. Best, *From Text to Sermon*, Edinburgh 1978, pp. 97–113.

22. *Op. cit.*, p. 113.

23. Cf. *A Kind of Folly*, Edinburgh 1976, p. 65.

24. *The Trouble with the Church*, Eng. tr., London 1966, pp. 63ff.

25. 'Sermon Forms', in *Journal of Theology for Southern Africa*, 36, 1981, p. 12.

26. Ian Pitt-Watson, *op. cit.*, p. 57.

27. H. W. Fowler and F. G. Fowler, *The King's English*, Oxford 1922, p. 1.

28. J. Bruner, *Toward a Theory of Instruction*, Cambridge, Mass. 1966, identifies three strategies of learning: the enactive, the iconic and the symbolic. Normally, intellectual development moves in a spiral through this sequence. To rush the learner too speedily to the symbolic may mean that he 'may not possess the imagery to fall back on when his symbolic transformations fail to achieve a goal in problem solving' (*op. cit.*, p. 49). Here we may find a rationale for the legitimate illustration: it anchors the thought in the iconic or concrete: the world of living people and events.

29. James Mackey, *Jesus – The Man and the Myth*, London 1979, p. 143. Cf. the discussion of the Lord's Prayer, pp. 142–144.

30. This list is somewhat indebted to that in Raymond Abba, *Principles of Christian Worship*, London 1957, pp. 87–96.

31. Cited in R. Abba, *op. cit.*, p. 107.
32. Cited in R. Abba, *op. cit.*, pp. 23–24.
33. *Bulla of Alexander VII*, 1661, in P. Guéranger, *Institutions Liturgiques*, Paris 1880, vol. 2, p. 118.
34. Pius XII, Encyclical *Mediator Dei*, 1947, London 1954, § 64.
35. Martin Luther, *Table Talk*, Eng. tr., W. Hazlitt, London 1895, p. 185.
36. C. S. Meyer, ed., *Cranmer's Selected Writings*, London 1961, pp. 90–91, cited in D. L. Frost, *The Language of Series Three*, Bramcote 1973, pp. 5–6.
37. See A. C. Thisclton, *Language, Liturgy and Meaning*, Bramcote 1976, p. 21.
38. W. D. Hudson, 'Some Remarks on Wittgenstein's Account of Religious Belief' in *Royal Institute of Philosophy Lectures* vol. 2, London 1969, p. 40, cited in Thiselton, *op. cit.*, p. 5.
39. Anon, *c.* 1935, in Donald Davie, ed., *The New Oxford Book of Christian Verse*, Oxford 1981, p. 292.

FURTHER READING

Karl Barth, *Prayer and Preaching*, London 1964.
E. Best, *From Text to Sermon*, Edinburgh 1978.
Colin Morris, *The Word and the Words*, London 1975.
E. A. Nida, *Message and Mission*, New York 1960.
D. Z. Phillips, *The Concept of Prayer*, London 1965.
Ian Pitt-Watson, *A Kind of Folly*, Edinburgh 1976.
A. C. Thiselton, *Language, Liturgy and Meaning*, Grove Liturgical Study No. 2, Bramcote 1975.

FOR DISCUSSION

1. Is there a difference between preaching and teaching? If so, what is it?
2. Is it more difficult to preach in the age of television and mass entertainment? Has the spoken word lost its power to communicate? Is there a future for preaching? If so, what characteristics must it have not only to survive but to fulfil its purpose?
3. What theological and social factors should influence the language of prayer?
4. Discuss the ways in which the Word is communicated in worship.

CHAPTER 6

BECOMING A CHRISTIAN

In most Churches, the rites of the Christian Initiation have traditionally been three: baptism, confirmation and admission to communion. Scholars agree that these rites are closely bound with one another, with the Gospel itself, with the life and purpose of the Church and with individual Christian identity. Yet, important as they are, they have been variously interpreted, variously combined and variously administered.[1]

In the Churches of today, the pattern of Christian Initiation is being questioned on theological and pastoral grounds. The crisis is a profound one. The Initiation theology we have inherited from the past is mostly *ex post facto* theology, that is, rationalisation of existing pastoral and liturgical practices seen in isolation both from the original motive forces that brought them into existence and from the subsequent historical factors that made them what they are. In discussing this sensitive and complex topic we must therefore begin with some basic historical considerations.

A—THE DEVELOPMENT OF CHRISTIAN INITIATION

Much has been written on the relation of early Christian initiatory practices to other known practices of the time such as the ritual washings of the Essene community of Qumran and the initiation rites of Hellenistic mystery religions. In spite of the long and acrimonious disputes of times past, the immediate roots of Christian initiation must be sought first and foremost in Judaism. Jesus himself underwent a baptism of water in the river Jordan. His baptism stood in obvious continuity with the ministry of John, who probably found his inspiration in Jewish proselyte baptism. The Jewish roots of the baptism of Jesus are particularly evident in the messianic and eschatological dimensions of the event as recounted by the evangelists. From the beginning, the Church was a baptising community. The continuity between the baptism of Jesus and the baptism of his followers has never been in doubt: as we know from Acts 8:16, early Christian baptism was a baptism 'in the Name of Jesus'.

For the pious Jew, the 'Name' was synonymous with 'divine power'. In turn, the concept of 'Name' was closely linked with the concept of 'God's

Word'. The relation of God to his People, the world and the eschaton is fundamental to the understanding of the Jewish religion. At the time of his choosing, God speaks to his People, sometimes through everyday events, sometimes through special happenings. His Word is a word of power. Every time the Word is uttered, God's purpose and design for the world is revealed more and more. The Word that 'saves' is the Word that 'sends out'. God's design for the world consists of making fallen mankind a People according to God's heart: creative and redemptive, the Word of God always makes a reality of what it says. It is an integral part of God's design that the divine Name (that is, Power) should be imprinted in the hearts of the hearers and imposed on the whole of their existence. When the Word is both spoken and heard, the hearers are made to identify with God's purpose and design and are consecrated to it as efficacious signs of God's coming universal reign. For the ancient Jews, effective belonging to the chosen People was a matter of collective and personal consecration to God's design for the world 'in the Name', that is through the imposition of God's own creative, redemptive and fulfilling power. The right to belong to God's People was a physical birthright and a matter of genealogies, but the power of the Name was not effectively imposed on anyone until circumcision, that is until the moment in which the covenant with the individual was struck and sealed.

In the New Covenant, belonging to the People of God is now the physical birthright of any human being. When, having heard the apostolic proclamation of the Gospel, the individual is ready to acknowledge Jesus as the Word made flesh, the power of the Word Incarnate who is of the same substance with the Father is imprinted in the heart of the believer and imposed on the whole of his existence. Made one with Jesus in the Body of the Saviour, the believer is identified with God's design for the world and consecrated to it as an efficacious sign of the coming kingdom of God. The action of God's Word on the believer is such that he is, at the same time, both 'saved' and 'sent out'. In baptism, the believer is caused to be reborn in the People of the New Covenant. Baptised 'in the Name of Jesus', he is made a son in the Son. Filled with the Spirit, he is admitted to the Eucharistic Community of those who, believing in God's purpose, are consecrated to it through God's power. To be baptised in the Name of Jesus is therefore synonymous with 'believing that Jesus is the Son of God', but in a context in which both 'belief' and 'knowledge' refer to the reality of an existence empowered by God towards the eschaton before they refer to mere intellectual adherence to any credal or doctrinal statement.[2]

Since the writing of the sixth chapter of the Epistle to the Romans, Christian baptism has increasingly been seen as a dying with Christ and a rising with him to life again. Much has been made of the points of similarity between Christian baptism and the initiatory ceremonies of Hellenistic mystery religions, and not enough of the fundamental difference between the two. In the initiatory ceremonies of mystery religions individual salvation was achieved by means of the physical performance of a rite the purpose of which was to bring the initiated to the full consciousness of his inherent divinity by means of the imparting of the true 'gnosis'. By mystically associating him with the god and his ordeal, the rite not only conferred on the neophyte an absolute guarantee of salvation, but actually bestowed on him the fullness of it in an anticipatory way. It was not a matter of magic, as many may be tempted to believe, but a simple matter of psychological awareness brought about by the 'gnosis' contained in the *rite*. In Christian initiation, on the contrary, what matters is neither the rite nor the gnosis, but the final result of the whole initiatory *process*: a Spirit-filled life in a Spirit-filled community consecrated to God's purpose.

In the New Testament, the initiatory *process* is constantly portrayed in this way: first comes the apostolic proclamation of the Word (obviously followed by conversion in the case of adults) and then come the water-bath and the outpouring of the Spirit, the latter not necessarily in that order. The initiated does not receive a personal guarantee of ultimate salvation, but an *arrabon*, a token, earnest and foretaste of it within a community of believers. Ultimate salvation will depend on the believer's continued obedience to God's will: for a Christian there is no final salvation apart from the eschatological Body and its purpose. No trace of such doctrines can be found in Hellenistic hermetic literature, though much of the latter is sometimes reflected in popular versions of Christian theology.

It would be a mistake to think of the New Testament data on Christian initiation as the raw material for immutable policies and practices. History teaches us a different lesson. In post-apostolic times, two different patterns of Christian initiation – each with its own theological emphases and nuances – slowly evolved by appropriating and indigenising the New Testament data in differing cultural milieux. The first of these patterns was geographically confined to East Syria (that is to that part of Syria which was outwith the Roman Empire) and to Armenia, as we learn from the *Acts of Thomas*, the *Didascalia Apostolorum* and the Armenian Order of Baptism (third to sixth century A.D.). The second pattern originated in Western Syria and the Graeco-Roman world, as we learn from Justin Martyr, Hippolytus and Tertullian.

Recent studies of the East Syrian-Armenian documents reveal that Christian initiation in those regions consisted originally of three different rites:

(a) a '*messianic anointing*' on the head known as 'marking' or 'signing';
(b) a *water-bath* with triple immersion in the Name of the Trinity;
(c) *admission to the eucharistic community* (an action which included the reception of Communion).

Later on, an anointing of the whole body for the purpose of 'healing' was added to the ceremonies before the water-bath, together with a solemn blessing of the oil to preface it all. Later on still a further anointing, this time with 'chrysm' (oil and balsam), was added as the conclusion of the specific rites. The later anointings responded to the common use of oil before a bath to loosen the dirt and after a bath to tone up and perfume the skin of the whole body. The final of these anointings was known as *hatma* or 'seal'.

The Western pattern of initiation, common to the Greek-speaking world, Rome and Carthage, contained initially six distinct moments:

(a) *formal instruction* in the faith, previous to any liturgical action;

(b) *formal renunciation* of Satan and his ways and *anointing* with the oil of exorcism;

(c) *water-bath* with triple immersion in the Name of the Trinity;

(d) *a further anointing*, explicitly associated by Tertullian with the reception of the fruits of the Spirit;

(e) *an imposition of hands with further anointing* in front of the gathered community which 'sealed' the initiated as members of the Body of Christ;

(f) the first *Kiss of Peace*, the first participation in the *Prayer of the Church* and the first admission to *Communion*.

With regard to this pattern, there is a discrepancy between Tertullian and Hippolytus. Tertullian knows of only one anointing after the water-bath, whilst Hippolytus mentions two. It would appear that the Hippolytan pattern of *two* anointings was characteristic of Rome and Milan, whilst the pattern of Tertullian, with *one* anointing, was to continue as characteristic of the rest of the Latin world until the enforced Romanisation of the latter. In either version of the Western pattern, the various elements are so organised as to make of the water-bath the *fulchrum* of the whole process and of the anointing or anointings its *climax*.

It would be a mistake to see these two patterns as polemically opposed the one to the other: they are both fruits of a natural growth, the seed of which is already in the New Testament. The East-Syrian-Armenian pattern is more 'Jewish' and archaic (a point generally true of the East Syrian Rites as a whole). It is more 'consecratory' than 'initiatory'. Its more immediate sources are to be found in the baptismal imagery of the third chapter of the Gospel of John and in the eschatological-messianic themes of the Gospels of Mark and Matthew. The Graeco-Latin pattern is 'later' in feel, more elaborate and more finely articulated. It is more 'initiatory' than 'consecratory' and, at least from the fourth century onwards, it leans more and more towards the baptismal imagery of the sixth chapter of the Epistle to the Romans.[3]

By the end of the fourth century, the two different patterns of initiation were well and truly established. A new problem confronted the Church then: that of making the traditional liturgical signs relevant to the lives of the newly converted masses. The new problem was solved in different ways in the different parts of the Christian world. So Cyril of Jerusalem, taking advantage of his privileged position on the scene where the life, death and resurrection of Christ took place, strives to show the vividness of Christ's offering in the liturgical signs. More than a little embarrassed by the tendency of a half-converted Empire to identify with Christ's Kingdom, John Chrysostom points to the reality of the past-made-present in the struggle of re-living the Lord's life, death and resurrection in the day-to-day conflict with the radical challenges which the secular city provides. Living at the edges of a rapidly decaying Western Empire, Ambrose of Milan points to the transformation of all creation constantly brought about by God in Christ: the cleansing water, the perfumed oil, the white-robed family of the faithful are for him the visible and tangible beginning of a new and incorruptible world to come. Member of a small and still persecuted minority, Theodore of Mopsuestia interprets the baptismal liturgy as a message of hope and the repository of the eschatological reality already begun and yet to be revealed. Not surprisingly, in explaining the East Syrian pattern of initiation Theodore insists on the role of the Christian community in the coming about of the promised future and on the total commitment of the individual to God's plan for the world.[4]

How successful or otherwise the great mystagogues of the time turned out to be in their struggle to make the liturgical signs relevant in the lives of the believers can be gathered from the actual reaction of the half-converted masses. Many, perhaps the majority, had become Christians for no more than appearance sake. Of those who had come to believe, the greater number went on as a rule to be more concerned about their own personal salvation than working for the coming of the Kingdom: for the majority, baptism was the known ritual way to obtain remission of sins. As in their opinion such remission was not guaranteed by any other means, it made sense for the many to delay the reception of baptism until the moment of death. The fact that some, like the Emperor Valentinian, occasionally miscalculated did not stop this delaying policy. In the view of the many, the Church had no other purpose than procuring by means of appropriate rites and ceremonies the individual salvation of all. The eschatological perspective was lost. Utilising in his own way the doctrines of Ambrose, Augustine tried to redress the balance and proposed that baptism should be administered as early as possible in the life of the individual. Baptism – he argued – was the way God himself had appointed to deal not so much with the reality of 'sins' as with the reality of 'original sin': should there be no baptism, there would be no regeneration and therefore no salvation. With minor additions and variations, it is Augustine's theology we have inherited in the Western Churches: the theology of a *rite* and not the theology of a *process*.

With the willing cooperation of the State, it did not take long for the Church to 'christianise' the known world of the West. In apostolic times, infants may or may not have been baptised. In the age of Hippolytus, infants were certainly being baptised, but in numbers sufficiently small for infant baptism to be considered the exception rather than the rule. The change from adult to infant baptism took in fact a long time. It was so gradual that the Church failed to notice it and continued to baptise infants with a rite originally devised to baptise fully responsible adults. Given Augustine's rationalisation of baptism, it was hardly surprising that the Church continued blissfully in her customary liturgical ways even after the historical situation that had caused those liturgical ways had long ceased to apply. The Church had now a cast-iron justification for doing nothing. Since baptism was seen as the way appointed by God himself to wash away original sin and only incidentally any other sin the individual might have committed, there could hardly be any cause for the upsetting experience of change. The actual wording of the service was no obstacle, since many no longer understood Latin and therefore did not expect to understand the service. The one change that took place, as we learn from the *Ordo Romanus XVIII*, was that the Church gave up the pretence of asking the infants to renounce Satan and believe in Christ and commanded that the infants' parents should be asked instead. Infant baptism may or may not be a legitimate practice, but infant baptism and adult baptism cannot possibly be one and the same thing.

From the point of view of the administration of the rites of initiation, the effect of the shift from adult to infant baptism turned out to be different in the two halves of the former Roman Empire. In the East, the whole of initiation came to be administered to infants. Inevitably, the number of baptisms was such that the administration of the whole rite was left to the local presbyter rather than to the bishop as had been customary before. In the West, the process of initiation was split in two. How and why the split came about can only be guessed at. We have already noted that in Rome and Milan, under the influence of Hippolytus, two different anointings were administered after the water-bath. It would appear that the local presbyter was encouraged to perform the first part of the total service, until and excluding the final 'sealing' which was then reserved for the bishop and left to be performed at a later date. It would appear that the rest of Europe, under the influence of Tertullian, knew only of one anointing after the water-bath and that initially their baptismal policy was identical with that of the East. As part and parcel of the enforced romanisation and standardisation of practices, the rest of Europe seems to have been compelled, at a later date, to administer *two* anointings after the manner of Hippolytus, and to accept the Roman splitting of the initiation Rites. This was not, of course, done without protest. In the rest of Europe, therefore, as a sign of unwilling obedience, the Northern Churches started to administer the second anointing a whole week after the administration of what was for them the *complete* process of initiation. Slowly, the gap between the two anointings grew to a gap of months and then whole years. As many bishops could not cope with the numbers of 'confirmations' and others simply did not care, the same kind of gap slowly occurred in Italy as well. It was not only that some of the bishops were slack in their duties to 'confirm': many of the candidates did not bother to turn up even when the bishop came. The result of all this was of course utter chaos, so that in 1281 Archbishop Peckham of Canterbury commanded that no person should be admitted to Communion until such time as he or she had been episcopally confirmed. The rest of the Church followed suit, standardising the practice in theory if not in actual life. With the theoretical standardisation of practices came the inevitable legitimation of *ex post facto* theology which reached its final and finest expression in Thomas

Aquinas: sacraments are the God-given ways of supplying grace for the crucial moments of change in the life of the individual. In initiation, there was a need for three distinct 'increases' of grace: there were therefore three distinct 'sacraments of initiation', namely baptism, confirmation and communion.

We should not forget that for mediaeval Christianity, to be a Christian and to be a citizen were one and the same thing. In these circumstances, the celebration of birth in the secular city was one and the same thing as the celebration of birth in the Church. In the same way, confirmation was at one and the same time the celebration of Christian and civil maturity. Communion was then seen as a consequence of one's responsible acceptance of adult duties in the Church and as a spiritual aid to one's duties in both the secular and religious sphere. The *ex post facto* theology of the time could do no other than see the three sacraments of initiation, together with the other sacraments, as liturgical actions instituted by Christ himself for the purpose of physically or morally 'causing' the grace needed by the individual at different times in his or her personal development within Church-Society as a whole.

At the Reformation, the mediaeval idea that only liturgical actions specifically instituted by Christ could properly be called 'sacraments' was accepted without question. Since Scripture could hardly provide a specific 'moment of institution' for confirmation, its sacramental status was gravely jeopardised in the eyes of the Reformers. Though unwilling to grant confirmation the status of a sacrament, Calvin saw the pastoral advantage of the practice and recommended that young people who had been baptised as infants should be given the opportunity to respond to the Word and make a conscious, public decision for Christ.

The initiation practice of the sixteenth century Churches has remained essentially the same until modern times. The first major change was introduced when Pius X allowed Roman Catholic children to receive Communion before they were confirmed. In more recent times, the Episcopal Church in the USA adopted a policy very similar to that of the Oriental Churches, with the added possibility of an optional and repeatable service of 'Affirmation' in later years.[5] The last notable change was the adoption by the Church of South India and the Roman Catholic Church of adult baptism as the implied norm.

B—THE LEGACY OF THE PAST

Daniel Stevick sums up the historical development of Christian initiation thus:

> It is striking how often in this process of adaptation the forms of Christian Initiation were shaped by extrinsic forces. Augustine derived his theology from current Church custom and defended it by a critical misreading of St. Paul. St. Thomas' doctrine of confirmation reflected the practice of confirming at a moment in

life subsequent to baptism. The Roman view that the bishop should retain the right to confirm prevailed in the West by a process that had little to do with the merit of the issue ... The rites of the sixteen century Reformation and Counter-Reformation were shaped without the historical data as to how initiatory practice had developed. Pragmatic, disciplinary and polemic considerations have dominated the history of Christian Initiation. Few new departures have stemmed from a fresh insight into the meaning of becoming a Christian.[6]

The legacy of such a confused past is a number of difficult and unresolved questions. Is confirmation a sacrament or not? If it is a sacrament, is it distinct from baptism, or are baptism and confirmation one sacrament celebrated in two distinct acts? When is the precise moment of the reception of the Spirit: at some point in baptism or in confirmation? Questions such as these used to be a great source of controversy. In a sense they still are, though in the light of our present knowledge we should indeed know better.

Our understanding of sacramental theology is now undergoing enormous changes. Whatever we might mean by 'sacrament', the history of Christian initiation should make it quite clear that baptism and confirmation as practised today belong together and that it is unjustified to speak of two sacraments. No Christian would deny that baptism is related to salvation. Salvation has two different aspects, one negative and one positive. We are saved *from* sin and alienation from God (the *negative* aspect). We are saved *for* God, that we might become his People and the instrument for the coming of his kingdom (the *positive* aspect). Immersion in the water that drowns, cleanses and gives life is a highly dramatic way of pointing to the 'negative' aspect of salvation (salvation 'from'). The laying-on of hands, with or without anointing, is a most apt way of pointing to the consecration to God's purpose within the community of the chosen (salvation 'for'). The two clearly belong together. There should be no question of two different sacraments, but it is up to the Church to decide, since the two aspects of salvation cannot be disentangled the one from the other, whether baptism alone is sufficient or not. The decision would remain a theological one, but that is not to say that the driving forces behind that decision would be other than pastoral and pragmatic. At the same time, we should remember that the Holy Spirit acts on the individual long before the individual comes to faith, let alone to baptism or confirmation, and that the Spirit will continue to act on that same individual long after he or she has been confirmed. Baptism and confirmation are so to speak two 'focus-moments' of a continuous process. In other words, in biblical and theological language an individual 'receives' the Spirit every time the Spirit acts, but some moments are more significant than others.

Is baptism of infants objectionable or not? If it is objectionable, is it so on theological or pastoral grounds, or both? How far are baptism of infants and adult baptism one and the same thing? Questions such as these depend on our answer to the more fundamental question of what a sacrament is. If we abandon the unnecessarily restrictive definition of Peter Lombard and subsequent mediaeval speculation, we should surely be free to maintain that true sacramentality resides in the Word's unique capacity to make a reality of what it says, and that a sacrament exists wherever the Word is uttered in any perceivable form. In his Baptismal Sermon of 1521, Luther taught that when we speak of baptism we speak not of a *rite*, but of the *whole life* of the baptised within the community of faith. From E. Schillebeeckx we learn that in a sacrament there always is a call from the Word, a call which both requires and empowers a human answer whilst at the same time giving a clear example of the type of answer required. Since, as Luther taught, we are not speaking of a moment in time, but rather of a whole life in which there are significant moments, we cannot restrict either the call or the answer to the moment of the administration of the rite. For the same reason, we cannot deny the supreme significance of the moment of the administration of the rite in terms of God's call and of our expected response to it. Many Churches today find it difficult to admit the obvious, namely that the mediaeval idea that the faith and promises of parents and god-parents can in some way make up for the infant's inability to respond is no more than a worthless juridical fiction. Since the baptism of infants can in no way be said to imply the infant's profession of faith, it should be plain to anyone that baptism of infants and adult baptism are not at all one and the same thing. That is not to say, of course, that the baptism of infants is theologically unacceptable. Initiation is about incorporation into the People of the New Covenant. That incorporation involves both a call from God and a response from man. There is nothing theologically unacceptable in the possibility of different liturgical timings for the different elements. The Word makes a reality of what it says, so there can be no objection to having the Word proclaimed over an infant, on the understanding that that infant, in the necessary process of growth and development, will be led and empowered by God, through life in the community of faith, to respond to God in the appropriate way whether or not that response is publicly celebrated in a liturgical action. There can be no theological objection to the public and liturgical celebration of that response either, when the time for it comes. On the other hand, children of Christian parents are born within the covenant. There should therefore be no objection to the possibility that the whole of the initiation rites should be reserved for later years in the case of children who by right of birth already belong to the People of God. The only possible objection would come from Augustine's rationale for the baptism of infants, but, as we know, that rationale was never accepted by any Church to the exclusion of any other possible explanation. Whatever decision is made should be on pragmatic and pastoral grounds, and not on theological ones. The real question is whether or not the Church has the right to make such decisions: the very history of Christian initiation shows that the Church obviously always thought that it had.

Should children of non-practising parents be admitted to baptism or not? Since at least the ninth century, as the *Ordo Romanus XVIII* testifies,

Western Christendom has requested parents and later, god-parents, to make promises on behalf of the infants. The right and duty to belong to the People of God is now, in the New Covenant, the right and duty of all who come into this world. Whether or not it is liturgically and sacramentally celebrated, the same call is made by the Word to every human being, the same power offered, and the same answer required. The whole point about the baptism of infants is a pragmatic and pastoral one, that is a consideration of their growth and development within a Body to which they belong. There would be no point in admitting infants to a Body in which they would have no opportunity to grow. On the other hand, should the parents relinquish their right and allow the child to grow within the Church though they, the parents themselves, were not prepared to do the same, what could be the possible theological, pragmatic or pastoral objection? A realistic prospect of growing in the Christian community should be the deciding factor, and not the fact that the parents may or may not be practising Christians. A sense of belonging is the only prerequisite for an infant's learning and growth. From this point of view, there would be little point in an infant belonging to a community within which he or she will never have a chance to grow. On the other hand, an infant will never grow in a community within which he or she does not belong. In this respect we should not dramatise: the difference between a child who is baptised and a child who is not is not the difference between a child who is saved and a child who is damned for eternity. Augustine thought so, but we are under no obligation to think likewise.

Can baptism be repeated or not? The mainstream Churches have been constant in their belief that baptism is first and foremost the action of God. On this basis they have always maintained that baptism cannot be repeated. Doubting the validity of a properly administered baptism would be tantamount to doubting the validity of the action of God: an action which, by its very nature, must of necessity be once and for all. However, it cannot be emphasised enough that becoming a Christian is a *process* of which the liturgical celebration of the sacrament is the *pivotal point*: the action of God on us both antedates and postdates the liturgical celebration, as well as being co-extensive with it. The action of God on us (before, during and after the celebration of the sacrament) consists of a call which empowers and demands the answer of our identification with God's plan of salvation and our consecration to it. What is said of the process as a whole can be said of the sacrament, but only in so far as the sacrament is the pivotal point of the process itself: as we shall see, it is in this way that we should see the relation of baptism to justification if we are to avoid the accusation of magic and superstition. Baptism is the moment in which the ever efficacious Word of God is visibly proclaimed to the individual. It is the moment in which the grace of God is visibly bestowed upon the neophyte, the moment in which he or she is visibly consecrated to God's plan of salvation and therefore incorporated into the visible Body which exists for the proclamation of the coming reign of God. Doubts about the *validity* of this action of God are therefore totally out of the question. The only possible doubts in these circumstances are not about the action of

God, but about the *response* of the individual. Mainstream Churches are therefore unanimous in teaching that, when an adult whose conversion is insincere is validly baptised, there is no need to celebrate his or her subsequent true conversion within a sacramental and liturgical act. It is precisely in this context that the whole doctrine of the indelibility of baptism was developed. Since we are speaking of a process and not of an instant in time, all that is needed in this case is the true conversion of the individual. No one validly baptised as an adult has therefore the right to ask for rebaptism, since the action of God is already and visibly complete. Must the same be said of necessity of a person who has been validly baptised as an infant? It would be wrong to ask for rebaptism on the grounds that one's baptism as an infant was *invalid*. It would be wrong to suggest that a service of 'affirmation' (which by its very nature could be repeated as many times as might be thought to be pastorally advisable) would in fact do *less* than was necessary to supply what was lacking to the original baptismal rite. Some might however argue that there is a crucial difference between the baptism of an adult and the baptism of an infant, not from the point of view of the action of God, but from the point of view of the response of the baptised: in the case of adult baptism, the individual is given a chance to make God's call coincide with his or her response, however insufficient or even insincere that response might be. *Providing no doubt was cast on the validity of God's call in one's baptism as an infant*, one might perhaps argue that the possibility of a liturgical act in which God's call was publicly repeated so that it might clearly coincide with the human response should not be discounted outright. Such an act would not *add* to the original baptism, but neither would it *detract* from it, and some pastoral advantage might conceivably be derived from the practice. However, should theological agreement be reached on this point, the individual Church would still have to contend with different but equally pressing pastoral considerations. For instance, such practice might be thought inadvisable in the circumstances, as it might – in the mind of many – lead to a serious misunderstanding of the nature of the sacrament. It would be perfectly within the competence of the Church so to decree, on the grounds that the good of the individual must be subordinate to the good of the whole.

Are baptism and confirmation rites of passage, or not? There is no doubt that pastoral experience suggests that rites of passage respond to a felt need of practising and non-practising Christians alike. All mainstream Churches are the heirs of that particular mediaeval adaptation of the understanding of baptism to imply also secular citizenship: the rite which conferred personhood in the Church also brought one into civil society and made one subject to its laws: as we have already noted, the universal Church was then synonymous with the universal political order. People are born, grow old and die. This passage through life has still for many today a distinctly religious dimension, though not all are prepared to adhere to a Christian creed. This religious dimension of life is something one can and indeed should celebrate. Should this dimension be celebrated by indiscriminate baptism? We have already answered in the negative to this question. The modern West is 'post-Constantinian': for more and more, Christianity is a religion of choice rather than a religion of growth. From the point of view of sociology, initiation is a 'border rite' marking the boundary between Church and non-Church. A change in the relationship between Church and society is bound to change the sense of appropriateness of initiation rites. Birth and maturity could and should still be celebrated, but it would be futile even for national Churches to maintain that baptism and/or confirmation can continue to be rites of passage in exactly the same sense as they used to be. One wonders where the forces for the conservation of the status quo really lie: in the inner core of the Churches or in the non-committed fringe? In either case there seems to be at large a great deal of suspect collusion and make-belief. When people of the non-committed fringe bring their children to be baptised, is it indeed baptism they are asking for, or some kind of passage rite? And yet, what else could they be asking for, since baptism is the only Christian rite of passage they know? Some Churches today offer a Service of Thanksgiving and Dedication for precisely such cases. One cannot help feeling, however, that at least for the moment the solution is an unsatisfactory one, since there is too much confusion and uncertainty in this respect both in the mind of the Churches and in the mind of parents.

The most serious legacy of the past on the subject of Christian initiation is perhaps the still unresolved problem of the relation of justification to the sacrament of baptism. Theologians of all denominations have tended to shy away from the problem in spite of the existence of Anabaptism, Quakerism and the Salvation Army. Is a believer justified by faith or by baptism? And if one is justified by faith, how can baptism be said to be necessary to salvation? The theology we have inherited from the past teaches us that there are three kinds of baptism, easily remembered by the Latin expression *baptisma fluminis, flaminis, sanguinis*: baptism of water, baptism of desire and baptism of blood. If a catechumen died before he or she had a chance to be baptised, there has never been any doubt in the Church as to his or her ultimate salvation just because the baptism of water had not been administered. In such cases, the Church taught that the catechumen had been baptised by baptism of desire. Now, whatever baptism of desire may be, it certainly is not baptism in the accepted sense. There was never any doubt either about the ultimate salvation of anyone, catechumen or not, who had actually been martyred for the faith. In such cases the Church taught that the martyr had been baptised by baptism of blood. Again, whatever may be said of baptism of blood, it certainly cannot be said that it is baptism in the accepted sense. In the case of a coerced insincere baptism, the Church has always taught, as we have already seen, that all that is needed in those circumstances is a sincere private conversion. It would therefore appear that when a truly converted person receives baptism, he or she is already saved by justification by faith and that baptism and justification would coincide chronologically only in the unlikely case of somebody coming to faith at the very moment in which the water is poured and the formula pronounced, that is by chance and not by virtue of the rite. We seem to be in a terrible dilemma: either salvation is through justification by faith and the Church was wrong in saying that baptism was necessary to salvation, or justification is by baptism and the Church was wrong in admitting the possibility of baptism of blood, the possibility of baptism of desire and the non-necessity of rebaptism in the case of insincere conversions. The dilemma, of course, is only an apparent one and the problem is successfully solved once one places the rite within the larger context of the process of becoming a Christian. Had many of the concepts peculiar to the ancient mystery religions not survived in Christendom, the apparent dilemma would not have arisen in the first place. The dilemma could never have arisen even in the light of mediaeval theology. The Schoolmen themselves taught without a shadow of doubt that God's call to salvation cannot be separated from God's call to become a visible instrument of God's grace in the community of believers. Since baptism was seen as the sacramental gate to the life of the Church, justification without the desire of baptism would have been totally unthinkable, not least because of what they saw as a flagrant violation of Christ's command in Matthew 28:18–20.

C—THE SHAPE OF THINGS TO COME

In his book entitled *Christian Initiation* Hugh M. Riley argues that the fundamental principle of any existing Christian community is that God truly addresses himself to us here and now, and that we, in view of this address of God, can answer his call in the individual circumstances of our actual lives. The central role of the liturgy is that of service to the mystery of God's encounter with his people. It is to guide them in their individual encounter with God, and to do so it must avail itself with the highest possible degree of awareness of all available means to give us the best opportunity to hear the call of God and to respond to it. God has chosen to reveal himself and to address us in many ways. Within the Church, he addresses us through the medium of certain signs which, we believe, derive their meaning and efficacy from the life, death and resurrection of Christ who is himself the primary mystery and sign of our encounter with God. These chosen signs, we believe, are the words and actions which comprise our worship. In the light of all this, our attitude to the liturgy must be one of enlightened conservatism. This demands creative and imaginative attention being paid to the fact that the signs of any given liturgy must be made meaningful to the individuals participating in it. Throughout the history of the Church we are confronted with a liturgy of initiation which is fundamentally the same, and yet, in view of the need of the particular participants and their worlds, each individual liturgy varies in genius and scope. The one common denominator apart from the fundamental signs – Riley concludes – is the necessity to make salvation history a real presence in the lives of the people.[7].

The time has now come for the Churches to make new departures and to gain fresh insights if the Word is to have free course and heal the nations. In the first place, all Churches – especially the powerful national and supra-national ones – must truly accept the fact that in the modern West Christianity is indeed becoming more and more a religion of choice and less and less a religion of growth. Pretending otherwise will not serve. Doing nothing about it will serve even less. In the second place, we must re-think our theology in the light of all we have discovered or re-discovered so far and strive to apply it within the context of today. In this hard and painful process we may well find that we have to rid ourselves of much unthinking conservatism. In particular, we must come to a viable decision on Christian initiation policy, as the status quo will certainly not do. In making this decision we will have to avail ourselves of all possible means including recent discoveries in psychology, sociology, education and other related fields, however partial and limited these discoveries might still be.

In broad outline, we have a choice of three possible decisions. We may decide to reserve the whole of initiation to adults in a single rite involving the three fundamental elements we read about in the Scriptures: proclamation of the Word, water-bath and reception of the Spirit. As we learn from the history of Christian initiation, we would have more than a certain latitude in the arranging of these three fundamental points. But the pattern of initiation of adults only cannot itself be said to be in tune with the real needs of today. Without added correctives it would at best do nothing to give our children a real chance to adapt to the forms of behaviour, the norms and the values of a truly mature Christian environment. Were we to choose this first possibility, the necessary corrective would have to be the reinstitution of something very akin to the ancient catechumenate, as modern Roman Catholic documents seem to advocate in the face of obstinate resistance from practically every quarter. The introduction of this corrective would not be without its major traumas. It would involve not only a major psychological change, but also a complete reappraisal of the legislation and of the very structures and self-understanding of the Church. The real root of the problem facing us is not in any one initiation policy, but in the moribund state of the local churches. Aidan Kavanagh, himself an advocate of the reinstitution of the catechumenate, writes:

> To begin a catechumenate is a fateful step, and thus an
> intimidating one for many. It is to set changes in motion on
> every level throughout the parish and to expose the real health in
> faith of the local church for all to see.

Kavanagh argues that there is no dearth of 'catechumenates' either in the Church or civil society, but none of these are in direct contact with the structures of Christian initiation. Re-introducing the catechumenate would not be as revolutionary a step as it might at first appear to be. In his opinion, the problem lies somewhere else:

> If there is really little or nothing into which catechumens can be
> initiated, it would be better for the local church not to have a
> catechumenate. The problem is in a sense self-solving, for such a

church will not be vigorous enough to generate much evangelical appeal in the first place. The circle is as closed as it is fatal.

Warning us against the dangers of a rigidly axiomatic approach which would continue to block renewal whilst going through the motions of reform, Kavanagh concludes that 'it is for the local church to put itself into the hands of the gospel and Christ's Spirit rather than under the safer and more manageable tutelage of conventions and programs'.[8]

A second possible choice would be that of giving the whole of initiation to infants. Such policy would certainly allow our children to grow and learn within a group to which they could feel they belonged. Yet, by itself, this policy would not suffice. In the first place, much would depend on the health of the local community of faith. In the modern situation, a child would need not only a sense of belonging, but also the possibility to learn and grow within a tightly knit, loving, supporting community of mature Christians. If there were little or nothing more to grow into than a habit of Sunday worship, this policy would ultimately fail. All the strictures applied by Aidan Kavanagh to some of the local churches would apply here with a vengeance. Moreover, there would be an added and equally formidable problem. The policy of full initiation of children would not work unless the local church started discriminating between the fringe and the inner core, the drivers and the passengers. Some kind of discrimination would become necessary. Children of parents who would be prepared to allow them to grow within the community of faith would have to be disentangled from children whose parents asked only for some kind of rite of passage vaguely connected with Christianity, full initiation into the Church being granted only to the former category. Moreover, new structures would have to be introduced to cater for children whose parents would not themselves be prepared to take full part in the life of the Church. These structures would have to be flexible enough to withstand the present state of mobility of the population. Effective methods of god-parenting would have to be taught and suitable candidates for this new role would have to be identified among the local congregation. Altogether, the implementation of this choice of policy would prove no less daunting a prospect than the re-introduction of the catechumenate.

A third possible choice of policy would be the splitting of initiation into two different stages. The great advantage of this policy, and at the same time its greatest danger, would be that for many Churches this step would in fact mean the continuation of much of the status quo. In choosing this policy, the Church would run a very real danger of having the local congregations continue blissfully in their old ways no matter who issued the new directives: Church Assemblies, General Synods or even Ecumenical Councils. In the best of all possible worlds, the Church would still have to discriminate more than it has done so far, and still avoid causing unnecessary offence. Children would still have to be granted a greater sense of belonging than they have been able to experience to date. The congregations would still have to try and provide a more mature environment for our children to grow in and more occasions to meet than for worship designed for adults. New structures would still have to be introduced to relate the children's parents, practising or otherwise, with the congregation at large. Such changes would meet with great resistance.

Whichever policy we choose, painful change awaits us. Let it be the painful but joyous change of a true *metanoia*. Whichever way we turn, our choice is fraught with dangers. Living with danger should be quite in character with the expectations of those who profess to follow the One who came not to bring peace, but the sword and yet promised a Comforter to lead us into all truth. We must all learn the lesson from the past in faithfulness to its legacy. We must be prepared to change our understanding of the Church and its very structures that we might be better tools for the spreading of the kingdom. We must be prepared for great changes in the life of our congregations. On the future of Christian initiation will depend at least in part the future of the Church.

NOTES

1. Stevick D., *Holy Baptism*, Supplement to Prayer Book Studies 26, New York 1973, p. 9.
2. Cf. Bouyer L., *Eucharist: Theology and Spirituality of the Eucharistic Prayer*, Notre Dame 1968, pp. 30–40.
3. Cf. Kavanagh A., *The Shape of Baptism*, New York 1978, pp. 3–78.
4. Cf. Riley H. M., *Christian Initiation: A Comparative Study of the Interpretation of the Baptismal Liturgy in the Mystagogical Writings of Cyril of Jerusalem, John Chrysostom, Theodore of Mopsuestia, and Ambrose of Milan*, Washington D.C. 1974, pp. 452–55.
5. Cf. Stevick D., *op. cit.*, pp. 22–35.
6. *Ibidem*, pp. 34–35.
7. Cf Riley H. M., *loc. cit.*
8. Kavanagh A., *op. cit.*, p. 169.

FURTHER READING

Kretschmar G., *Recent Research on Christian Initiation*, in: Studia Liturgica 12:2/3 (1977), pp. 87–103.
Fisher J. D. C., *Christian Initiation: Baptism in the Medieval West*, SPCK, London 1965.
Fisher J. D. C., *Christian Initiation: The Reformation Period*, London 1970.

FOR DISCUSSION

1. In what ways should patterns of Christian initiation be affected by the modern post-Christendom situation?
2. Is it possible to have a rite of confirmation or admission to communion which does not suggest an incompleteness in baptism?
3. What is the connection between baptism and faith?

CHAPTER 7

THE MEAL FOR THE LIFE OF THE WORLD

A—THE MEAL IN THE UPPER ROOM

It all began when Jesus, on the evening of his arrest, gathered his disciples together for a meal in an upper room in the city of Jerusalem. The earliest written account of that meal which we possess is in Paul's First Letter to the Corinthians, chapter 11, verses 23–36. Here Paul speaks of having given the Corinthians, on his first arrival the tradition, the story, of this meal, which he had himself earlier received from the Lord. Paul was first in Corinth about the year 51, and he must have received this account at the time of his conversion. Thus we have here a story which goes back to the very early days of the Church, indicating a conviction that the church's obedient following of the command and example of the Lord in taking the bread and the cup was vital to its life and worship and witness.[1] Paul was insisting that the Church's meals must have been seen as continuous with the supper in the upper room on the night of Jesus' betrayal; he is imposing a 'Last Supper' motif on existing practices. The synoptic gospels were written later than 1 Corinthians, and each has an account of the last supper. These passages agree with 1 Corinthians 11 and with each other in the broad outlines of what happened in the upper room, but they differ in numerous details, some of which we will notice later (Matthew 26:26–38; Mark 14:22–24; Luke 22:17–19). John's Gospel has, in chapter 13, an account of the Last Supper which differs substantially both from Paul and from the synoptic stories. In John there is nothing about the bread and the cup, or Jesus' sayings about them; instead there is the narrative of the footwashing and a discussion between Jesus and the disciples about service, the coming betrayal, and the destiny of Jesus, leading into the farewell discourses of chapters 14–16 and the prayer of chapter 17.

All the sources are agreed that Jesus met with his disciples for a familiar ceremonial meal on that fateful night. The disciples were a mixed bunch; former zealots together with a reformed quisling; a handful of fishermen; Peter who was going to deny in a few hours' time having had any involvement with Jesus; and Judas, who was about to betray him to the authorities for a paltry fee. None of them were excluded from fellowship with Jesus as he approached his ultimate crisis. It was in a way a family occasion; Jesus and his family of disciples gathered for the ritual meal just as every pious Jewish family came together for such festivals. Despite the gathering clouds, it was in paradoxical fashion a festive occasion, and a ritual so familiar to the disciples that they must have found security in the midst of stress as they heard the familiar words and took part in the well-remembered actions, so rich with associations and speaking so powerfully of the things of God.

Jesus took this comfortingly familiar rite, and he must have startled and disconcerted his disciples by giving it a new meaning and a quite unexpected and puzzling significance. When he performed the traditional ritual of taking the bread he said (whether it was in addition to, or instead of, the customary words we are not told; Jesus' words made such an impression that they alone were remembered and passed down), 'This is my body which is for (or, broken for) you.' And when he took the cup he said, 'This is my blood of the new covenant which is poured out for many.'[2] In doing and saying these things, Jesus was linking together in the strongest and most dramatic of ways what happened at the Supper and what was to happen on the cross the next day. The two events interpreted one another and remain indissolubly linked. In the Supper Jesus proclaimed to his disciples that the death on the cross was to be the inauguration of a new covenantal relationship between God and his people; that he was to die for the disciples and 'for many' – a term which must be understood in the inclusive rather than exclusive sense as meaning 'everyone'. He is giving up his life for them; they are to be nourished unto eternal life by his broken body and outpoured blood. The rite of the footwashing, which takes the central place in the Johannine account, should be understood as another way of describing the linkage between the Supper and the Death. The footwashing speaks of the servant-role of Jesus. The narrative is not simply exemplary – though it is that: 'If I, then, your Lord and Teacher, have washed your feet, you also ought to wash one another's feet. For I have given you an example, that you also should do as I have done to you.' (John 13:14–15). It may well have awakened associations with the Old Testament figure of the Suffering Servant and passages such as Isaiah 53 may have come to mind, along with sayings of the Lord like, 'The Son of man ... came not to be served but to serve, and to give his life as a ransom for many' (Mark 10:45). Thus the Lord's Supper and the Lord's Sufferings were linked permanently and closely together, so that each lights up the mystery and the significance of the other, and neither can be properly understood in isolation.

The accounts of the Last Supper in 1 Corinthians, Luke, and John all suggest that in the course of the Supper Jesus indicated to his disciples that they should regard what he did and said at that time as an example to be followed frequently; in Paul and Luke it is an explicit command to take the bread and the cup, in John it is the suggestion that the disciples should serve one another in days to come as Jesus had served them by symbolically washing their feet in the upper room. And both the New Testament and other sources for the practice of the early church make it quite clear that the regular and distinctively Christian mode of worship was the repeating of the Supper that the Lord had celebrated with his disciples, thereby being obedient to his explicit command, becoming aware of his continuing presence with his people, and being nourished and sustained by his body and blood signified and conveyed in the bread and the wine.

The repetition of the Supper was to be 'in remembrance of me' (*eis ten emen anamnesis*). This phrase is more difficult to interpret than it might seem at first sight. While it clearly includes the idea of remembering Jesus and what he did, the Lord's Supper has never been a commemoration of a dead Jesus, or a wake for a dead God; it has always been a celebration of the living presence of the resurrected Lord. Perhaps a better translation into modern English would be to speak of 'recalling' Jesus and his work, for in the Supper he is present according to his promise, and the fruits of his self-offering are given to his people.[3]

Was the Last Supper a Passover meal, or some other kind of ritual fellowship meal? The Passover was an annual feast, celebrated whenever possible in Jerusalem, but throughout the *diaspora* as well, in small groups, and typically in the family. It commemorated and symbolized God's deliverance of his people from death by the blood of the passover lamb smeared on their lintels and doorposts, and their hasty departure from Egypt and safe passage through the Red Sea. The synoptic accounts suggest that the Last Supper was indeed a passover meal; John, however, indicates that it took place *before* the Passover, and Jesus was crucified as the Passover lambs were being sacrificed; while the epistles do not indicate whether it was understood as a Passover feast or not. The argument is complex, but not of crucial importance for our understanding of the Lord's Supper.[4] As we have argued earlier, the Last Supper, the crucifixion and the resurrection were tied together intimately and inextricably, and all the sources are agreed that this three-sided event took place at Passover time and must be understood in the light of the Passover. The Jesus who gave himself on the cross for his people and who gave and gives himself to them in the Supper may be understood as the Passover lamb: 'Christ our Passover lamb has been sacrificed for us; therefore let us keep the feast', cries St Paul (1 Corinthians 5:7). Christ died for the deliverance of all: this was a 'new exodus', the fulfilment and completion of the old. In Luke's account of the Transfiguration, Moses and Elijah spoke with Jesus of his '*exodus* which he was to accomplish at Jerusalem' (Luke 9:31). It is thus clear that the Supper, whether its origin was a Passover feast or not, must be understood along with the death and resurrection of Jesus in the light of the Passover – i.e. that it relates to a sacrificial death through which liberation is achieved, and through this Supper the people of God participate in the fruits of the sacrifice, in the liberation that has been won for them. They encounter God's purpose for all mankind and respond with joy to his call.

If the Lord's Supper inherited from the passover tradition an emphasis on looking back to Christ's acts of sacrifice and liberation which were real once again in the rite, it also took from the Passover the idea that the Supper looked forward, not just to the cross and resurrection but to the culmination of all God's purposes. Just as the Passover nourished and aroused a thirst for freedom and a longing for God's future, so the Lord's Supper looked forward with eager anticipation to a future which was often described by the image of the messianic banquet: 'On this mountain the Lord of hosts will make for all peoples a feast of fat things, a feast of wine on the lees, of fat things full of marrow, of wine on the lees well refined' (Isaiah 25:6). The synoptic gospels record that Jesus at the Last Supper looked forward to renewing the festivities with his disciples in the kingdom: 'I tell you I shall not drink again of this fruit of the vine until that day when I drink it new with you in my Father's kingdom.'[5] From the beginning, then, the Lord's Supper has been a feast of hope and expectation, pointing to the future, a kind of appetizer (*antepast*) for the messianic banquet. Thus the Lord's Supper should be seen as stimulating a thirst, a longing, for the immediate presence of God and an eagerness for the Kingdom and its justice. It therefore is also an act of commitment to the work of the Kingdom, the work of justice, liberation and peace. To share the bread and the cup is to share a destiny.[6]

B—EATING WITH JESUS

Other memories of Jesus enriched and fertilized the early Christians' understanding of the Lord's Supper; indeed it is possible that as these memories influenced the way the early Church celebrated the Supper, so the liturgical experience of the writers may have shaped the way certain gospel narratives were committed to writing. It is, first, necessary to remember that Jesus ate many times with his disciples before the supper in the upper room on the night of his betrayal. Many of these earlier meals would certainly have had a ritual element in them. They were celebrations of friendship, in which the disciples learned the meaning of love. It should not be necessary to argue that it matters a great deal whom one eats with and the way eating is organized. A radically segmented society like Hindu India had multitudinuous strict rules concerning who could eat what with whom, rules which preserved the segmentation of the society by ensuring that people from castes far apart in the social hierarchy could never meet as friends around the one table. Commensalism, eating together, is a sign and a source of friendship. If a family, or a group of friends, always 'eat on the trot', never sit down around a table to eat, and drink, and talk, they have lost one of the greatest sources of friendship and caring.

Jesus ate often with his disciples. He got a reputation as one who enjoyed eating and drinking, not at all a gloomy ascetic: 'This man's a drunkard and a glutton', they said, scandalized that eating and drinking should play so large a part in his life. But what really shocked the religious people of the time was not that Jesus enjoyed eating and drinking with his disciples, but that he was willing to share table-fellowship with all sorts of people. He received prostitutes and quislings and other notorious sinners, the outcasts of society, at his table. He refused to put up the fences that were so beloved of pious Jews. 'This fellow welcomes sinners and eats with them' (Luke

15:2 N.E.B.), they said in horror. For them the idea that a devout believer should eat with Gentiles, or with known wrongdoers, was unthinkable; the very possibility aroused deep-seated fears not very different from those of a high-caste Hindu afraid of the pollution incurred by sharing table-fellowship with an untouchable. But Jesus mixed freely with all sorts of people and was generally considered to keep the most undesirable of company at his table. He welcomed people who were known wrongdoers or had the most dubious of reputations.

The example – the shocking precedent – of Jesus' table-fellowship was only established in the early Church after bitter controversy. Jewish Christians found it desperately difficult to share at the Lord's Table, or at the common table, with Gentile Christians. Many of them said that the issue did not matter, that separate celebrations of the Supper for Jews and Gentiles would in no way compromise the Gospel. But Paul thought otherwise. For him the universality of the Gospel and the work of Christ in tearing down barriers among people must be displayed in celebrations of the Lord's Supper at which there was no discrimination, no recognition or sanctioning of the old-age suspicion and hostility between Jew and Gentile. He withstood Cephas to his face because he had equivocated on this vital issue (Galatians 2:11ff.). Paul battled on until he won. And the controversy was of no little moment; henceforward, wherever the church was established, there was to be one common table at which all, as equals, received and shared the things of God. And this principle of eucharistic commensalism shaped not only the Church but the whole of western society, as Max Weber recognised.[7]

Not that it has been sustained consistently within the church; the tradition in the Reformed Churches to 'fence the tables' in order to exclude the unworthy seems strange when measured against the practice of the Lord himself. And the refusal of one denomination to allow believers of another to join them at the Lord's Supper contrasts glaringly with Jesus' welcome to his table of a whole assortment of disciples, including the one who lost faith in him and betrayed him, and the one who denied any knowledge of him when the going got rough.

The narratives of the feeding miracles and the account of the Last Supper also shed light on one another. Consider, for instance, this narrative:

> As he went ashore he saw a great throng, and he had
> compassion on them, because they were like sheep without a
> shepherd; and he began to teach them many things. And when it
> grew late, his disciples came to him and said, 'This is a lonely
> place, and the hour is late; send them away, to go into the
> country and villages round about and buy themselves something
> to eat.' But he answered them, 'You give them something to eat.'
> And they said to him, 'Shall we go and buy two hundred denarii
> worth of bread, and give it to them to eat?' And he said to them,
> 'How many loaves have you? Go and see.' And when they found
> out, they said, 'Five, and two fish.' Then he commanded them

all to sit down by companies on the green grass. So they sat down in groups, by hundreds and by fifties. And taking the five loaves and the two fish he looked up to heaven, and blessed, and broke the loaves, and gave them to his disciples to set before the people; and he divided the two fish among them all. And they all ate and were satisfied. And they took up twelve baskets full of broken pieces and of the fish (Mark 6:34–43).

We may note the resonances between such an account as this, the narratives of the Last Supper, and the Church's celebrations of the Lord's Supper. For instance, the context of the feeding, and its immediate prelude, is teaching; it is not isolated, but must be understood as the consequence of the teaching, the two having a very significant linkage. Here we see quite clearly a theme we discuss in chapter four – the complementarity of Word and Sacrament and their inseparability the one from the other. Both the teaching and the feeding are instances of Jesus' care for the people, but neither on its own is an adequate expression of that boundless compassion. Next, the relation between Jesus and the disciples in the story must have reminded the early Christians of the activities of the various ministers at the Lord's Supper, suggesting both that the host is always Jesus, and that even faithless and mundane disciples have an important function in the distribution of the Lord's largesse to his people. The companies sitting in orderly fashion may have reflected more accurately than the image of the twelve disciples with Jesus, gathered around the table, the actual experience of the Lord's Supper in the churches in which the Gospel was read. But the most impressive similarity between this miracle and the Last Supper was the action of Jesus: he took the food, blessed it (*eulogesen*), broke the bread, and gave it to the people. These are precisely the four actions at the heart of the accounts of the Last Supper, and the actions repeated from the very earliest days every time Christians have celebrated the Supper of the Lord. There are differences, of course, and they are of no little importance. Fish are mentioned in the narrative along with the bread, and there is no wine; there is no explicit connection with the sufferings of Jesus, or suggestion that the bread is his body. But some of the differences give a new depth to the understanding of the Lord's Supper. There is for example, a strong emphasis on the prodigality of God's gracious provision for his people; there is wondrously enough food to satisfy everyone, and when the food had been shared among the multitude the remaining plenty was not wasted or thrown away but gathered together in baskets – sufficient for all Israel, enough for the whole world.

Similar light is cast upon the Lord's Supper by the Johannine story of the marriage at Cana of Galilee: Jesus is present at a festive occasion, a party, and he miraculously provides abundant wine as his contribution to the celebration. Here the emphasis is not so much on the meeting of human needs as on the importance of festivity. And in the sixth chapter of John after a miracle of feeding, Jesus speaks of himself as the bread that comes down from heaven to nourish a pilgrim people just as the manna was given in the wilderness. God provides for the material and spiritual needs of his people with infinite and wonderful generosity.

Finally, the Lord's Supper has been interpreted in the light of the meals which the resurrected Jesus had with his disciples, recounted in Luke and John. The story of the Emmaeus road (Luke 24:13–32) stresses the hidden presence of the Lord with the two disciples on their way, and how when 'he took the bread and blessed, and broke it, and gave it to them ... Their eyes were opened and they recognized him' (vv. 30–31). Once again, we have the four actions, and table fellowship with the Lord so that 'he was known to them in the breaking of the bread' – an experience which has been repeated countless times down the ages as the Church has broken the bread in obedience to her Lord's command and example. Another instance of recognition of the risen Lord in the context of a meal is the breakfast on the lakeside recounted in John 21:12–13. As they ate together, 'none of the disciples dared ask him, "Who are you?" They knew it was the Lord.' (v. 12). In a meal, the presence of the risen Lord is recognized; this table-fellowship of the first disciples is continued every time the Church celebrates the Supper of the Risen Lord.

C—THE LORD'S SUPPER IN THE EARLY CHURCH

And so it was from the beginning of the Church. In Acts we hear that the early Jerusalem Christians 'devoted themselves to the apostles' teaching and fellowship, to the breaking of the bread and the prayers' (2:42). Almost certainly this indicates the main features of the early gatherings for worship, which appear to have taken place alongside attendance at the temple, and very frequently, in the homes of the Christians rather than in any special buildings (Acts 2:47). It is suggested later in Acts that the Breaking of the Bread, the name in all probability for the Lord's Supper (and still used as such by sects like the Brethren), was the normal way of marking the first day of the week, the feast of the Resurrection. This frequency is at first sight a little strange, particularly if the Last Supper had been a Passover, for the Passover was celebrated only once a year. But in view of the influence of Jesus' regular table-fellowship on the understanding of the Lord's Supper, and the fact that from very early indeed the Christians observed the first day of the week as the feast of the Resurrection, weekly or even more frequent celebration is easy to explain, despite the Passover connection.

In 1 Corinthians 11 Paul is commenting on a situation where the Lord's Supper – a rite involving bread and wine and specifically connected with the death and resurrection of Jesus – is part of a full meal for the congregation. This meal had become scandalous and divisive because the better-off Christians were bringing plenty of food to eat themselves and refusing to share with the poorer Christians who went hungry. Hence Paul proclaims that 'when you met together, it is not the Lord's Supper that you eat' (v. 20). For the rich despise and humiliate the poor and divide the Body of Christ, making a parody of the sacred rite, a practical denial of its significance. (This may illumine the meaning of v. 29: 'For any one who eats and drinks without discerning the body eats and drinks judgement upon himself.') 1 Corinthians 11 and other Pauline passages, along with the references in Acts, remind us that the Lord's Supper was in fact a real meal, not an isolated ritual whose association with meals, or with the continuation of table-fellowship with Jesus, had been forgotten. This point remains valid even if Paul was insisting on a distinction and even separation between the eucharist and the *agape* meal. The emphases in the Acts and the Pauline accounts are rather different, but they seem to be complementary descriptions of a form of worship which was in essentials the same. Acts does not connect the Breaking of the Bread explicitly with the death of Jesus and makes no mention of wine, but sees the supper as a festive continuation of the table-fellowship the disciples enjoyed with Jesus before his death and after the resurrection. And it is worth remembering that the author of Acts also wrote the Gospel of Luke which has a special interest in Jesus' meals, and contains the story of the supper at Emmaus. In Paul we see the connection with the Last Supper and the linking with the dying of Jesus spelled out in very explicit terms. The interest of Paul and Luke may be slightly different, but they both enrich our understanding of the early and perennial forms of the Supper, without fundamental conflict.

As we move out of the New Testament period, we find evidence that the churches strove to follow the command and example of the Lord as closely as possible, celebrating the Lord's Supper weekly or more frequently, to recall Jesus and his death, to rejoice in his resurrection, to continue a real fellowship with him and with one another around the table, and to nourish faith and hope and love. Writing about the year 110, Pliny the Younger, who was a Proconsul in Asia Minor, reported to the Emperor Trajan on the activities of the strange new sect of Christians. Among their suspicious activities was the fact that they met together on a fixed day each week – clearly Sunday – for a common meal. This must have been the Lord's Supper, or the Eucharist or 'Thanksgiving' as it became increasingly commonly called, and which is mentioned in other early Christian sources. The *Didache* (probably early second century) gives evidence of weekly eucharistic worship:[8]

> On the Lord's Day of the Lord, come together, break bread, and give thanks, having first confessed your transgressions, that your sacrifice may be pure (chap 14:1).

There is an account of a common meal with explicit sacramental practices. Thanks is given over the cup as follows:

> We give thanks to you, our Father, for the holy vine of your child David, which you made known to us through Jesus. Glory to you for evermore.

Then thanks is given over the bread – the order is rather unusual:

> We give thanks to you, our Father, for the life and knowledge
> which you have made known to us through your child Jesus;
> glory to you for evermore. As this broken bread was scattered
> over the mountains, and when brought together became one, so
> let your Church be brought together from the ends of the earth
> into your Kingdom; for yours the glory and the power through
> Jesus Christ for evermore (chap 9).

After the meal there follows a magnificent prayer of thanksgiving. The
motifs are participation in the vine of David, gratitude for the life and
knowledge and immortality which believers have received through Jesus,
the 'sacred name' which is lodged in the hearts of the faithful, and the
eschatological gathering together of the church. The strange thing is that
there is no mention of the passion or the resurrection, of the body and
blood of Christ, or of the Last Supper. Accordingly some scholars regard
this passage as an account of an *agape*, or perhaps a very eccentric
eucharist. The *Didache* should remind us of the rich plurality of theme and
imagery which goes into the making of the Christian eucharistic tradition.

Justin Martyr was converted to Christianity about the year 130, and his
First Apology was probably written about 150. Here he gives two accounts
of the Lord's Supper. In the first, a baptism is followed by prayers of
intercession, the 'kiss of peace', and

> Then bread and a cup of water and of mixed wine are brought
> to him who presides over the brethren, and he takes them and
> offers praise and glory to the Father of all in the name of the
> Son and of the Holy Spirit, and gives thanks at some length that
> we have been deemed worthy of these things from him. When he
> has finished the prayers and the thanksgiving, all the people
> present give their assent by saying, 'Amen'.

> ... And when the president has given thanks and all the people
> have assented those whom we call deacons give to each one
> present a portion of the bread and wine and water over which
> thanks have been given, and take them to those who are not
> present.[9]

The second account relates to an 'ordinary' Sunday celebration –
incidentally making it quite clear that the eucharist was the main Sunday
service. On this occasion the service starts with the reading of 'the records
of the apostles or writings of the prophets', followed by a homily.
Thereafter the service proceeds much as before, except that there is no kiss
of peace, it is mentioned that the president prays 'to the best of his ability'
i.e. he is not tied to a text, and there is a collection for the needy.

Hippolytus's *The Apostolic Tradition* was probably written in the early
third century. It contains the earliest text of a eucharistic prayer and comes
before the development of the varied families of liturgies in east and west.
Its account of the eucharist is closely similar to that of Justin, but there is

considerably more detail. The text of the eucharistic prayer was probably a specimen rather than a mandatory form and it has been highly influential on all modern liturgical revisions. It contains all the major sections and emphases which most scholars regard as important in a eucharistic prayer. The eucharist follows the consecration of a bishop with the Peace and the offering of gifts, on which the new bishop 'with all the presbytery' lays hands and gives thanks:

Greeting
> The Lord be with you.
> And with your spirit.

Sursum Corda
> Lift up your hearts.
> We hold them towards the Lord (Greek: Let us pray to the Lord).
> Let us give thanks to the Lord.
> It is worthy and right.

Thanksgiving
> We give thanks to you, O God, through your beloved servant Jesus Christ, whom in the last times you sent to us as saviour and redeemer and messenger of your will; he is the Word inseparable from you, through whom you made all things, and on whom your favour rested. You sent him from heaven into a virgin's womb; he was conceived, made flesh and revealed as your Son, born of the Holy Spirit (and a virgin). As he gave full expression to your will and created for you a holy people, he stretched out his hands in suffering in order to free from suffering those who put their trust in you. And after he was handed over to suffering, which he freely accepted, that he might destroy death and break the bonds of the devil, tread down hell and give light to the righteous, fix the limit and manifest the resurrection,

Narrative of Institution
> he took bread, gave thanks to you and said, 'Take, eat; this is my body, which is broken for you.' Likewise also the cup, saying, 'This is my blood, which is shed for you; when you do this, do it to remember me.'

Anamnesis, or Remembrance
> We remember therefore his death and resurrection, and

Oblation
> we offer to you the bread and the cup, giving you thanks because you have accepted us as worthy to stand before you and serve you.

Epiclesis, or Invocation of the Holy Spirit
> And we ask you to send your Holy Spirit upon the offering of your

Holy Church; to unite all your saints, and to grant them, as they partake, that they may be filled with the Holy Spirit and that their faith may be confirmed in the truth;

Doxology
so that we may praise and glorify you through your servant Jesus Christ, through whom be glory and honour to you, to the Father and the Son with the Holy Spirit, in your Holy Church, both now and for ages and ages.

Assent of the People
Amen.[10]

All these early sources indicate that while there was a good deal of flexibility in the way in which the Supper was conducted and no form of words was mandatory, there was a close similarity in the *shape* of the rite, clearly determined by the intention of following the command and example of the Lord as closely as possible in taking, blessing, breaking and sharing. The great prayer was always one of thanksgiving over the elements and commonly, but not universally, included a narrative of the institution – as the story of the Last Supper tends to be called. The connections with the cross and with the resurrection are clearly affirmed by the explicit linking of the elements with the death of Jesus and the fact that the most appropriate day for the Lord's Supper was recognized to be Sunday, the weekly celebration of the resurrection.

D—SOME DEVELOPMENTS

We cannot here give more than the sketchiest of outlines of the development of the Lord's Supper. Readers who wish to know more are referred to some of the books listed in the bibliography. Certain developments which took place gradually over a period of centuries require, however, to be noted.

1. As we have suggested above, the Lord's Supper became disjoined from the common meal of the congregation, and the latter apparently disappeared in most places. The kind of situation of which we read in 1 Corinthians 11 was no longer to be found; perhaps partly because in other places, as in Corinth, the meal had become an occasion for disorder, gluttony, drunkenness, and faction in the church. It is also difficult to see how, as the size of congregations increased, a weekly or even more frequent common meal could have been sustained. With this change there went a change of title: the Lord's Supper, which clearly connotes a meal at which the host is the Lord himself, became known as the Eucharist, a word which quickly became a technical term for a rite. Whereas the earliest Church had seen one of the marks of distinction between itself and the pagan cults of the ancient world as being that the church had no altar but a

table around which they met for a meal, the way was now open to the Eucharist being understood as a sacrifice on an altar rather than a meal at a table.

2. We have seen earlier that the death of Jesus was interpreted, among other ways, as a sacrifice in the New Testament period, and that there was from the beginning a very intimate connection between the cross and the Lord's Supper. There was thus a necessary link between the Supper and the sacrificial death of Christ, and the Supper could never be freed from sacrificial connotations. But the precise relationship between the Supper and the Sacrifice needed to be spelled out. At the beginning the Lord's Supper was never referred to as being itself a sacrifice, but gradually in the second century it became common to refer to it as a sacrifice. Justin Martyr refers to the Eucharist as the sacrifice of the Church, and Tertullian describes it in terms of a sacrifice at an altar. This development may have been partly in response to an environment where a religion meant to most people a sacrificial system, and Christians had to be able to point to their sacrifice or be despised as atheists. It is a vast leap from this, but one that the Church found it fatally easy to make, to regard the Eucharist as a repetition or continuation of the sacrifice of Christ, under the control of the Church and implying some sort of incompleteness in what Christ did on the cross. No adequate interpretation of the Lord's Supper is possible without recourse to the language of sacrifice; but this language has to be used with a discretion and care that was not always obvious, particularly in popular understandings of the eucharist; and if the category of sacrifice is given so prominent a place in the understanding of the Supper that other complementary concepts are all but forgotten, a radically distorted understanding ensues.

3. In 1 Peter and in Revelation the community of believers is referred to as a royal priesthood, and the term used for pagan or Jewish priests was never applied in the New Testament to anyone in the Church. The Church was regarded as a corporate priesthood, but it had no individual priests who could act in isolation from, or on behalf of, the community. The whole body of believers had access through the blood of Christ to the holiest of all, and needed no other intermediary. But the Church as a whole stood in a priestly relationship to the world: they represented God to the world and the world to God, on the grounds of the Church's participation in the sacrifice of Christ.[9] Accordingly worship, and especially the Lord's Supper, was seen as an activity of the community of believers, in which each had a role to play; and that role was priestly. As, however, the corporate priesthood of the whole body of believers was gradually overshadowed by a new understanding that there were individual priests within the community whose primary responsibility for worship was strongly stressed, the people tended to become more and more passive in worship. Two indications of these processes are the fact that after the early Christian centuries until the Reformation, the people 'heard Mass', but communicated only once or twice a year. In other words, the people

watched and listened to a priest doing and saying intricate and
unintelligible things, and only very infrequently participated as far as to
receive communion. And when they did receive communion, they were
denied the wine; only the priest received in both kinds; the people were
disfranchised by being made passive observers, or partial participants.[11]

4. There was an increasing tendency to concentrate attention on the
elements of bread and wine rather than the rite as a whole, and to narrow
down the understanding of Christ's presence by affirming his presence in
the bread and wine and underplaying his presence as the host and master of
the feast; his presence, according to his promise, whenever two or three are
gathered together in his name; his presence in the Word; his presence in his
Body, the Church; and his presence in the needy neighbour. And this
concentration on the bread and wine led to people asking about 'the
moment of change' – when the bread and wine ceased to be what they
appeared to be and became the Body and Blood of Christ. The two
commonest answers – that the moment of change is when the words 'This
is my body' and 'This is my blood' are said by the priest, or that the
elements change at the *epiclesis*, the invocation of the Holy Spirit to bless
and sanctify the elements – make one suspect that the question itself is
inappropriate, and remind us of the dangers of a magical and mechanical
understanding of the sacrament.

5. From early days the Lord's Supper has commonly been called the
Mystery of the Holy Mysteries – a useful reminder that every encounter
with God must be mysterious and that Rudolph Otto was right in defining
the Holy as *mysterium tremendum et fascinans*. But in the case of the Lord's
Supper it is possible for the authentic and necessary mystery to be
obscured by a contrived and misleading kind of mystery. As elaborate
ceremonial and ritual gathered around the Lord's Supper, particularly
after Christianity became the official religion of the Roman Empire under
Constantine, the structure which tied the Lord's Supper to the Last Supper
and conveyed the authentic Christian mystery often became obscured. It
was not only the steady proliferation of additional rituals and the inclusion
of all sorts of extra prayers and private devotions which hid the structure
of the rite, but also the fact that the Mass was said in Latin, at crucial
points in an inaudible murmur, which reduced people's involvement in,
and understanding of, the service and encouraged stupid or superstitious
misunderstandings. In addition it was impossible for the people to see
what was happening; in the East because the major part of the service was
performed behind an elaborate *ikonostasis* (or screen covered with pictures
of the saints) totally obscuring the view, and in the West at a distant altar
and often behind a heavy screen, the priest standing with his back to the
people.
   The Reformation saw itself, in worship as in doctrine and ethics, as
endeavouring to recover the beliefs and practices of the New Testament
Church. In the Lord's Supper, the Reformers tried to strip away what they
regarded as the distortions of practice and doctrine and the accretions of

ritual which obscured the true nature of the sacrament instituted by the Lord. Like the earliest Christians, they tried to follow, as simply and directly as possible, the command and example of the Lord, and as a consequence they recovered something of what had been lost. They sought a simple, biblical shape for the sacrament; they believed it should always be allied with the preaching of the Word, for Word and Sacrament were seen as complementary and neither could stand on its own; they wanted the full participation and communion in both the bread and the wine of all present; and they wished the Supper to be frequently celebrated, and certainly every Sunday. Calvin spoke of the custom, which had arisen in the Middle Ages, of annual communion as a 'veritable invention of the Devil', for 'The Lord's Table should be spread at least once a week for the Assembly of Christians.'[12] So also Bucer wrote, 'I could wish that all would communicate at the Table of the Lord every Lord's Day.' And Richard Baxter, the great English Puritan pastor and divine wrote, 'The Lord's Supper is a part of the settled order for Lord's Day worship, and omitting it maimeth and altereth the worship of the day.'[13] Indeed, the 'right administration of the sacraments' which the Calvanist Reformers saw as one of the three marks of the true church must certainly be seen as including frequent celebrations of the Lord's Supper.

The Reformation was a corrective to what it denounced as 'the idolatry of the mass'. Like most correctives, it went too far, so that many Protestants tended to see the Lord's Supper as no more than a commemoration, to deny the real presence, and to refuse to consider any sacrificial or eschatological connotations whatsoever. In practice the Protestant churches were not able to carry through the changes that they wished and became, despite themselves, captives to the mediaeval traditions. For example, strong resistance from the people made frequent communion impossible in most situations. From the Reformation until recent times the Protestant and Roman Catholic traditions of eucharistic theology and practice tended to polarize and, as is common in such situations, each pole represented an unbalanced, one-sided and partial understanding and practice of the Supper which Jesus had commanded his disciples to keep.

E—THE LORD'S SUPPER TODAY

The twentieth century has been a period of remarkable convergence in eucharistic theology and renewal of eucharistic practice in almost all branches of the Church. The roots of the liturgical movement lie in the nineteenth century, but there is no space here to tell the fascinating story of its development and spread. Both in theology and in liturgical practice recent developments have arisen from the determination to get back to fundamentals. It has been realized on all sides that relevant liturgy must be faithful to the Church's Lord and take account of historical continuity. But this does not mean getting stalled in the debates of the Reformation, or the Enlightenment, or the Middle Ages, or absolutizing the doctrine and practice of the Council of Trent, or Thomas Aquinas, or Calvin or Luther. The asking of more fundamental theological questions in the now much broader ecumenical context has led to the careful development of a truly remarkable theological consensus in the understanding of the Lord's Supper. The most notable fruit of this process is probably the document produced by the World Council of Churches' Faith and Order Department as a result of some forty years' work by a large number of theologians, including many Roman Catholics, *Baptism, Eucharist and Ministry*. This was published in 1982 and sent to the Churches for comment, but already it indicates a very broad-based agreement.

In this document the eucharist is seen, first, as Thanksgiving to the Father for all his goodness and mighty acts, in which the church offers through, with, and in Christ a sacrifice of praise on behalf of the whole of creation. The Lord's Supper thus 'signifies what the world is to become: an offering and hymn of praise to the Creator, a universal communion in the body of Christ, a kingdom of justice, love and peace in the Holy Spirit.' It is, secondly, a memorial of Christ: 'the living and effective sign of his sacrifice, accomplished once and for all on the cross and still operative on behalf of all humankind', and thus the proclamation of God's mighty acts and promises. The Church recognizes 'Christ's real, living and active presence' in the Supper. Thirdly, the eucharist is seen as the Invocation of the Spirit who sanctifies, renews, leads into justice, truth and unity, empowers the church for mission, and gives a foretaste of the Kingdom. Fourthly, the eucharist is communion with Christ and within the Body, in which the true nature of the church is made manifest and a 'hunger and thirst after righteousness' is stimulated. It is, therefore 'a constant challenge in the search for appropriate relationships in social economic and political life.' And, finally, the eucharist is the meal of the Kingdom, which brings into the present age a new reality. It 'is precious food for missionaries, bread and wine for pilgrims on their apostolic journey.' Other notable recent statements of agreement on the eucharist include the Windsor Statement of the Anglican-Roman Catholic International Commission in 1971, and the 1967 American Lutheran and Roman Catholic Statement on the Eucharist as Sacrifice.

Along with the development of a theological consensus has gone a remarkable convergence in eucharistic practice. Much impetus was given to this by the measures of liturgical renewal laid down by the Second Vatican Council, but many of the non-Roman churches had already produced new liturgical orders, much influenced by new work on theology and the liturgical studies of scholars such as Dom Gregory Dix and J. A. Jungmann. The Liturgy of the Church of South India (1951) was one of the most interesting and influential of the new wave of liturgies. Since then almost all new eucharistic liturgies have virtually the same structure and although there is much diversity in language and in theological emphasis there is a strong common tendency to greater simplicity, more participation by the people, a proper balance between Word and Sacrament, and much greater flexibility and variety than was common in most traditions. But the eucharistic liturgy is essentially an integrated

whole, moving through all or most of these elements, with some variety as
to the sequence and emphasis:

> Hymns of praise
> Act of penitence
> Declaration of Pardon
> Proclamation of the Word of God
> Confession of faith
> Intercessions for the Church and the world
> Preparation of the bread and wine
> Thanksgiving to the Father for the marvels of creation,
>   redemption and sanctification
> The words of Christ's institution of the sacrament
> The *anamnesis* or memorial of the great acts of redemption,
>   passion, death, resurrection, ascension and Pentecost
> The invocation of the Holy Spirit on the community and the
>   elements of bread and wine
> Consecration of the faithful to God
> Reference to the communion of saints
> Prayer for the return of the Lord and the definitive manifestation
>   of his Kingdom
> The Amen of the community
> The Lord's Prayer
> Sign of reconciliation and peace
> The breaking of the bread
> Eating and drinking in communion with Christ and with each
>   member of the Church.
> Blessing and sending.[14]

In every conceivable situation in every land men and women seek to
obey the Lord's command by taking, and blessing, and breaking and
sharing the bread and the wine. Outwardly there is immense variety in the
ways they do this, but basically it is always the same: a festival of praise and
thanksgiving for God's great love in Christ, a celebration of our fellowship
with Christ and with one another, nourishment for a pilgrim people, and
stimulus to seek God's ways of justice and of peace. Here we encounter
God in Christ; he gives himself to us, and we to him. He gives himself for
the life of the world.

NOTES

1. Cf. I. Howard Marshall, *Last Supper and Lord's Supper*, Exeter 1980,
   pp. 32–33.
2. There is no space here to go into the variations in the words of Jesus in

the various sources. For detailed discussions the reader is directed to J. Jeremias, *The Eucharistic Words of Jesus*, London 1966 & I. Howard Marshall, *op. cit.*

3. For Jeremias' controversial interpretation of the *anamnesis* see *The Eucharistic Words of Jesus*, pp. 237–255.

4. Readers may follow the argument in Jeremias, *op. cit.*, pp. 15–18 and I. Howard Marshall, *op. cit.*, ch. 3.

5. Matthew 26:29; cf. Mark 14:25, Luke 14:16, 17. For detailed discussion of these texts, see Jeremias, *op. cit.*, pp. 218ff.

6. On this para. see Geoffrey Wainwright, *Eucharist and Eschatology*, London 1971.

7. Max Weber, *The Religion of India*. Trans. Hans Gerth and Don Martindale, New York 1958, pp. 37–38.

8. Cited from R. C. D. Japser & G. J. Cuming, *Prayers of the Eucharist – Early and Reformed*, London 1975, pp. 14–16.

9. First Apology, 65, 3: cited in Jasper and Cuming, *op. cit.*, pp. 18–19.

10. Hippolytus, *The Apostolic Tradition*, ch. 4. Translated from text L, taking into account text E, in B. Botte's, *La Tradition Apostolique de saint Hippolyte*, Paris 1963, pp. 12–16.

11. On this see especially J. A. Jungmann, *The Early Liturgy*, London 1960, ch. 2: 'The Church as a Worshipping Community'.

12. *Institutes*, IV.17.46.

13. Cited in G. W. Sprott, *The Worship and Offices of the Church of Scotland*, Edinburgh 1882, p. 99.

14. Slightly adapted from *Baptism, Eucharist and Ministry*, Geneva, World Council of Churches, 1982, pp. 15–16.

FURTHER READING

Josef A. Jungmann, *The Early Liturgy*, London 1960.
I. Howard Marshall, *Last Supper & Lord's Supper*, Exeter 1980.
Joachim Jeremias, *The Eucharistic Words of Jesus*, London 1966.
Nicholas Lash, *His Presence in the World*, London 1968.
Gregory Dix, *The Shape of the Liturgy*, London 1945.
    Geoffrey Wainwright, *Eucharist and Eschatology*, London 1971.

FOR DISCUSSION

1. How do you understand the presence of Christ in the Lord's Supper?
2. Is it important that bread and wine rather than, say, tea and biscuits are used in the Lord's Supper?
3. How should we understand the Eucharist as a *memorial* of Christ?
4. Should the Lord's Supper be an experience of liberation?
5. Can we speak of the Lord's Supper as 'The feast of the future'?

CHAPTER 8

TIMES AND SEASONS

A—INTRODUCTION

In some contexts, as Paul reminds the Thessalonians (1 Thessalonians 5:1ff.), it is not relevant to speak of times and seasons. If we ask, with the apostles, when the reign of God will be fully established in Israel, we are told, 'It is not for you, to know times or seasons, which the Father has fixed by his own authority (Acts 1:7). In one of the most astonishing statements in the New Testament, Mark reports Jesus as saying: 'But of that day or that hour no one knows, not even the angels in heaven, nor the Son, but only the Father' (Mark 15:32). The last Day may be regarded as something of a special case: it is not so much an historical event as the climax of history. Paul, however, also enters a caveat about over-zealous concern with 'times and seasons' of a different sort. When he fears that the Galatian Christians are falling back into old ways from which his gospel should have set them free for ever, he writes: 'You keep special days and months and seasons and years. You make me fear that all the pains I spent on you may prove to be labour lost' (Galatians 4:10f. N.E.B.). The Colossians are told not to accept censure in matters of food or drink or the observance of festival, new moon or sabbath, for 'these are only a shadow of what is to come ... the substance belongs to Christ' (Colossians 2:16f.).

Not that it is only the New Testament which makes critical noises about times and seasons: the prophets can be more extreme than anyone.

> New moons and sabbaths and assemblies,
> Sacred seasons and ceremonies, I cannot endure.
> I cannot tolerate your new moons and your festivals;
> they have become a burden to me,
> and I can put up with them no longer   (Isaiah 1:13f. N.E.B.).

Yet here the prophet's (or Yahweh's) rejection of 'new moons and sabbaths' is bound up with his rejection of Israel's sacrifices, prayers and worship – because 'there is blood on your hands' (1:16). The observance of 'times and seasons' is valid only if the cultic action is coupled with righteous living.

> Wash yourselves and be clean.
> Put away the evil of your deeds,
>   away out of my sight.
> Cease to do evil and learn to do right,
> pursue justice and champion the oppressed;
> give the orphan his rights, plead the widow's cause   (1:16f.
> N.E.B.).

This emphasis on *praxis* is the main thrust whenever the validity of liturgical action is considered. It remains a factor even when Paul is arguing that one cannot be saved by good works, any more than one is saved by keeping special days, months, seasons and years: when the context demands it, Paul can cite catalogues of vices (cf. Romans 1:29ff.) and virtues (cf. Galatians 5:22) and insist on well-ordered worship (cf. 1 Corinthians 14:40). Hence, just as the prophets' rejection of the kind of worship that is unrelated to the moral demands of the Torah should not be taken as a rejection of worship itself (a covenantal obligation), so apostolic criticism of those members who relapsed into observances unrelated to the gospel should not be taken as a rejection of the notion of recurrent patterns in church life and practice. Indeed, the weekly cycle is established and presupposed in Paul's churches: 'On the first day of every week, each of you is to put something aside ...' (1 Corinthians 16:1). Since many of the early Christians were Jewish, it is not surprising that they continued to keep the hours of prayer (cf. Acts 3:1) or to observe the times of festival (cf. Acts 2:1).

What importance attaches to this recognition of 'times and seasons' in the life of the church? How important is it for the believing community as a whole and for the individual? How deep are its roots in human existence? To attempt an answer, we must begin with the origins of the Jewish year.

B—THE CYCLE OF THE JEWISH YEAR

To appreciate the cycle of the Jewish year, one must distinguish two different understandings of time: the circular and the linear. The forefathers of the people of Israel were nomadic shepherds or semi-settled farmers, whose lives were bound up with the cycle of nature. Their religious observances therefore followed the pattern of cyclic repetition, involving day, week, month and year, each event being marked with appropriate rites. Most obviously, the seasons are marked by reference to events of economic importance to the people. Thus the first-born lamb, the sowing of crops, the early and the later harvests, and the ingathering of fruit are all celebrated annually, with appropriate rites.

The revolution which prompts the emergence of the idea of 'linear time' is compounded of a number of factors. One is the dynamic and dialectic relationship that is recognised to obtain between the transcendent God and the events of his people's history. God is no longer simply the power immanent in nature: the power that makes the crops grow and gives increase to flocks and families alike. He is the 'God who acts' to elect and save his people in their historical situation: the God who 'heard our voice, and saw our affliction, our toil and oppression' and who 'brought us out of Egypt with a mighty hand ... and brought us into this place and gave us this land, a land flowing with milk and honey' (Deuteronomy 26:7ff.). Such a view is tantamount to a doctrine of providence. It presupposes the notions of covenant relationship and divine election. Above all, the 'salvation history' (*Heilsgeschichte*) which it reflects effects the transition from 'circular time' to 'linear time'. There is now a story to tell. The recollection of the past is now important for understanding God's nature and purpose in history and helps to interpret present and future. History enshrines a revelation of the divine purpose, a teleological motif from the influence of which, as S. G. F. Brandon pointed out, history has never since been able completely to emancipate itself. The God who thus acts in history is none other than the Creator, by whose express will and creative action the universe itself was born. He is also the God in whose hands the future, the End, lies: the 'Alpha and Omega' who is active in providence.

What is the relation between the old circular view and the linear concept of time? Even in revolutions and conversions, not all aspects of one's self-understanding undergo transformation: there is identity within difference. The Old Testament suggests the danger of a ritual and ideological bifurcation. Those who lived close to the soil were vitally concerned with the fertility of fields and cattle, with which the old cyclic view dealt directly. In the new situation, they might be tempted to make verbal confession of the *Heilsgeschichte* while carrying out the ritual acts and following the life-style of fertility cults which impinged on their basic economic concerns and world-view. Hence the persistence of Baal-worship, even among those, like Gideon's family, who considered themselves loyal to Israel. This kind of synthesis was unacceptable to the prophets. The prophetic attack on the baals, however, must be seen in context with the teaching of Deuteronomy 26 which combines the offering of first-fruits with the recital of the *magnalia*, 'the mighty acts of God', and acceptance of the Lord's commandments in terms of covenantal obedience. That is to say, in the liturgy of Israel, Yahweh – God of Sinai, God of the Exodus – is seen both as the driving force of the nation's history *and* as the power which gives the increase in field and flock. *This* is the synthesis which the champions of Yahweh urged. It means that the rites and celebrations of circular time are incorporated in the programme of linear time. The cycles retain importance and find expression in the liturgical year. But human history is now seen as more than simply a succession of cycles. The past, present and future are interconnected; their significance is made evident in the 'story of salvation' (*Heilsgeschichte*), narrated, enacted and celebrated by the community in cult and liturgy.

This dual nature is evident in the Jewish year. Time may be linear, but in each year as it comes round the Israelite is commanded to keep three recurring feasts (Exodus 23:14); and each of these feasts has a dual reference. Thus the three great pilgrim festivals, *Pessach, Shavuot* and *Succot* not only recall God's mighty acts of salvation in Israel's history, but also celebrate times of agricultural significance. *Pessach* marks the early harvest, *Shavuot* the second harvest and *Succot* the ingathering of the fruit. The week is marked by the *Shabbat* or sabbath: the 'very soul and being'[1] of Israel. It is concerned with a cycle of six days of dignified labour and on the seventh a day of rest.

> The holiness of the Shabbat should pervade the Jew's action and thought throughout the whole week. True to this injunction the Jew has never ceased to declare expectantly before the recital of the Daily Psalm, 'this is the first day towards Shabbat', and so on, thus daily and regularly preparing himself for the Holy Day.[2]

Each day is thus related to the seventh, *Shabbat*. So basic is this pattern that even the years follow it: every seventh year is a 'sabbatical' year, and every seventh sabbatical is the Year of Jubilee.

In the cycle of liturgical observance, the Temple had an important place and function. Following Josiah's reform (621 B.C.), it was the sole place of sacrifice and the centre of pilgrimage. Pilgrimages were made at the great annual festivals noted above. Apart from the sacrifices themselves, there were prayers and psalms of praise; instruction was given by the priests, and recitals of the *magnalia* (the 'mighty acts') were incorporated in both teaching and worship. New moons and sabbaths were also observed, and prayers and sacrifices offered three times daily: in the morning (*Shacharit*), in the afternoon (*Minchah*) and in the evening (*Maariv*). After A.D. 70, the Temple ceased to operate, but it left its mark on the liturgy. As a prominent rabbi put it,

> Why did they say that the *Shacharit* could be recited till midday? Because the regular morning sacrifice could be brought till midday. And why the *Minchah* up to the evening? Because the regular afternoon offering could only be brought till the evening. And why did they say that for the *Maariv* there is no limit? Because the limbs and the fat which were not consumed on the altar by evening could be brought for the whole night.[3]

The local shrines throughout Israel were no longer places of sacrifice after 621 B.C. but possibly served as centres of congregational worship.[4] At any rate, it is more likely that they continued for a while to retain their function as the focus of local religious observance, even without the sacrifical cultus. We find the husband of the Shunamite woman expressing surprise that she was proposing to visit the holy man since 'it is neither new moon nor sabbath' (2 Kings 4:23). At such times, a visit to him was recognised procedure. After the exile, however, the synagogues came into their own as the focus of community life and worship. Central to them was the Torah as scripture. Basic procedures were the reading and interpretation of the sacred scrolls. Other elements were the reciting of the shema, prayers, psalms and benedictions. Lectionaries developed to regulate the reading of the Torah, together with the prophets and later books at sabbath assembly. Weekday services were also held (on Mondays and Thursdays). Worship, social and community concerns, and finally education came under their purview. Yet the hub of Jewish life was the family. This too had its daily, weekly and festive rituals. With the final destruction of the temple, public and private prayers in synagogue and home – following the times and seasons of 'liturgical time' – became the standard 'sacrifice of praise' to God.

C—THE DAWNING OF THE NEW AGE

The coming of Jesus the Messiah 'in the fullness of time' had major implications for *Heilsgeschichte*. The End or Telos of 'significant time'[5] had come: not, as it transpired, at the end of chronological time, but in mid-course. Hence the story (*Geschichte*) of the Christ event (including Incarnation, Ministry, Cross and Resurrection) became focal for Christian worship. The scriptures of Israel were now 'the Old Testament', prefiguring, interpreting and witnessing to Jesus as Messiah (cf. John 5:59). In time, the 'memoirs of the apostles' (Justin) were added, and the New Testament grew to canonical status alongside the Old.

Different emphases are apparent in the New Testament presentation of Jesus as the Christ, but all witness to his work as epoch-making. The Matthaean emphasis on the Messiahship of Jesus is seen in the Sermon on the Mount, which is not so much a new Torah as the Torah and Prophets brought to full expression by the Messiah (cf. Matthew 5:17). John the Baptist marks the transition from the old dispensation to the new (cf. Matthew 11:11–14). Peter's confession at Caesarea Philippi ('You are the Christ ...') is celebrated as a divine revelation (Matthew 16:17ff.), though Peter has still to learn that the Cross is an inseparable part of that revelation (cf. Matthew 16:22f.). The crucified and risen Jesus is the focus of the Church's faith. He is worthy to be worshipped. All authority is given to him. From now on, his commission is that his followers should make disciples of *all* nations. His presence will be with them to the close of the age (cf. Matthew 28:17–20).

The focus of Paul's proclamation is the crucified Messiah (1 Corinthians 1:23ff.). This is the basic substance of his preaching (*kerygma*) and the content of apostolic tradition (*paradosis*).

> For I delivered to you as of first importance what I also received, that Christ died for our sins in accordance with the scriptures, that he was buried, that he was raised on the third day in accordance with the scriptures, and that he appeared to Cephas, then to the twelve ...   (1 Corinthians 15:3f.)

Paul seems to put special emphasis on 'words of the Lord', which speak to the moral problems experienced in the young churches,[6] and he also uses this dominical tradition to regulate liturgical practice. Thus, the tradition of the last supper – 'received from the Lord' (1 Corinthians 11:23) – provides the definitive pattern for the celebration of the Lord's Supper at Corinth, a proclamation of 'the Lord's death until he comes' (1 Corinthians 11:26). To Paul and the Church is given the ministry of the new covenant, in sharp contrast to the old (cf. 2 Corinthians 3:6). The Messiah has come; there is a new creation: 'the old has passed away, behold, the new has come' (2 Corinthians 5:17). The transformation that the Messiah brings revolutionises one's understanding of time. The decisive event has already occurred. We look back to it, through the *kerygma* and the *paradosis* of the Church, in order to find the future, the consummation of all God's work in Christ (cf. 1 Corinthians 15:20–28).

The writer of the Letter to the Hebrews is particularly concerned to show that, because of Christ's work, temple sacrifice is superseded and that all prayer and worship must now be made 'through Christ', our intercessor with the Father. In an elaborate argument, he develops a high christology which is relevant to his purpose. Jesus, Son of God, who was human like us and knows full well our human weaknesses (Hebrews 4:15), is 'a high priest for ever after the order of Melchizedek' (6:20), superseding the old Levitical priesthood and inaugurating the new covenant.

> For it was fitting that we should have such a high priest, holy, blameless, unstained, separated from sinners, exalted above the heavens. He has no need, like those high priests, to offer sacrifices daily, first for his own sins and then for those of the people; he did this once for all when he offered up himself (7:26f.).

The Temple ministry was but 'a copy and shadow of the heavenly sanctuary' (8:5). Christ has entered once for all into the Holy Place (9:12), 'into heaven itself, now to appear in the presence of God on our behalf' (9:24). Repeated sacrifices are now no longer required, for the perfect self-giving of Christ is 'once for all', bearing the sin of many (cf. 9:25–28). The new covenant, established through him, brings assurance that God has forgiven sin (10:16–18). Any further sin offering is therefore redundant.

If Temple worship, with its sacrificial cultus, is at an end, what kind of liturgical action is appropriate to the people of the new covenant? The writer to the Hebrews has his answer ready:

> Since we have a great priest over the house of God, let us draw near with a true heart in full assurance of faith ... Let us hold fast the confession of our hope without wavering ... and let us consider how to stir up one another to love and good works, not neglecting to meet together, as is the habit of some, but encouraging one another ... (cf. 10:21–25).

In short, he points to a confessing, mutually supportive, worshipping community – meeting together *regularly*, and sustained by the intercessory ministry of the Son of God himself. But what of 'times and seasons'? Do these belong to the shadow rather than the substance? (cf. Colossians 2:17). Or perhaps to elementary rather than mature understanding? (cf. Hebrews 6:1). What answer did the churches give in their practice?

D—TIMES AND SEASONS IN THE EARLY CHURCH

The practice of the early Christians as described in Acts represents that of a Messianic sect on the fringe of Judaism. They observed the times of prayer in the Temple and were active in the synagogue, especially in a missionary capacity (the manner in which sectarians tend to work). The break with Judaism was probably inevitable in the long run, even if it was effected by voluntary action rather than compulsion exerted by either party. Important factors leading to it were the Christian proclamation of Jesus as the Christ and the Jewish rejection of that claim; together with the rejection by the Christians of the Old Testament Torah as the focus of God's salvation (cf. Acts 6:11). Later, when a curse on deviant Messianists was inserted in the daily benedictions in the synagogue the rupture was complete. Nevertheless, the Jewish origins of the Christian movement predisposed the Christians to accept a cyclical liturgical practice, even if the centre of the circle was Christ rather than the Mosaic Torah.

The writer of Acts suggests that *daily* observances were important in the lives of the early Christians.

> And day by day, attending the Temple together and breaking bread in their homes, they partook of food with glad and generous heart, praising God ...   (Acts 2:46f.).

Such daily observance was linked at this early stage with Temple worship and presupposed the hours of Temple prayer. There is also emphasis on Christian fellowship (*koinonia*), centred on common table in house groups. In the Didache (8:2f.), the Lord's Prayer with the Doxology is enjoined, to be recited three times daily: doubtless another echo of the Jewish practice of morning, afternoon and evening prayer. In Tertullian (*De Oratione*), prayer is said at the third, sixth and ninth hour, because this is held to be scriptural practice: but the scriptural warrant is now derived from the New Testament. The Spirit was given at the third hour (Acts 2:15); Peter prayed at the sixth hour (Acts 10:9); and Peter and John went to the Temple at the ninth hour (Acts 3:1).

Hippolytus gives a more elaborate justification of the Christian hours of prayer. The third hour marks the time when Christ was seen nailed to the wood, while the Old Testament provided the typological precedents of the offering of the shewbread and the slaying of the lamb (*Apostolic Tradition* 36:2, 3). The sixth hour marks the time when darkness fell as Christ hung on the Cross (36:4). At both times, the Christian if at home should pray and praise God; if elsewhere, he should pray in his heart to God. At the ninth hour, Christian prayer should be lengthier and characterised by praise, for this is the hour when Christ was pierced and shed his blood. The approach of evening leads on to the dawning of another day, a symbol of the resurrection (36:5, 6). In addition, Hippolytus bids all faithful men and women, on rising and before beginning work, to wash their hands and pray to God (35:1). However, if there is a teaching session that morning (i.e., an explanation of the Word), they should go there to be strengthened against whatever evil the day may bring (35:2, 3). If no such instruction is available, one should read 'a holy book' at home (36:1). One should also pray before lying down on one's bed at night (36:7). At midnight, however, one should rise, wash one's hands and pray: a domestic observance, if both partners are believers; otherwise one prays alone. No doubt the prayers on rising, on retiring and at midnight might be described as moments of prayer rather than 'hours'. The weight is put on the three traditional hours, and especially on the ninth. One may pray alone, but the fellowship of the Church has also an important place, as has family prayer. Here then is at least a plea for a full daily cycle of prayer and worship for all Christians. Hand-washing, we note, is part of the ritual: Jewish antecedents are not hard to trace. As Gregory Dix has observed,

> Hippolytus reveals clearly for the first time how firmly the Jewish liturgical basis persisted in the Catholic cultus after a century and a half of Gentile Christianity'.[7]

The paradox is that the basis of the Christian Year represents a sharp differentiation from Judaism. '... The Lord's Day, the first day of the week, is the foundation of the entire structure'.[8] Even in the New Testament, 'the first day of the week' was the day for congregational and eucharistic worship (Acts 20:7). It was the day for exercising stewardship in relation to giving (1 Corinthians 16:2). It was, above all, the Lord's Day (Revelation 1:10), the day of the resurrection. All four Gospels make much of the time of the resurrection: early on the first day of the week (Mark 16:2; Matthew 28:1; Luke 24:1; John 20:1). And as the Risen Christ was known to them in the breaking of bread (Luke 24:35), the Lord's Day was the time for celebrating the Lord's Supper. 'On every Lord's Day – the day that belongs specially to Him – come together and break bread and give thanks' (Didache 14:1). It was a day of joy and praise, when fasting and penitential kneeling were out of place and indeed came to be expressly forbidden. As the first day of the week, it recalled the Day of Creation. Thus Justin –

> We all hold this common gathering on the day of the sun, since it is the first day, on which God transformed the darkness and matter and made the universe, and Jesus Christ our Saviour rose from the dead on the same day.[10]

It was also called 'the eighth day', described in the *Epistle of Barnabas* (so-called) as 'the beginning of another world'. For that reason 'we also celebrate with gladness the eighth day in which Jesus also rose from the dead, and was made manifest, and ascended into heaven'.[11] Noile M. Denis-Boulet comments,

Thus what impressed the early Christians was the new beginning, the renewal of the cycle, symbolised in music by the octave. In conformity with the mysterious significance of cyclic time, which we have mentioned in connection with primitive man, it is the first day of the week, but inasmuch as it recurs and is identical with the eighth day it represents both the eternity of God and eternity shared by redeemed mankind.[12]

The Lord's Day was thus rich in symbolism and characterised by joy. It was totally distinct from the sabbath that ended with dusk in the seventh day, even if Jewish Christians such as the Ebionites observed both.[13] Ignatius probably spoke for most Christians when he said that they ceased to keep the Sabbath and lived for (or by) the Lord's Day (*Magnesians* 9:1). The latter was, as Justin makes clear, the day for the reading of the scriptures, for the preaching of the Word and for the celebration of the eucharist.

On the day called Sunday there is a meeting in one place of those who live in cities or the country, and the memoirs of the apostles or the writings of the prophets are read as long as time permits. When the reader has finished, the president in a discourse urges and invites (us) to the imitation of these noble things. Then we all stand up together and offer prayers. And, as said before, when we have finished the prayer, bread is brought and wine and water ....[14]

It was a day that focused on the great realities of the faith and celebrated God's salvation in thanksgiving and joy.

Thus, as Thomas Talley has observed, 'the earliest community found the week a sufficient frame for the ordering of its prayer and fasting'.[15] Wednesdays and Fridays are singled out by the *Didache* as fasts, in contradistinction to the Jewish fasts on Mondays and Thursdays. Later, we find Wednesday linked to the day of betrayal and Friday to the crucifixion. Thus the cycle of the week relates to the cycle of the individual days: each of them to be lived as in the presence of God, in thankful recollection of his saving work in Christ. Two of them came to be characterised as fast days, in whole or in part. The Sabbath or seventh day carried an obligation to rest, although not all Christians could have found it possible to observe it literally. The Lord's Day was the celebration of the resurrection, when in Word and Sacrament the fullness of the Lord's work was proclaimed and received, and his *parousia* awaited with expectation.

Since the weekly cycle appears to encompass all that is vital in Christian life and liturgy, what prompted the emergence of the Christian *Year*? Several features encouraged the process. The early Jewish Christians were already so familiar with the annual Jewish festivals that they could not simply ignore them as markers of 'significant' time. Instead, they defined their significance in Christian terms. The beginning of the process can be seen in the New Testament. If Paul could say, 'Christ *our* paschal lamb has been sacrificed. Let us, therefore, celebrate the festival ...' (1 Corinthians 5:7f.), it is difficult to see how Christians, especially of Jewish background, could fail to associate Passover time with the death of Christ and the sealing of the new covenant. Again, when Paul writes, 'I will stay in Ephesus until Pentecost' (1 Corinthians 16:8), he and the Corinthians whom he addressed were clearly still using the Jewish feasts as points of reference, if not of celebration; and it was only a matter of time before Pentecost acquired a definitive Christian connotation, viz., the giving of the Spirit and the birth of the Church as in the Book of Acts. 'A matter of time' is, of course, the operative phrase in this context. As long as intense eschatological expectation focused on the *parousia* as an imminent event, chronological time (as opposed to 'significant' time) was of relatively little concern. But with the passing of the years, the perspective was so adjusted that a yearly cycle became increasingly meaningful.

An important indicator of change is the Quartodeciman Pasch. It followed the Jewish (i.e., lunar) calendar. While the Jews celebrated their festival, the Christians fasted on 14 Nisan in remembrance of Christ's Passion. As far as we can deduce, there was a vigil from 14 to 15 Nisan, in the course of which the Passover recital in Exodus 12 was read (with or without Christian *midrash* or commentary). Baptisms may have their place at this point, and at cockcrow the fast was broken with the *agape* or love feast and eucharist. Finally, there was a sermon on the Passion of which Melito's *Peri Pascha* is a good example.[16]

The transition to the Good Friday-Easter observance is not difficult to imagine. The Church came to adopt the solar calendar of the Roman Empire, rather than the Jewish lunar year (the Council of Nicea had to rule on this matter). The celebration of the eucharist seemed much more appropriate on the Sunday, the day of the resurrection. To Friday, already a fast day, was added – exceptionally – the Saturday as a prolongation of the fast, which terminated about cockcrow on Sunday morning. The whole observance, with its movement from suffering and death to the new life of the resurrection, commemorated Christ's passion.[17] It came to provide the context, *par excellence*, for baptism.[18] It 'established the year as a liturgically sensitive cycle for Christianity'.[19] Moreover, since the passion of Christ was thus observed at a specific date, it seemed appropriate that the Christian martyrs be similarly honoured as participating in the Lord's suffering, and a rash of commemorative feasts began to spread over the calendar.

Pentecost in the early Church was used not only of the fiftieth day but of the fifty days of 'exultation' (so Tertullian) following the Pasch: 'days of rest and joy' (according to the Council of Nicea), when fasting and kneeling in penitence were out of order. Pentecost itself or Whit Sunday was said by Tertullian to be a happy occasion for the administration of baptism (next after the Pasch itself), and his references suggest that the themes of resurrection, ascension and the second coming were appropriate to it. A. A. McArthur, commenting also on Eusebius' references to it, writes:

In view of the direct evidence it cannot be doubted that early in the fourth century the Day of Pentecost was a unitive festival, commemorating both the Ascension of our Lord and the Descent of the Holy Spirit. The season of the fifty days was 'sealed', completed, by this Day, for this was the culmination of the rejoicing in the eternal Kingdom of God which began with the Pascha.[20]

The third ancient Christian festival, according to the fourth century Egyptian *Canons of Athanasius*, was Epiphany (6 January). It was associated with the baptism of Jesus by John, but it was also a new year's feast at the ingathering of harvest among the Egyptians. They linked it also with the wedding at Cana and the story of water into wine. In Jerusalem, however, it was apparently the feast of the nativity. Other themes found associated with it include the adoration of the Magi, the transfiguration and the loaves and fishes. T. Talley comments:

Here, evidently, we are confronted with a feast celebrating not an event on the known date of its original occurrence, but rather the manifestation of Christ's divine power, the appearing of divine glory in history, as a concept exemplified in a plurality of events in the gospel. Indeed, in Gaul the feast will regularly celebrate the *tria miracula* of the adoration of the Magi, the baptism and the wedding at Cana.[21]

A. A. McArthur noted that John 1:1–2:11 presents just such a theme as the manifestation of the glory of the Son of God, and tentatively but intriguingly suggested the feast of Epiphany at Ephesus towards the end of the first century as the *Sitz im Leben* of this part of the Fourth Gospel.[22]

Christmas was observed at Rome on the winter solstice, 25 December, from at least A.D. 336, and celebrated the nativity of the 'Sun of Righteousness'. Previously, this date had been 'the birthday of the unconquered sun' (*natalis solis invicti*), and the Christian signification did not by any means completely displace the older reference for several centuries. It was also resisted in some parts of the Church, including Jerusalem and Alexandria, where the nativity continued to be celebrated at Epiphany.

However, the framework of the Christian Year is now beginning to emerge. It remains only to add the forty days of preparation for the Pasch (Lent), which we find in Athanasius, and within this period to designate the Monday and Thursday in Holy Week as of particular significance; and also a six-Sunday Advent, which is found in Gaul in the fifth century. Within the period of Pentecost, Ascension Sunday is singled out in deference to the Lukan presentation. These may be regarded as the essentials. There are many elaborations, some of which deserve to be described as deformations.

But the last word on this subject may be given to Origen. He has

suggested that Christians cannot observe the pagan holidays and
continues:

> If anyone makes a rejoinder to this by talking of our
> observances on certain days – the Lord's Day which we keep, or
> the Preparation (i.e., the Friday stations), or the Passover (i.e.,
> the Pasch) or Pentecost – we would reply to this that the perfect
> man ... is continually observing the Lord's Day. Moreover, since
> he is always making himself ready for the true life and
> abstaining from the pleasures of this life which deceive the
> multitude ... he is always observing the Preparation (i.e., the
> stations). Furthermore, if a man has understood that 'Christ our
> passover was sacrificed' and that he ought to 'keep the feast' by
> eating the flesh of the Logos, there is not a moment when he is
> not keeping the Passover (i.e., the paschal feast) ... In addition
> to this, if a man is able to say truthfully 'we are risen with
> Christ' ... he is always living in the days of Pentecost.[23]

In modern jargon, we might speak of the need to *internalise* the liturgical
cycle, so that it is one with the cycle of our own living and being: a sobering
thought to all who are tempted to be over-fascinated with formal
observance. It also means, however, that the liturgical cycle, properly
conceived, is the notation of the music of heaven, celebrating and
proclaiming the salvation which God has wrought for mankind in Christ.

E—THE DAILY OFFICES

The apostolic injunction was to 'pray constantly' (1 Thessalonians 5:17).
How are Christians to respond to such a requirement? At Thessalonika,
there was a tendency for them to fill all their hours with fervent spiritual
activity, to the detriment or abandonment of the responsibility to work. To
that line of thinking an official disclaimer was administered (2
Thessalonians 3:6–13; cf. 1 Thessalonians 5:14). The Christian life is one of
constant prayer, joy, thanksgiving ... and responsible action. 'If anyone
will not work, let him not eat' (2 Thessalonians 3:10). Another extreme
view, of good pedigree, is to identify work and prayer. The crucial question
is how a balance is to be achieved. One attempt was through the ordered
life of religious community, with its daily cycle of observance. 'It is a
matter not of producing a certain quantity of prayers said at any moment
within the space of twenty-four hours but of the existence of as continual a
prayer as possible based on the support of celebrations spaced at regular
intervals.'[24]

Indeed, one support which the ordinary Christian could have, distracted
as he often was with the responsibilities of worldly existence, was that of
the worshipping community. Prayer in the fellowship of believers was
generally acknowledged as the best practice for everyone; prayer *en famille*

was the next best thing; individual prayer, while always important, should
not be regarded as a substitute for corporate prayer, except in emergency.
Hence it was common practice, in East and West, for believers to gather at
least twice a day – i.e., morning and evening – for liturgically ordered
prayers, with psalms or hymns.

The monastic orders observed a much fuller cycle, related to the division
of the day into four parts (marked off by prayers at the third, sixth and
ninth hours, following scriptural warrant) and to major points in the daily
cycle: dawn, sunrise, sunset, nightfall. Thus, in the fourth century
Apostolic Constitutions, probably from the Syrian Church, we find the
following offices: the night office (at cockcrow), *orthros* (at daybreak), the
third, sixth and ninth hours, and the evening office. Chrysostom gives a
vivid account of the Superior awakening the monks for the night office at
cockcrow, followed closely by morning prayers at daybreak. Basil
comments that *orthros* marks the point at which the monks and the local
community associated with them praise God before leaving for their place
of work: a deliberate incorporating of the monastic and lay traditions. The
community reassembles, if possible, for the office at the third hour. Basil
also mentions an office when the day's work ends, another when night
begins, and finally prayer in the middle of the night: after all, did not Paul
and Silas in prison pray and sing hymns to God about that hour? (Acts
16:25). The ideal is not simply that the monk should keep set times of
prayer, but that his whole life – day and night – should be one of continual
prayer and reflection on the scriptural word.

In the West, monasteries came to base their cycle of daily offices on the
Rule of St. Benedict, and from about the eighth century the canonical 'day
hours' were as follows: (i) *Lauds*: the early morning office; it derives its
name from the recurring 'praise ye' (*laudate*) in Psalms 148–50, which were
part of this order until 1911. (ii) *Prime*: (iii) *Terce*: (iv) *Sext*: (v) *None*: the
offices appointed for the first, third, sixth, and ninth hours. (vi) *Vespers*:
the office appointed to be read in the evening. Having undergone
modifications in the course of its life, it consists today of a hymn, two
psalms, a N.T. canticle, a lesson, responsory, the Magnificat with
antiphons, and prayers. (vii) *Compline*: the last office of the day, recited
before retiring. With a hymn and psalms, the Nunc Dimittis is said. (viii)
Matins: the night office. Its characteristic element was the 'Te Deum'.

The eight offices comprise the 'sacred sevenfold' ('seven times a day I
praise thee' – Psalm 119:164) and the night office ('at midnight I rise to
praise thee' – Psalm 119:62). With the passage of time, the keeping of the
daily offices tended to become an end in itself; practice requires to be
constantly related to the original intention of continual prayer, praise and
reflection. The need for revision has therefore been felt from time to time.
The Breviary, in which the divine office for the Roman Catholic Church is
set out, underwent major revision in 1568, 1911 and 1971.[25] The 1971
revision, prompted by Vatican II, was thorough-going and 'went well
beyond a simple return to the Rule of St. Benedict'.[26] Prime dropped out
for the most part, and other changes simplified the structure of the daily
cycle. As Adalbert de Vogüé has observed:

The hours of prayer are only the infrastructure of continual prayer, the accented moments in a melody which aspires to be uninterrupted. Their aim is to realise the continuous consecration of time in a figurative and inchoate way. The Christian who observes them finds in them a reminder, staggered over shorter or longer intervals, of his call to pray without ceasing, a safeguard against immersion into temporal anxieties and forgetfulness of the Lord, a renewal of his converse with God.[27]

It remains only to note that since the Reformation, the Anglican communion has used the service of Morning Prayer (Matins) and Evening Prayer (Evensong), as set out in the various Books of Common Prayer (esp. 1662). Matins combines material from the mediaeval office of that name with additions from Lauds and Prime. Evensong combines Vespers and Compline. Although the 1662 B.C.P. provided the standard for centuries, various attempts at revision were made (and sometimes frustrated) in the twentieth century. Since 1965, 'alternative' services have introduced a measure of variation and abbreviation of traditional forms. What is significant, however, is the emphasis upon the Word. The basic structure of these offices is that of the mediaeval 'liturgy of the porch': services of worship which were a prelude to but not a celebration of the eucharist, and which made extensive use of scripture in reading, singing and meditation. In Lutheranism also, morning and evening Sunday services derive from this same basic structure and origin.

F—FAMILY AND PERSONAL PRAYER

It is not, of course only in congregations and religious communities that worship is offered to God. Private devotions and family worship are just as much the necessary context for public worship as are the offices of religious communities. Indeed, with the Reformation's general rejection of monasticism there came a renewed emphasis on the importance of family worship and private prayer. All Christians equally were now seen as belonging to the 'spiritual estate', and this involved for everyone the need to give time to nurturing the relationship with God.

There was, of course, nothing novel in this emphasis. Jewish worship, as we have seen, gave a major place to the rituals of the home. Of these Passover was certainly the greatest, but in a real sense every family meal was an occasion for worship. And when Jesus urged his hearers to go into their closets and pray to God in secret he was not introducing the notion of private prayer for the first time, but simply calling for authenticity in the practices of private prayer to which all pious Jews were accustomed. And in the case of Jesus himself, the Gospel accounts suggest that he gave much time to private prayer and prayer with his disciples in addition to attendance at the worship of temple and synagogue.

Patterns of family and private prayer vary widely across the spectrum of the Christian Church. Roman Catholic, Anglican and Orthodox clergy are obliged to say daily offices. The laity may take part in these offices when they are said in church, and they hold up before all Christians a strenuous and bible-centred pattern of praying. The Rosary and many other forms of popular devotion developed as helps to prayer for individuals and small groups who wished a simple structure for their praying. As long as the Mass involved little more than the physical presence of the laity, they were trained to occupy themselves with private devotions while present at Mass. In all these traditions there developed a fairly sharp distinction between the spirituality of the clergy and religious, who were regarded as people set aside for prayer, and the laity, of whom much less was expected by way of prayer.

It was the churches of the Reformation which, in radically reinterpreting the distinction between clergy and laity, expected most of the laity. On Sundays, before and after public worship, and morning and evening on weekdays, families were to assemble for worship, and in addition each individual was expected to devote time daily to private devotions. On Sundays the church met in the church building; on weekdays it met in families, the father playing the role of the minister on Sundays. Family worship centred on the Bible, and consisted of systematic Bible reading, the singing of psalms, and extempore or conceived prayer. In the Scottish *Directory for Family Worship* (1647) a concession is made to the weaker brethren:

> As many as can conceive prayer, ought to make use of that gift of God; albeit those who are rude and weaker may begin at a set form of prayer, but so as they be not sluggish in stirring up in themselves (according to their daily necessities) the spirit of prayer, which is given to all the children of God in some measure: to which effect, they ought to be more fervent and frequent in secret prayer to God, for enabling of their hearts to conceive, and their tongues to express, convenient desires to God for their family.

The ideal was the cultivation throughout the congregation of a Bible-centred piety by the encouragement of family and personal devotion, with the Sunday worship as the culmination in one place of the dispersed devotions of the week. And the whole was impregnated with Scripture and at its best closely integrated into the whole pattern of life.[28]

There are thus two main alternative patterns of personal and family worship, which we might label the monastic and the Reformed. Both are strenuous and in each the Scriptures have a major place. Each fits into an overall structure of worship which reminds us that, strictly speaking, there is no such thing as private prayer: all praying is in unity with the whole Church and its Lord. In prayer no one should feel isolated for he or she is joining with the faithful of every age and land, and with angels and archangels and the whole company of heaven in praising God and offering our prayers to him.

Each pattern is an exacting ideal which, for a variety of reasons, is peculiarly difficult to sustain today. The monastic pattern was meant for monks and clergy, not for people 'in the world', and it is hard for anyone with varied family, work and social responsibilities to live a life of prayer designed for monks or celibate clergy. The Reformed pattern was intended for laity and ministers alike, but changing modes of family life and the pressures of modern industrial society have made it almost impossible to sustain in the twentieth century a pattern of spirituality which was feasible from the sixteenth to the nineteenth centuries. Besides, modern understandings of the Bible make it difficult to use it in prayer in just the same way as it was in the past in the Reformed tradition.

Such difficulties lead to a sense of guilt and even of despair on the part of many Christians who feel that they should follow one or other model of prayer in its exacting detail. Others become depressed because, so far from finding that they make progress in prayer, they seem to lose ground. The first, and most important, thing to say to such people is this: what really matters is the relationship with God, which God himself establishes and sustains. Our prayers are simply our response. Their excellence does not earn us God's favour, nor do our faltering prayers lose us God's love. In our relationship with God, as in our relationships with our fellows, guilt can be a very disabling thing, and guilt at being unable to sustain some great ideal of prayer is quite unnecessary guilt. What we have elsewhere spoken of as 'the Abba principle' in prayer suggests that we should pray to God in the way that is natural to us and not force our prayers into the straitjacket of some inherited pattern that we cannot really make our own. And we should be flexible as well as disciplined in prayer, realizing that a pattern of devotion that is appropriate in one situation may not fit another at all, and should be modified or changed.

There is wisdom in the Hindu teaching on the four *ashramas*: each major stage of life has its own pattern of spirituality. The youngster (*brahmacharya*) learns of God from his *guru* and is introduced to prayer and meditation. The married (*grihasthva*) serve God in bringing up their children and working in the world. When the children are flown from the nest husband and wife together devote more and more of their time to the things of God (*Vanaprasthya*). Finally, to prepare for death, the individual renounces the world and goes off into the jungle to devote himself entirely to the things of the spirit (*sannyasa*). It is often like that, too, in the West and for Christians. No one should feel upset that the pattern of spirituality which served well at one stage in life is not appropriate at another, or that the life of prayer has to be kept under constant review, and changed from time to time. Rigidity is the foe of relationship, and prayer is a central part of our encounter with God.

NOTES

1. Cf. Y. Vainstein, *The Cycle of the Jewish Year*, 2 ed., Jerusalem, p. 87.
2. *Ibid.*, p. 95.
3. *Ibid.*, p. 22.
4. Cf. J. Weingreen, *From Bible to Mishna*, Manchester 1976, pp. 115–28.
5. Cf. S. de Vries, 'Time in the Bible', in *The Times of Celebration* (ed. D. Power), *Concilium*, February 1981, pp. 4–10.
6. Cf. 1 Thessalonians 4:15; 1 Corinthians 9:14 (cf. 9:4); 1 Corinthians 7:10f.; 1 Corinthians 11:23–34. For a discussion of such passages, see J. I. H. McDonald, *Kerygma and Didache*, 1980, pp. 112–25.
7. *The Treatise on the Apostolic Tradition of St. Hippolytus of Rome*, London 1968, p. xliii.
8. A. A. McArthur, *The Evolution of the Christian Year*, London 1953, p. 13; cf. T. Talley, 'A Christian Heortology', in *Concilium* (as above), p. 15 f.
9. So Tertullian, *Concerning Prayer* 23; *On the Soldier's Chaplet* 3.
10. I Apol. 67:3f.
11. *Epistle of Barnabas*, XV.
12. *The Christian Calendar*, London 1960, p. 38f.
13. Cf. Eusebius, *Ecclesiastical History*, III, 27.
14. I Apol. 67:2f.
15. *Art. cit.*, p. 16.
16. Cf. O. Perler, *Méliton de Sardes Sur la Pâque*, 1966, p. 24f.
17. Talley, *art. cit.*, p. 17.
18. *Ibid.*
19. *Ibid.*, p. 18.
20. A. A. McArthur, *op. cit.*, p. 151f.
21. Talley, *op. cit.*, p. 19.
22. McArthur, *op. cit.*, p. 69.
23. Origen, *Contra Celsum*, VIII, 22; translation adapted from H. Chadwick, *Origen: Contra Celsum*, Cambridge 1953, p. 468.
24. A. de Vogüé, 'Monastic Life and Times of Prayer in Common', in *Concilium* (cited above), p. 73.
25. On 1568, cf. P. Janelle, *The Catholic Reformation*, Milwaukee 1971, p. 86f.
26. A. de Vogüé, *art. cit.*, p. 72.
27. *Art. cit.*, p. 73.
28. A good, and not untypical, instance of this kind of Reformed piety is to be found in Owen Chadwick *The Reformation*, Harmondsworth 1964, pp. 180–3.

FURTHER READING

N. M. Denis-Boulet, *The Christian Calendar*, London 1960.
A. A. McArthur, *The Evolution of the Christian Year*, London 1953.

A. A. McArthur, *The Christian Year and Lectionary Reform*, London 1958.
Nathaniel Micklem, ed., *Prayers and Praises*, London 1954.
David Power (ed.), *The Times of Celebration* (*Concilium* 1981).
G. S. Stewart, *The Lower Levels of Prayer*, London 1939.

FOR DISCUSSION

1. Luther said: 'Days and times should not control Christians. Rather, Christians freely exercise control over days and times'. Given this freedom, is there any need to set aside special times for worship, prayer and devotion?
2. In what way should Sunday be observed by Christians, and how can its benefits be shared with the secular world?
3. 'Christian worship is not about timeless truths, nor is it primarily concerned with times and seasons. It is about the timely action of God for our salvation.' Discuss.
4. What special problems face family and personal prayer today? How may they best be responded to?

CHAPTER 9

WORSHIP AND PASTORAL CARE

A—INTRODUCTION

Worship and pastoral care – here, surely, we have two central activities of the Christian Church, two indispensable aspects of Christian praxis. The two are interdependent, and each illumines the other. When Christians treat worship as an escape from caring for the neighbour and being responsive to the needs of the world, when worship becomes an alternative to the doing of justice, when clergy attempt to avoid the role-ambiguity of the pastor by affirming their professionalism as 'experts in liturgy', then worship is being radically distorted by the dissolution of the necessary partnership between liturgy and pastoral care. The two share a whole range of common themes: grace, guilt, forgiveness, new beginnings, dialogue, communication, fellowship, reconciliation, healing are obviously the concern both of worship and of pastoral care. In its own fashion, each attempts to help men and women to cope with reality, open themselves to truth, and grow towards a mature relationship with God and their fellows. Of course they overlap and flow into one another; they are complementary – and more, for it would be fair to say that liturgy is a dimension of Christian pastoral care, and pastoral care is a dimension of Christian worship.

We are not suggesting that there is in worship *nothing but* pastoral care going on, and certainly not that pastoral care can be absorbed entirely into worship. There is more to worship than pastoral care, and *vice versa*. Worship is not just a kind of group therapy or corporate pastoral counselling, but none the less it plays an important, perhaps indispensable, part in the processes of healing, restoring, reconciling, purifying, growing, and forming fellowship. In other words, there is a highly significant overlap between the two activities; worship has a pastoral dimension and pastoral care has a liturgical dimension.

We are not arguing that worship is a good thing because it is psychologically beneficial or socially useful. It may well perform such functions, well or ill (indeed there is no doubt at all that it does), but that is not the reason why people worship. We glorify and praise God because 'it is our duty and our joy', not because we seek some personal or collective benefit. That such benefits can flow from worship and are promised in worship should not be forgotten. But that is not the point of worship, and it would become mechanical if such expectations were to come to the fore. Worship used simply as a means of psychological hygiene or emotional manipulation is perverted and loses its authenticity; but we should expect participation in the worship of God to affect profoundly the deepest levels of our personality and emotions and relationships, and to shape and disturb the life of the worshipping community. Yet these fruits of worship are not its justification.

There is more to worship than the pastoral dimension – that is most certainly true. But if that element is lacking, worship is defective and inadequate. And likewise with pastoral care; there must be a dimension of worship or its integrity as *Christian* pastoral care has to be called into question.

B—THE PASTORAL DIMENSION IN WORSHIP

'For centuries,' wrote A. J. Jungmann, a leading Roman Catholic liturgical scholar, 'the liturgy, actively celebrated, has been the most important form for pastoral care.'[1] One could demonstrate the truth of this remark by drawing up a list of the rites and elements in worship which clearly have a significant and necessary pastoral content: penance, confession, funerals, baptism, confirmation, the 'Peace', marriage, and so on. But Jungmann means more than that; the pastoral should be a dimension in all worship, not simply a characteristic of certain moments or types of worship. Because the church, the community which worships, is a pastoral fellowship, pastoral care should be the context, content and consequence of its worship. The God who is worshipped is the Shepherd of his people, and it is as Shepherd that he deals with his people in worship, enabling them to exercise a mutual pastoral care and outreach to all mankind.

This mutuality in pastoral caring deserves some emphasis. Worship considered as a human activity is something in which the whole people of God participates actively; it is not the acts and speech of 'professionals', of experts, which the people observe and listen to passively and without personal involvement. Similarly, the pastoral care that takes place in worship is not provided by the priest, pastor or minister for a passive people, but something in which every worshipper should participate both as provider and as recipient. And in the reciprocity of this kind of worshipful pastoral care, God's people encounter his care through their care for one another.

There is such a thing as a *pastoral* theology of worship, reminding us of the important fact that in worship God is dealing with *people*, both as individuals and in their collectivities. As soon as this is lost sight of, and the pastoral dimension in worship is neglected, worship becomes mechanical and impersonal and ultimately degenerates into magic. But such worship is defective in that it does not express God's concern for the individual and his communities, God's care for people, and the Christian fellowship's reflection of that care.

In worship that is authentically Christian, believers should experience God's loving care in and through the mutuality of caring within the fellowship, and find resources of insight and sensitivity to deepen and enrich their care. Those who encounter the Lord in worship should learn there how to discern his presence in the neighbour and in the needs of the world.

C—THE LITURGICAL DIMENSION IN PASTORAL CARE

When worship and pastoral care become separated from one another, pastoral care easily becomes secular, theologically empty and rooted in the latest theories of psychotherapy without reference to the Christian tradition. A kind of individualism takes over, suggesting that pastoral care has nothing to do with the flock or the fellowship, but takes place in one-to-one therapeutic sessions or small encounter groups. The pastor then becomes the expert, whose skills disable mutual pastoral care within the fellowship. The emphasis is increasingly on crisis intervention: care is less and less seen as an ongoing process of support, encouragement, learning and growth, and more and more as the solving of problems, the healing of sickness. These medical or psychiatric models can only take over if worship is pushed to the periphery.

It is easy for pastoral care to conform to secular models of counselling and therapy so that clergy are regarded – and sometimes see themselves – as counsellors and therapists and a great gulf opens between what happens in the counselling session and what happens in worship. It is even possible to find clergy who regard what goes on in the worship of the Christian community as an anachronistic distraction from the 'real business' of counselling individuals. There is in such cases a theologically suspect split between the sanctuary, which takes on the quality of a museum, and the study, office, or vestry, which is regarded more and more as a clinic. In the one the community gathers for rituals which its leaders no longer believe significant; in the other the weak, bruised, or sick individual meets the professional problem-solver or therapist.

The liturgical dimension protects three particular emphases in pastoral care. First, it expresses and reminds us of God's primary role in caring for people. Pastoral caring, in other words, has to do with grace; the pastoral activities of the Church, like its worship, are participation in the ongoing work of God. Secondly, we are reminded that the whole community is involved in caring, as it is involved in worshipping. Pastoral care is not something that can be delegated to a few or monopolized by an elite within the Church. When caring is concentrated in the person of the pastor and the community becomes dependent on his skills and competence, we have a new kind of sacerdotalism, which like all sacerdotalism deprives the People of God of their true functions and responsibility, reducing the laity to the status of 'clients' or 'patients' of a falsely professionalized clergy.

Pastoral care is a responsibility of the whole household of faith which constantly interacts with worship, the central praxis of that fellowship. Thirdly, it follows that there must be an ongoing dialectical interaction between theology and pastoral care. Pastoral care dare not cut loose from theology and attempt to root itself exclusively in psychological and sociological theory. Nor is it merely the application of an already established theology. Pastoral care which is Christian must both listen to theology and ask theology hard questions which arise out of the caring experience.

Worship is a collective activity, something that the Christian fellowship does. More than mutuality is involved here: the members of the community of faith care for one another and for their needy neighbours, that is true, but this care must also concern the structures of society which so deeply affect people's lives and happiness. Thus there is a necessary interaction and movement between the pastoral and the political. Since the Church may aptly be described as the sacrament of the unity of all mankind, we should not be surprised that the Church's worship is full of signs of those structures of community which sustain fraternity and harmony. In other words, Christian worship is a political act, making statements and symbolic demonstrations concerning the nature of the Kingdom. Worship is prophetic to the world; it expresses the nature of Christian community, and thus proclaims what true fellowship is and what society should be. It makes the Gospel clear and visible. When Christians exchange the sign of Peace, or share the bread and the cup, or offer themselves to God, they are symbolically affirming God's care for them, their responsive caring for one another and the care for the world God loves, which is at the heart of mission.

D—PASTORAL THEMES IN WORSHIP

(i) *Fellowship*
In worship fellowship is both expressed and strengthened. The symbols which we use effect what they express, like the kiss which simultaneously shows and confirms love. In worship God and his people open themselves to one another in love and service, so that worship involves mutual commitment to one another and to God, the whole being grounded on the self-giving of God in Christ. And worship is a pledge, a binding commitment to God and his people and purposes. In worship we enroll anew in the household of faith.

Worship is meeting, encounter with God and with our fellows. In worship fellowship is made, sustained, confirmed. Karl Barth was right when he said, 'It is not only in worship that the community is edified and edifies itself. But it is here first that this continuously takes place. And if it does not take place here, it does not take place anywhere'.[2] The Church is edified by the Word encountered and received in worship, by the challenge, strengthening, encouragement, enlightenment, affirmation, direction, forgiveness, hope, conviviality received in worship, and above all by the awareness mediated through worship of acceptance and incorporation into a supportive, understanding and purposive community. Worship gives us a sense of belonging.

Worship is also concerned with the restoration of fellowship. There has recently been a recovery of the understanding that sin is primarily a breach in relationship with God and with one's fellows, rather than violation of law. Sin divides people from God and from one another; forgiveness means reconciliation, the healing of estrangement and the restoration of fellowship: 'where sin has divided and scattered, may your love make one again', runs part of one of the prayers in the new Roman *Rite of Penance*. In worship, or sometimes as part of the preliminaries to worship, sin is recognized and confessed, and with forgiveness the worshipper knows himself to be accepted fully and without condition into fellowship with God and the Church. General confession and absolution have a place in almost all forms of worship. In the Middle Ages these corporate acts of confession became increasingly overshadowed by an even more complex system of individual sacramental confession in which penances were carefully allocated to particular sins, and the performance of these penances was the condition for the receiving of absolution. The wilder shores of penance, particularly the system of indulgences, attracted the wrath of the Reformers, and they attacked the system as legalistic, sacerdotalist (because of the power of the priest over the penitent) and shot through with justification by works rather than grace. To replace the individual penitential process, the Reformers emphasized two things: corporate confession as an indispensable part of congregational worship and the system called by the Calvinists 'ecclesiastical discipline'. The former frequently developed into a repetitive and verbose part of the service of worship, the emphasis often being more on long catalogues of sins than on God's gracious forgiveness. The latter, as developed in Geneva, Scotland and other Calvinist countries, involved the minister and elders having special responsibilities for the oversight of morals. Offenders were brought to trial before the Session or Consistory, and a whole range of penalties from private admonitions to excommunication were available to help to bring offenders to repentance. The more heinous offences involved several appearances in church at the 'stool of repentance', there to be publicly rebuked before forgiveness was proclaimed. In the form for Public Repentance used in Scotland in the sixteenth and early seventeenth centuries, absolution is pronounced with great authority and the penitent is then received back warmly to the congregation: 'The minister shall say, in manner of absolution: If thou unfeignedly repent of thy former iniquity, and believe in the Lord Jesus, then I, in his name, pronounce and affirm that thy sins are forgiven, not only on earth, but also in heaven, according to the promises annexed with the preaching of his word, and to the power put in the ministry of his Church.

Then shall the elders and deacons, with ministers (if any be), in the name of the whole Church, take the reconciled brother by the hand, and embrace him, in sign of full reconciliation.'[3]

Although in such exercise of discipline the whole congregation is encouraged to join in confession and seeking forgiveness, the system quickly became legalistic and hard, often becoming a public spectacle in which some of the 'godly' rejoiced at the discomfiture of the sinners. The note of solidarity sounded clearly in Knox's Liturgy, ceased to be heard: 'We all here present join our sins with your sins; we all repute and esteem your fall to be our own; we accuse ourselves no less than we accuse you; now, finally, we join our prayers with yours, that we and you may obtain mercy, and that by the means of the Lord Jesus Christ.'[4] Instead, self-righteousness, judgementalism and gossip were engendered.

The remnants of 'ecclesiastical discipline' and the practice of private sacramental penance have been very properly criticized by those who seek a renewed and living experssion of confession and forgiveness in the life and worship of the Church. Alastair Campbell, for instance, argues that the fact that 'we rightly shy away from an *imposed* penitence, from a heavy-handed judgement on others which reduces them to the status of errant children requiring interrogation and hard discipline ... should not prevent us from pointing the way and leading the way to a positive form of penitence, which goes *through* the complexity of human motivation not away from it.'[5] Justifiable impatience with the neat distinctions and tidy classifications of the older penitential system led to its sharp decline in modern times. All Christian traditions are now seeking, with variable success, to encourage communal and flexible rites of confession and reconciliation as integral parts of worship, and more informal and personal ways of confession, counselling and mutual support.[6] Through reconciliation and forgiveness, fellowship is restored.

(ii) *Wholeness*
Precisely because it engages the whole personality, worship has a role to play in the integration of the personality. Worship can help in the overcoming of the great splits engendered by our culture, between reason and the emotions, the body and the spirit; but sadly it sometimes reflects and accentuates these cleavages.

If worship speaks to the heart as well as to the head, if it communicates to the feelings and plays a part in what John Macmurray called 'the education of the emotions'[7] there should be an accepted place for the expression of emotion in worship. Take, for instance, grief. In western cultures it is often felt that strong emotion should not be expressed in public, that even at a funeral service it is 'not done' to weep. This attitude persists despite the increasing popular awareness that bottled-up grief is often destructive, and shows itself in other ways which can be persistent and disabling. Even among Christians many would see public grieving as a sign of emotional instability or spiritual weakness and inadequacy. But the Gospels record that Jesus wept over Jerusalem, the city that he loved, and over his dead friend Lazarus.

It is similar with the split between body and spirit. Although views which depreciate the body have been repeatedly labelled heretical, and William Temple could speak of Christianity as the most materialistic of all the great religions, despite the fact that Christians believe that the Word became flesh, that in Jesus, God was embodied, the body has often been despised. But in authentic Christian worship the body is accepted as an integral and splendid aspect of the person; spiritual worship is also, and necessarily, bodily worship, in which the body is an agent of celebration in harmony with mind, spirit and heart.

(iii) *Liberation*
Listen to James Cone speaking of the significance of worship for American Blacks:

> The eschatological significance of the black community is found in the people believing that the Spirit of Jesus is coming to visit them in the worship service each time two or three are gathered in his name, and to bestow upon them a new vision of their future humanity. This eschatological revolution is ... a change in the people's identity, wherein they are no longer named by the world but named by the Spirit of Jesus ... The Holy Spirit's presence with the people is a liberating experience. Black people who have been humiliated and oppressed by the structures of white society six days of the week, gather together each Sunday morning in order to experience a new definition of their humanity. The transition from Saturday to Sunday is not just a chronological change from the seventh to the first day of the week. It is rather a rupture in time ... which produces a radical transformation in the people's identity. The janitor becomes the chairperson of the Deacon Board; the maid becomes the president of the Stewardess Board Number 1. Everyone becomes Mr. and Mrs., or Brother and Sister. The last becomes first, making a radical change of self and one's calling in the society. Every person becomes somebody, and one can see the people's recognition of their new found identity by the way they walk and talk and 'carry themselves'. They walk with a rhythm of an assurance that they know where they are going, and they talk as if they know the truth about which they speak. It is this experience of being radically transformed by the power of the Spirit that defines the primary style of black worship. This transformation is found not only in the titles of Deacons, Stewardesses, Trustees and Ushers, but also in the excitement of the entire congregation at worship. To be at the end of time where one has been given a new name requires a passionate response with the felt power of the Spirit in one's heart.[8]

All round the world, in all sorts of contexts, one finds this exhilarating experience of Christian worship as liberating. Polish shipyard workers, striking for free trade unions and free expression in an authoritarian society, are sustained in their search for liberty by daily celebrations of the mass in the yards. Groups of the victims of dictatorship in South Korea find that their thirst for freedom and justice is totally dependent on regular meetings together for prayer – and for those who are in prison, the knowledge that their brothers and sisters are praying for them gives them new courage.[9] In Latin America even traditional forms of piety such as the stations of the cross have often come to be regarded as protests against oppressive regimes which deny liberty to the people. As the sufferings of Christ are remembered the words, 'As you did it to one of the least of these my brethren, you did it to me', come to mind.[10] That Archbishop Romero of El Salvador was murdered while presiding over the worship of the people of God was no accident, for he and the Church he led had often shown that worship was central to their concern for the oppressed, at the same time a protest against oppression and the nourishing of a thirst for liberty.

Enough has been said to show that in our day there has been a remarkable recovery of the experience of Christian worship as liberating. But one must enquire as to the authenticity of this understanding of worship. Is it, perhaps, that people turn to worship for the stimulant or tranquillizer most in demand at any given time, and in an age of liberation movements fighting for political emancipation, or women's liberation, and gay liberation, and so on, they naturally seek liberation in worship? Are we in danger of speaking not of worship in the Spirit, but of worship in the *Zeitgeist*? The question is a real one, but the answer is quite clear: what has happened is in fact the recovery of a central emphasis of Christian worship which has in the past often been all but lost.

It is not, of course, as if worship as such, in isolation as it were, is liberating. Christian worship is the re-presentation of God's mighty deliverance of his people, the recapitulation of salvation history, in which the people of God appropriate and enter into the salvation or liberation wrought by God himself, express their gratitude and delight in freedom, are nourished to work for liberty and stimulated to yearn for freedom's final consummation. It is God who is the liberator; in worship we respond to his act, enter into the freedom he has given us, and are nourished to share in his continuing work of deliverance. As the psalmist puts it:

When the Lord delivered Sion from bondage,
It seemed like a dream.
Then was our mouth filled with laughter,
on our lips there were songs.

The heathens themselves said: 'What marvels
the Lord worked for them!'
What marvels the Lord worked for us!
Indeed we were glad.

Deliver us, O Lord, from our bondage
as streams in dry land.[11]

Passover above all was the celebration of God's liberation of his people. The rite expressed, and continues to express, the present liberty of God's people, reclining as free men and women around the table, as totally dependent on God's gracious act of deliverance. Had God not acted, Israel would still be in bondage, not yet a People (*laos*), without name or dignity. The rite repeats and re-enacts the story, reminding the people of their roots, of their dependence upon God, of their dignity, and celebrating the liberty they have been given. And it does more than represent a past deliverance; it gives the resources for living as free men and women now, and provides an appetiser and a foretaste of the joys of the fully consummated liberty that is to come. Each Passover points forward – 'Next year in Jerusalem' – and beyond that to the messianic banquet.

It is hardly surprising that Passover became a time when a peculiarly intense thirst for liberty was commonly in the air, a time when Jews were usually liable to protest or revolt against contemporary oppression, being nourished at the feast of liberty. And it was this rite that Jesus took, re-shaped and attached for ever to the 'exodus' that he was to accomplish in Jerusalem. In the Lord's Supper, at the centre of Christian worship, there is accordingly this inescapable focusing on liberation. We remember, recapitulate, and participate in the liberty won and given to us by Christ. Here we receive food for living as free men and women, and a thirst for the banquet in the Kingdom of heaven when many will come from north and south and east and west and sit down with Abraham and Isaac and Jacob. And in this Supper not only do we receive liberty and a thirst for liberty, but our understanding of liberty is clarified and refined, our vision enlarged and our hope stimulated.

Authentic Christian worship, then, cannot be separated from a concern for liberation, for this would be to detach it from its rooting in the mighty acts of the God who delivers his people from bondage. For freedom Christ has set us free; in worship we appropriate, enjoy, proclaim and express this freedom; and the freedom celebrated in the cult must infect the life and structures of society if we are to avoid a quite blasphemous separation between the sacred and the secular.

(iv) *Growth*

Christianity has to do with maturity understood as 'the measure of the stature of the fulness of Christ' (Ephesians 4:13), and worship is related to the growth of the Body and its members towards this goal. Worship has its part to play in challenging Christians to seek a deeper and more intelligent faith and in strengthening them for living lives which show forth the qualities of Christian maturity. But over against this emphasis on maturity there is a balancing stress on the need for childlikeness: 'At that time the disciples came to Jesus, saying, 'Who is the greatest in the kingdom of heaven?' And calling to him a child, he put him in the midst of them, and said, 'Truly, I say to you, unless you turn and become like children you will never enter the kingdom of heaven' (Matthew 18:1–3; cf. Mark 10:13–16 and parallels). Christian maturity, it would seem, is also a return to the simplicities of childhood.

Thus worship, which is an aid and stimulus to Christian growth, is at one and the same time education and play, work and relaxation, the most serious of all activities and also the most lighthearted, a duty which is delightsome and almost frivolous – children romping at their parents' feet, chattering inconsequentially the while, listening to stories, and curling up to relax in a father's arms. Playtime is also story-time, and for many today worship is the only time they hear the Christian story – and more than hear: in worship we enact and celebrate the story, and graft together this story and our own story. Play is essential for growth and education and the development of a capacity to relate. In worship God nurtures his family, and this is most fully expressed in liturgy which is playful not solemn, serious but joyful. Children are right to be restless with grave and didactic worship or punctilious liturgical performances in which the presence of children is regarded as a disturbance rather than an enhancement. One may suspect that those who think worship is for adults only have a distorted understanding of Christian maturity and might find the worship of the Kingdom not at all to their liking!

Play and education are not incompatible with one another, and both are present in worship as necessary parts of its function of enabling growth. Playfulness is perfectly compatible with a deep seriousness – note the total absorption of the tennis player in the game – and engages the whole personality. Children deprived of play are stunted in their development; and adults who have lost the capacity for spontaneity and laughter are altogether too solemn for the celebrations of the children of God! In worship as in play we move into another world; the rules and the time-structure of the 'ordinary world' are suspended and replaced with something different: it is the second movement, not 8.35 p.m.; one's whole being is concentrated for a moment on getting the ball into the net; one is sitting beside old Mrs. Smith, but joining with angels and archangels and all the company of heaven in singing God's praises. Both play and worship are joyful, and in this joy we seem to know eternity.[12]

In this chapter we have been arguing that there is a pastoral dimension in the whole of Christian worship. But some forms of worship have a heavier 'pastoral loading' than others. In particular those services which may be reckoned as 'rites of passage' have particular pastoral significance. A rite of passage is a ritual which invests with meaning an individual's change of status, gives public recognition to the new situation, supports those going through a crisis of change, and proclaims the community's understanding of the significance of what has happened.[13] Rites of passage are associated particularly with birth, puberty, marriage and death. Elsewhere in this book we deal with baptism and confirmation, the two central rites of Christian initiation. In this chapter we will say something aout marriage and funerals, two rites of passage which clearly require to be discussed in a pastoral context. They are also by far the most popular Christian rituals in secularized western societies.

E—MARRIAGE

(i) *Theories of Sexuality*

'Sexual intercourse' said St. Jerome, baldly stating the dominant view for centuries in Christendom, 'is impure.'[14] A strongly negative attitude to sexuality, borrowed initially from the Stoicism of late antiquity which saw sexual intercourse as 'a little epilepsy', flourished in a Christian setting, so that Origen could say that during intercourse the couple lost the Holy Spirit, for 'the matter does not require the presence of the Holy Spirit, nor would it be fitting.'[15] This belief in the impurity of sexual intercourse led to the assertion of celibacy as a superior and purer state, and the gradual development in the West of compulsory clerical celibacy.

It also made more difficult a positive assessment of marriage. Gregory of Nyssa dismissed marriage as 'a sad tragedy',[16] while Jerome could find little positive to say about marriage save that it was necessary for the production of virgins![17] Augustine's theory that original sin was transmitted through sexual intercourse was widely held. Marriage was seen by many as a kind of compromise through which lust could be controlled. Even Luther could speak of marriage as 'a hospital for incurables, which prevents its inmates from falling into graver sin,'[18] although elsewhere he takes a much more positive view of marriage.

Such grudging admission that marriage may be acceptable for Christians as a lesser evil than fornication and promiscuity, as a recognition that many people are incapable of sustaining a life of celibacy, as a way of disciplining sinful passions, as necessary for the procreation of the human race, jars strongly with the main thrust of the Bible's teaching. Little is left of the Song of Song's magnificent celebration of sexual love, or even of St. Paul's daring analogy between Christ's love for the Church and the love of a husband and wife. As Jack Dominian writes: 'The sexual union with its own physical and temporal limitations cannot exhaust the mystery of Christ and his Church. But by making this particular analogy, Paul continues the familiar symbolism of marriage between God and his people found in the Old Testament and thus brings the sexual union into the very centre of the history of salvation.'[19]

(ii) *Theologies of Marriage*

There have been two types of theology of marriage in the Church – sacramental and non-sacramental. The sacramental interpretation stems from Augustine, who built on the Pauline analogy between marriage and the relation between Christ and the Church. Because marriage reflected this profound and permanent unity between Christ and the Church, it was of its nature indissoluble. Augustine also built on the occurrence of the word *sacramentum* in the Vulgate translation of Ephesians 5:32 to argue that like the soldier's *sacramentum* or pledge of loyalty, marriage involved an irrevocable commitment to one another on the part of the bride and groom. Prominent among the blessings of marriage were children, the others being fidelity and the indissoluble sacramental bond. The relation between these three – *proles, fides*, and *sacramentum* – was much discussed. Thomas Aquinas laid down his position as follows:

> Marriage has as its principal end the procreation and upbringing of children, which end belongs to man by reason of his generic nature and hence is common to other animals; in this way we get offspring as the blessing attached to matrimony. But as a secondary end, as Aristotle says, we have, in man alone, a common sharing in tasks which are necessary in life, and from this standpoint, husband and wife owe faith to each other, and that is another blessing attached to matrimony. Marriage, as it exists among believers, has yet another end, and this consists in its signification of the union between Christ and the Church and thus we get the sacrament as a matrimonial good. Hence the first end is found in human marriage, in as much as man is an animal, the second in him precisely as man, and the third in him *qua* believer.[20]

The sacramental view gradually gained wide acceptance in the Church. Interestingly, the ministers of the sacrament were, and are, the couple themselves; the priest does no more than bless a sacrament which they perform, and declares publicly that they have entered into the married state. A strength of the sacramental understanding of marriage is that it founds the relationship of husband and wife on an objective basis, *ex opere operato*, rather than upon feelings or the subjectivity of the couple: but a consequence is the absolute indissolubility of a sacramental marriage – a rigidity which raises serious pastoral issues.

The Reformers attacked with great vigour the sacramental understanding of marriage. For a rite to be a sacrament they required dominical institution, and concluded that there were only two true sacraments – Baptism and the Lord's Supper. The exegetical basis for a sacramental interpretation based on Ephesians 5:32 was easily demolished. Sacraments are means of grace, but, Luther argued, 'It is nowhere written that he who takes a wife receives the grace of God.'[21] Marriage remained an ordinance of God, a permanent commitment of a man to a woman, providing the ideal context for companionship and the procreation of children. In certain extreme cases of breakdown in relationship, divorce became a possibility. A Christian marriage is a parable rather than a sacrament of the love which Christ has for his Church. There may, according to the Reformers, be a distinction of quality between a Christian marriage and marriage as such, but there is not a difference of kind. Marriage is, therefore, basically a secular thing, subject to the civil law; it belongs to the order of creation, worldly, but at the same time a divine institution.[22]

The contrast between the two types of theology of marriage must not be overstressed; they share a remarkable amount in common, and are different ways of saying similar things: that marriage involves a permanent, exclusive and unconditional commitment to one another on the part of husband and wife; that this is the proper context for the full expression of sexual love; that it provides the most secure environment for the upbringing of children; and that God's blessing is good, if not essential, for a Christian marriage. In marriage people encounter the love of God, whether they recognize it as such or not, and a Christian marriage may be a demonstration of the reality and power of that love, a sign of the love of God.

(iii) *The Pastoral Context of Marriage*
The observant reader will have noticed that our discussion of the theology of marriage moved to and fro between consideration of marriage as a prolonged relationship between a man and a woman, normally terminated only by the death of one of the partners, and the wedding service, the initiation, blessing, and celebration of that relationship. The two belong together, of course: the wedding is the rite of passage into the married state. Accordingly, even in a book on worship, we should not go very far in talking about wedding services without asking questions about the understanding of marriage that is expressed and confirmed in a particular rite. But it is also true that the wedding service has a specific role to play in the Church's pastoral care for married couples. Sometimes couples are married in church with minimal or non-existent preparation for marriage, and preliminaries to the service consisting of the legal formalities, the choosing of hymns, and an indication of how much should be paid to whom. Even when a more personal approach is taken and the couples are given opportunities to discuss the meaning of Christian marriage and explore their relationship as well as participating in the planning of the service, that is sometimes the total of the Church's pastoral care directed to them as the married couple or a Christian family. Jack Dominian, the lay Roman Catholic psychiatrist, argues that compared to the preparation and continuing support given to the celibate religious, the married have been profoundly neglected. He traces this neglect of care for marriage as an unfolding relationship to 'the conceptualization of the sacrament as an entity which was complete in the exchange of rights over each other's bodies followed by sexual consummation.'[23] The wedding service accordingly ought to be from the pastoral point of view one moment, and an immensely significant moment, in an ongoing process of care and support for the growth of love in marriage. And it is only thus that the wedding service can proclaim an adequate understanding of marriage.

(iv) *Wedding Rites*
The early church combined considerable concern with Christian marriage with a singular lack of interest in wedding rites. A marriage was initiated by the couple entering into a contract which was regulated by the civil authorities rather than by the Church. Churchmen might criticise legal possibilities of divorce or other details of the law, and when the Roman Empire began to break down the Church took an increasingly detailed interest in the regulation of marriage. But still a wedding was regarded as basically a legal affair. That is not to say that rituals might not

appropriately be appended to the legal marriage: according to Tertullian, for instance, a blessing and a celebration of the eucharist were appropriate in weddings.[24] Sometimes the bishop's consent to betrothal was sought, and many ceremonies of secular or pagan origin became associated with the weddings of Christians – e.g., the giving of a ring and dowry, the crowning of one or both parties, and the veiling of the bride. The giving of a blessing by priest or bishop was considered something of a special honour; Christians were often married without the presence of a priest. From about the fifth century in various parts of Christendom the clergy began to be more regularly involved in the conduct of weddings, and a variety of local rites gradually emerged. These rites were legally recognized as valid marriages, but for centuries it remained optional even for Christians whether they should have what we would today call a 'Church wedding' or a purely civil ceremony. Only with the Council of Trent did a uniform wedding service come into use in the West.

Prolonged confusion about what is essential in a Christian wedding service has not yet been satisfactorily resolved. The sacramental interpretation of marriage, stemming as we have seen from St. Augustine, gradually heightened the liturgical significance of the wedding service (or the service, together with the subsequent consummation) so that it stood on a par with the other sacraments, particularly baptism and the Lord's Supper. Almost all traditions, whether or not they regard marriage as a sacrament, would today view this kind of 'liturgical inflation' of the wedding as a mistake. At the heart of rites of matrimony lies the public commitment of a man and a woman to one another, the public recognition of their new status, God's blessing on their relationship, and the celebration of their love for one another. Around this core prayers, scriptural readings, exhortation and the celebration of the eucharist are appropriately arranged, together with the use of symbols such as the ring which, while not specifically Christian, are apt, evocative and sanctioned by long usage.

F—FUNERALS
(i) *The Pastoral Context*
Strictly speaking, there is no such thing as a theology of funeral services, but just as behind wedding services there lies a theology of marriage which relates both to the rite and to the pastoral care of which it is a central expression, so funeral services relate to a theology of death and resurrection on the one hand, and to the Church's care for the grieving on the other. In the New Testament one finds much material on death and eternal life, and discussions about grieving and the Christian hope, but virtually no indication whatsoever that the early Christians had some kind of distinctive burial rite. Since virtually all religions have a solemn rite of passage to mark the fact that a death has taken place and to dispose of the body reverently, we may suppose that the early Christians also had something of the sort, but it does not seem to have had importance enough for it to have left its mark on the pages of the New Testament. We do have

evidence from the early centuries that Christians had funeral rites which were essentially Jewish or pagan rituals adapted to express the Christian belief in resurrection. Services of prayers, praise and Bible readings took place around the body, usually in the home, but sometimes in church. The cortege to the place of burial took place in daylight, with the Christians dressed in white robes with lights and palm branches, singing psalms of triumph and hope. All this was in stark contrast to the sombre funerals of classical paganism, which took place in darkness because death was regarded as an ill-omened threat to life. From quite early on the Lord's Supper was often associated with funerals – a reminder of the reality of continuing fellowship with the departed.

These practices continued well into the Middle Ages, although the atmosphere of hope and joy was gradually superseded by a strong emphasis on sin, judgement and purgatory, all reflecting an uncertainty about the destiny of the departed soul, well expressed in the *Dies irae*. It is hardly surprising that, particularly in the popular mind, the main intention of the funeral was seen as earning some remission for the departed in Purgatory, or some easing of the awful judgement. All such attempts to influence the fate of the dead were strongly resisted by the Reformers, Anglican, Lutheran and Calvinist. Masses for the dead, vigils, requiems and virtually all the mediaeval funeral observances were dismissed by Luther as 'papistical abominations', but both Lutherans and Anglicans quickly developed purged funeral services which omitted prayers for the departed and quite clearly had a pastoral intention – to speak to the mourners of the hope of the Gospel. For Luther, the intention of a funeral was to 'strengthen our faith and encourage the people to true devotion. For it is right and fitting that a funeral should be performed honourably, to the praise and honour of the joyful article of our faith, the resurrection of the dead.'[25]

The Calvinists went far further. They saw a pressing need to prepare people for death, but when all superstition had been swept away from funeral rites and Scripture consulted for guidance, they found virtually nothing left, or permissible, by way of funeral services. In Knox's *Liturgy*, for example, after a long and impressive section on the Visitation of the Sick, itself a striking instance of the pastoral use of prayer and worship, the whole section on burial is as follows: 'The corpse is reverently to be brought unto the grave, accompanied with the congregation, without any further ceremonies; which being buried, the minister, if he be present, and required, goeth to the church, if it be not far off, and maketh some comfortable exhortation to the people, touching death and resurrection.'[26] Nearly a century later, the *Westminster Directory for the Publick Worship of God* (1645) advocates a similar paucity, indeed absence, of ritual at the time of burial: 'And because the custom of kneeling down, and praying by or towards the dead corpse, and other such usages, in the place where it lies before it be carried to burial, are superstitious; and for that praying, reading, and singing, both in going to and at the grave, have been grossly abused, are no way beneficial to the dead, and have proved many ways hurtful to the living; therefore let all such things be laid aside.'

But even where all burial ceremonials and funeral services were explicitly rejected, they soon came back, and probably never entirely disappeared. There seems to be a very basic need for this particular rite of passage. And as an act of worship relating to death, a funeral service is a time when the Church affirms her beliefs about death and the hope of eternal life; and expresses her pastoral care for the bereaved.

(ii) *Theology of Death*

Death is a problem to which Christianity gives no slick or simple answer. But it is also a problem that Christianity does not evade. The apostle Paul, who speaks of death as a friend, so that we long through death to put on our heavenly dwelling, is also aware of the bitterness and threat of death 'the last enemy', even for those who know that Christ has given us the victory over death. A general theodicy does not always help in explaining this particular death – and all deaths are particular and specific. C. S. Lewis's *The Problem of Pain* has much clear, reasoned Christian discussion of death and suffering; but his later *A Grief Observed*, written while he was himself mourning the death of his wife, has a profundity which many people find more helpful, for in it his Christian hope has been shaped and forged on the anvil of experience.

Death is the completion of life. This is most easy to accept in the case of the death of one who is full of years and honour, who welcomes death as a goal and a fulfilment, who sees worldly finitude as something to rejoice at. 'Do not seek death,' wrote Dag Hammarskjöld, 'Death will find you. But seek the road which makes death a fulfilment.'[27] Yet death cannot always be seen as the natural completion of life; death is a foe, bitter and destructive, to be feared as 'the wages of sin', to be resisted and rebelled against. Here we may note the contrast between the death of Socrates and the death of Jesus. For Socrates, death was to be embraced, as liberation from the tomb of the body, as the beginning of real life; it was to be accepted with equanimity and without fear. Jesus, on the other hand, prays in agony in the garden that the cup may pass from him, and finally dies in anguish, alone, forsaken ('My God, my God, why have you forsaken me?') and with loud cries. Here we see how terrible death can be – and how God could draw its sting and set us free from its power. Thus Christians believe that Christ has triumphed over death, and have cause for rejoicing and the opportunity of entering into eternal life now, an adventure which has its culmination beyond the grave.[28]

(iii) *Grief*

Christians have a strange ambivalence in face of death, well expressed by Thomas Becket in T. S. Eliot's *Murder in the Cathedral*: 'Beloved, as the World sees, this is to behave in strange fashion. For who in the world will both mourn and rejoice at once and for the same reason?'[28]

A death means grief and mourning for those who are left behind. Commonly grief goes through stages such as these. First, shock, when the initial impact of the loss often leads to erratic and uncharacteristic behaviour. Secondly, control, a short period, usually ending with the funeral, in which there is a socially recognized and accepted pattern of grief behaviour. Thirdly, regression, pretending that nothing has changed, desperately trying to recover the past – a time of acute loneliness. Fourthly, adaptation: life must be taken up again, but now the pattern must be changed. Grieving takes time – far more time than many people recognize. And grieving is commonly accompanied with strong and discordant emotions; anger, remorse, recrimination, fear, regret, emptiness. Pastors must learn to respond appropriately to a range of deep feelings, and to support people throughout the time of grieving.

The funeral is a stage – and a vital stage – both in the grieving process and in the pastoral care of the mourners by the community. It is worship addressed to God, in which the community hold up the bereaved before God, and it is also a part of an ongoing process of pastoral care, exercised by the community as well as by the pastor. The mourners are held in fellowship, accepted in their new status by the community. Their grief is expressed, shared, publicly recognized, accepted. And thus the funeral plays its part in care, comfort and healing. The death of someone close to one is commonly experienced as a threat to the meaning of one's own life and disturbs structures of support and significance on which one has come to rely. The reverence for the body and the memory of a dead companion which is expressed in the funeral service helps to assure the mourners of their own worth. Christians can be realistic in face of death, because its awfulness and its finality is understood in the context of hope. Christians do not 'grieve as others who have no hope' (1 Thessalonians 4:13). But Christians do and should grieve, even as they hope. And at the funeral service they are reminded not only of the grace and mercy of God, but also that there is a fellowship which cares for them and will mourn them when they come to die.

NOTES

1. *Pastoral Liturgy*, NYC 1962, p. 380.
2. Karl Barth, *Church Dogmatics* IV/2, Edinburgh 1958, 638.
3. *The Liturgy of the Church of Scotland, or Knox's Book of Common Order*, ed. John Cumming, London & Edinburgh 1840, p. 150.
4. *Ibid.* p. 145.
5. *Rediscovering Pastoral Care*, London 1981, p. 8.
6. See, for instance, the Roman *Rite of Penance*, 1974.
7. *Reasons and the Emotions*, London 1935.
8. J. H. Cone, cited in Geoffrey Wainwright, *Doxology: The Praise of God in Worship, Doctrine and Life*, London 1980, p. 419.
9. Julio de Santa Ana, ed., *Towards a Church of the Poor*, Geneva 1979, 11–12.
10. J. Moltmann, *The Crucified God*, London 1974, p. 53.

11. Psalm 126, Grail Version.
12. Cf. Peter Berger, *A Rumour of Angels*, London 1970, and J. G. Davies, *New Perspectives on Worship*, London, SCM Press, 1978, ch. 1.
13. The classic treatment of rites of passage is Arnold Van Gennep, *Les Rites de Passage*, Paris 1909; E.T. *The Rites of Passage*, London & Chicago 1960.
14. Jerome, *Ad Jovinianum*, I.20: PL23. 238, cited in E. Schillebeeckx, *Ministry: A Case for Change*, London 1981, p. 88. Cf. other references on p. 161.
15. *Homilies on the Book of Numbers 6*, cited in J. Martos, *Doors to the Sacred*, London 1981, p. 408.
16. Cited in J. Dominian, *Christian Marriage*, London 1968, p. 26.
17. *Ibid.*
18. *Collected Works*, vol. 44, pp. 1–14, cited in A. V. Campbell, *op. cit.*, p. 74.
19. *Op. cit.*, p. 119.
20. S.T. III (Suppl.) q. 65 art. 1, cited in Dominian, *op. cit.*, p. 30.
21. *Babylonish Captivity*.
22. For more detailed discussion, particularly of Luther's position, see H. Thielicke, *Theological Ethics*, vol. 3, pp. 125ff.
23. Jack Dominian, *Marriage, Faith and Love*, London 1981, p. 119.
24. Ad. Ux. 2.6.
25. WA 35, 479, cited in *Dict. Lit. & Worship*, 102.
26. *Knox's Liturgy*, p. 105.
27. *Markings*, p. 136.
28. This paragraph is indebted to an essay by Dr. Alan Lewis.
29. T. S. Eliot, *Murder in the Cathedral*, London, Faber & Faber, 1968, 51.

FURTHER READING

William H. Willimon, *Worship as Pastoral Care*, New York 1979.
Alastair V. Campbell, *Rediscovering Pastoral Care*, London 1981.
Jack Dominian, *Marriage, Faith and Love*, London 1981.
J. Spiegel, *The Grief Process*, London 1978.

FOR DISCUSSION

1. In what ways can worship stimulate and encourage personal growth?
2. Is Christian worship defective if it is not experienced as a liberation?
3. How effectively may marriage or funeral services perform their pastoral function?

CHAPTER 10

WORSHIP IN THE MODERN WORLD

A—THE CRISIS OF WORSHIP

'There is a crisis of worship', proclaimed the Uppsala Assembly of the World Council of Churches in 1968. Since that time there has been a deeper and more widespread conviction that something unprecedented is happening to worship, particularly but not exclusively in the industrialised countries of the West. Quite simply, societies seem to be emerging in which worship of any sort occupies only a marginal position, in which many people regard worship as an optional extra, hardly more than a hobby for the small minority of people who 'like that sort of thing'. Are we perhaps seeing the emergence of societies in which there is no place for worship, of people who have no need or inclination to worship?

We must be careful, however, not to overstate things. There have been crises of worship before. To mention but three examples: some of the Old Testament prophets launched devastating onslaughts on the pattern of worship of their day; Jesus' attitude to the temple and its cult was, to put it mildly, ambivalent; and the Reformation denounced 'the idolatry of the Mass' and virtually the whole apparatus of mediaeval worship. But all these protest movements saw the issue as a choice between true and false worship; they did not envisage the possibility of having no worship at all. They did not look benignly on worship *as such* – false worship, they suggest, is worse than no worship at all, but true worship is of vital importance to individuals and to societies. In itself, worship is regarded as problematic and constantly liable to perversion; it is not seen (as it is by many modern sociologists) as something necessary, good and useful for the smooth and proper functioning of societies and individuals. False worship is harmful and destructive and immoral; true worship is a duty and a delight – and probably useful in all sorts of ways as well, but its utility is merely a by-product of its truth.

The contemporary crisis of worship arises from the fact that so many people see the acids of modernity eating away all kinds of worship, true and false, useful and harmful, so fast that soon only vestiges will remain. There is no doubt that many people in western societies look on any manifestation of worship as quaint, disposable and infantile, an irrational

163

activity from which increasing numbers of people are successfully emancipating themselves. All worship, in this view, is false. Grudgingly it may be admitted that for a time at least, and for some people, worship may be useful or necessary. But worship belongs to the nursery, and the human race has come of age.

Like all such problems, this crisis penetrates deep into the life of the Church. There is genuine puzzlement about the place of worship in the Christian faith and life. Even in the Christian scheme of things, worship appears to occupy a far less significant place than it did in the past. A gap has opened in many places between theology and the practice of worship; it is forgotten that in the past worship generated much of the problematic of theology and provided one criterion of theological truth. Some of the best and most thoughtful of Christians, as Charles Davis has pointed out,[1] have withdrawn from participation in worship because they find it archaic, formal and unrelated to the context in which they are endeavouring to live out their faith. Others continue to attend worship, but find it jarring or quaint rather than enlightening, stirring and relevant.

The crisis is no superficial or transient matter, capable of being solved by tinkering with liturgical forms. Doubts about the principles and meaningfulness of liturgy are integrally connected with the modern crisis of faith, and this in its turn cannot be separated from the contemporary cultural, social and intellectual confusion and uncertainty. 'If worship constitutes a problem in our secularised society,' writes Raymond Panikkar, 'the principal reason is not that the liturgy is outmoded or boring (it was almost equally so 200 years ago), but rather that the principles of the liturgy are themselves in crisis. Fashion or boredom are not in the main obstacles, but the fear of meaninglessness. All too often theological reflection about this problem remains superficial, considering it mainly as a practical or pastoral problem, while basically it is theological.'[2] Great issues are at stake, and it is important that we should try to understand in some general way at least what is happening. Worship, after all, is concerned with the search for meaning, with renewing, affirming, reordering our view of reality, of God, the world, and our relations with our neighbours. Worship is therefore necessary for the sustaining and proclamation of the Christian vision, because it is an encounter with the living God, that is, with Reality. And that is why the crisis of worship has to be taken with the most profound seriousness.

B—THE CHANGING PLACE OF WORSHIP

The most obvious and easily documented change in recent times is the decline in attendance at worship. This type of data is easily quantifiable and although there are problems in interpreting its significance, and dangers that a decline in attendance at public worship should be seen as necessarily indicating a decline in religious belief or commitment, the trend in almost all industrial societies is unmistakable; there has been a prolonged, very substantial and probably unparalleled decline in participation in public worship over the last century or so. This decline has not been uniform over time; it has tended to accelerate since the middle of the twentieth century. It is more marked in urban than in country areas, among the working classes than the middle classes, and among Protestants than among Roman Catholics. All these factors suggest some kind of incompatibility between worship and modern industrial society. Exceptions to this rule which have been suggested include the United States of America and Poland. In the case of the United States it is true that attendance at worship is markedly higher than in most West European situations, but even there religious observance has been declining since the 1950s. In Poland the close association of national sentiment and the Catholic Church complicates the picture, but here, too, attendance at worship has been decreasing – or was, prior to the conflict between the Solidarity trade union and the government. In most of the less industrialized countries, attendance at worship remains high, but falls off markedly as industrialization makes itself felt.[3]

Certain types of worship, however, survive more strongly than others in an industrial, secular society and continue to attract large numbers of people. For instance, even in situations where attendance at the 'normal Sunday service', whether that is Mass, Parish Communion, 'hymn sandwich', or a sermon with preliminaries, is low, surprisingly large numbers of people wish to be married in church, bring their babies for baptism, and want a Christian funeral. Motivations in this matter are clearly complex and do not directly concern us at this point. But the resilience of these *rites of passage* is such that strongly anti-religious regimes such as that of East Germany feel the necessity to provide secular alternatives.

The rituals of folk religion also continue to flourish and even increase in popularity, existing in an increasingly uneasy and often confusing symbiosis with Christian worship. Folk religion has to do with locality and the soil, with one's sense of belonging in a particular place and a specific community; with bonding to neighbour, and home, and a particular history. It is a religion of sacred places, sacred buildings, and special communities. Sometimes folk religion takes the form of a religion of national identity, as in Poland, or Scotland where some perfervid patriots are presbyterian atheists. The church building often is a focus of primordial sentiments shared by many who never worship there; it is good to have it there to stay away from; the existence of this sacred space within the area confers some unspecifiable benefit upon the community. When a church building is closed, vandalised or demolished it is not only those who worshipped there who are disturbed, but many others as well often show signs of uneasiness that this reassuring physical presence is no longer securely among them. Subconsciously the building and what goes on within it are felt to continue to play a vital role in the folk religion of social cohesion and social continuity; a focus for the sense of belonging. The harvest festival is an example of a rite of folk religion, part harvest home, part fertility ritual, which has in modern times by popular demand become one of the main peaks of the church's year for many – even in city churches where the most that any member of the congregation cultivates is a back garden. Christmas, the pagan mid-winter festival long-since Christianized, is well established as by far the most popular Christian feast, but to judge by the tone of many sermons on Christmas it is in danger of reverting to its pagan, folk-religious origins. Be that as it may, amazing numbers of people go to church to worship at Christmas time, and if one counts, as one must, hymns and carols as forms of worship, each Christmas is a veritable bonanza of worship, much of it combining in subtle and significant ways elements of folk religion and more explicitly Christian forms. Christian worship and the rituals of folk religion have mingled and grown together so closely through many centuries that it is hard to disentangle them from one another and often difficult to distinguish what is Christian and what is folk religion in a particular act of worship. It is fairly clear that as soon as Christianity became the religion of the majority, or even of a substantial proportion of the people, it had to fulfil the functions of folk religion, and baptize at least some of its rituals. The interaction between the two over many centuries has left its mark on each so that one may reasonably argue that the two are now interdependent. Interestingly enough, one line of criticism of the Anglican liturgical reforms represented by the Alternative Service Book has been that the attempt to produce theologically and liturgically more adequate forms of worship endangers the delicate balance between Christianity and English folk religion in which the Book of Common Prayer has, rather strangely, become the pivot. In other words, the endeavour to make worship more explicitly and unambiguously Christian in a modern idiom makes it less capable of being a vehicle of folk religion as well.

The rites of civil religion flourish exceedingly, probably increasingly, in a secular context. These rites (like civil religion as a whole) legitimate, sacralize and conserve the authority structure of a society; they encourage and extol the civic virtues such as patriotism; and they assuage concern about the propriety of the behaviour of governments and the society as a whole. Some form or other of religion is the most widespread agency of legitimation, and where there is no recognized, established or suitable religion to hand for these purposes, a quasi-religion has to be developed. Since Constantine Christianity has played the role of the civil religion in most of Europe. Macchiavelli recognized long ago that Christianity by its very nature does not make a wholly satisfactory civil religion, and he yearned to exchange it for the lustier religion of ancient Rome. But, for all that, Christian worship has doubled as the ritual of civil religion, and continues to do so. Armistice Day, now Remembrance Sunday, in Britain fulfilled and continues to fulfil a variety of needs – to recollect those who have died in the service of their country, to revive memories of the camaraderie of the forces, to give thanks for deliverance from enemies, and also to set at rest doubts about the wasteful carnage of war and questions about the justification of it all – by a ritual which at its worst becomes a celebration of chauvinism rather than of Christianity. Compulsory chapel in boarding schools, whatever the actual content of the worship, often gives the pupils the impression that worship is good for one in some rather unspecific way, like other compulsory items of the life-style: cold baths, cross-country runs, and the Combined Cadet Force. It is hard for it not to be seen as a rite of civil religion, the celebration and sanctification of the public school ethos and the kind of society that ethos is intended to sustain.[4]

Civil religion and its rituals have been as unpopular with the theologians as they have been central to many sociologists' concerns. The theologians have regarded civil religion with suspicion because of the belief that the liberal *Kulturprotestantismus* of nineteenth century Germany led directly to the sacralizing of blood and soil under Hitler and the difficulty many Christians found in disengaging themselves from Nazism. The sociologists, on the other hand, see the provision of what Peter Berger calls a 'social theodicy' as a primary function of religion, and if Christianity cannot or will not provide what is necessary, an alternative must be found. Typical of such an alternative is the strange ritual of viewing Lenin's embalmed body in his tomb in Red Square in Moscow. As the long queue edges forward reverently towards the tomb one knows that one is observing a ritual of civil religion, a rite which has a significant function in the Soviet atheistic scheme of things. The accusations that Stalin encouraged 'the *cult* of personality' denotes at least an incipient awareness that ritual has a place in politics, or tends to return surreptitiously whenever it is cast out.[5] One could hardly wish for a better instance of civil religion than this account of a rally in China which appeared in *China Reconstructs* in 1976:

> At ten o'clock in the morning, to the majestic strains of 'The East is Red', Chairman Mao, the reddest, reddest sun in our hearts, appeared on the Tien An Men rostrum. 'Chairman Mao is here! Chairman Mao is here!' Thousands of emotion-filled eyes turned towards Chairman Mao! Thousands of people waved their gleaming red *Quotations from Chairman Mao Tse-tung* and shouted again and again: 'Long live Chairman Mao! Long, long live Chairman Mao! Oh, our respected and beloved Chairman Mao, how we have longed to see you. It is you who have given us new life. It is you who have lighted the flame in our fighting youthful hearts. It is you who have led us from victory to victory. We knew that just one glimpse of you would give us greater wisdom and courage – and today our wish has come true!'[6]

Peter Berger is probably right in suggesting that when the Christian world-view is no longer generally accepted, a specifically Christian legitimation of the social order cannot be maintained for long.[7] But that is not to say that the church may not continue to be used as an agency of civil religion, increasingly evacuated of Christian content. And problems also arise in situations of religious pluralism, of which the United States is probably the classic instance. Here, as Will Herberg showed in his classic *Protestant-Catholic-Jew* (New York, 1955), there has emerged a kind of 'establishment' of the three types of mainstream religion. It is this triple religion which interacts so closely with the American Way of Life, and performs the functions of a civil religion. And in countries like England and Scotland where there are established churches in situations of increasing religious pluralism, it is notable that in recent times on great national occasions – coronations, royal weddings and the like – the established churches have given up their monopoly and the other main churches share in the service, suggesting a gradual move in a similar direction to that already taken by the States. In the more ecumenical atmosphere of today the rituals of civil religion suggest an establishment of Christianity rather than of a particular denomination. And this is almost inevitable, because the rites of civil religion must express unity rather than division and partiality. They are a matter of adaptation, compromise and alliance between Christianity and civil society's need for ideological support and ritual articulation.

The importance of the rites of civil religion may help us to understand why most western societies have attempted, until modern times, to enforce uniformity of worship. Diversity of cult was seen as politically dangerous as well as theologically suspect, and the uneasiness about a variety of forms of worship being tolerated reflected an awareness of the need for one particular denomination to be the civil religion of the state; other cults were potentially or actually seditious. Diversity of worship was seen as theologically unacceptable, socially divisive, and politically disruptive. As time went by the conviction that worship makes a vital contribution to social order and the legitimation of authority was not abandoned, but the limits of tolerance were gradually extended: first, in northern Europe, Protestant worship in any of its major forms became acceptable; then any mainstream mode of Christian worship; and now secular as well as religious ritual is seen as capable of performing the functions of a civil religion. This expansion of tolerance has gone *pari passu* with a decline in the significance generally attributed to worship and with the increasing religious pluralism of society. In addition to the rich variety of Christian sects and denominations, most cities today have places of worship for the major world faiths, and also for some of the huge and ever changing diversity of cults and groups of devotees. But large numbers of people, including many who seldom if ever darken the doors of a place of worship, continue to believe that worship, whatever the kind, is in some very general way 'a good thing'. Worship has become a matter of choice and not compulsion; there are no Acts of Uniformity or of Conformity remaining on the statute books; and there is much to be said for this 'free market' in forms of worship. But undergirding the new pluralism is a general public assumption that all worship is really the same thing, and rather a good thing at that; in such a relativistic atmosphere it becomes rather bad form to speak in terms of true and false worship any longer. Liturgical syncretism, patching together ersatz forms of worship without any coherent theological rationale out of the nicest and most moving bits collected from every quarter, or liturgical fundamentalism, rigid adherence to a specific denominational tradition, so that worshippers may continue in the comfortable delusion that nothing has changed, nothing been challenged, are the two easiest responses to pluralism. Each is a trap, and fortunately there are far more exciting possibilities of mutual enrichment, theological rediscovery, and a refreshing of worship presented by the modern diversity of forms of worship.

Worship occupies a less central place in the life of most modern societies, there is less of it and fewer people participate. But worship is not dispensable. If people are deprived of the traditional forms of worship, or find they have gone moribund, they seek alternative forms for creating and sustaining meaning and solidarity, they find surrogates for worship. Mary Douglas, the social anthropologist, writes:

> If ritual is suppressed in one form it crops up in others, more strongly the more intense the social interaction. Without the letters of condolence, telegrams of congratulations and even occasional postcards, the friendship of a separated friend is not a social reality. It has no existence without the rites of friendship. Social rituals create a reality which would be nothing without them ... It is impossible to have social relations without symbolic acts.[8]

The prevalence of worship surrogates, sometimes of rather bizarre sort, at a time when worship seems to be in decline suggests the continuing existence of a fundamental human need which is not being met adequately by the worship of the churches. The vacuum is filled by a strange medley of rituals which attempt to convey meaning and significance to human existence. Astrology, with its suggestion that the details of earthly life are governed by the stars and given significance thereby, occupies at least as much space in the popular press as 'serious religion'. The occult, spiritualism, even witchcraft and black magic seem not only to continue but to flourish in secular societies where organized religious worship declines in significance. Some worship surrogates are essentially debased and suspect quasi-religious forms; others, like the rituals of the football match or the political demonstration are avowedly secular (although hymns are sometimes sung by football crowds!). Television commercials not infrequently exude an unction or an awe which might suggest that they are central rites of the acquisitive society. And some religious programmes on radio and television, notably the daily service, Songs of Praise and Stars on Sunday, are clearly intended to fulfil a felt need for worship on the part of many people who may have only the faintest connection with the organized churches.

Some worship surrogates appear to be ethical alternatives to the worship of the churches. Bodies such as Amnesty International, the Anti-Apartheid Movement, C.N.D., and many other radical or idealistic groups, attract to their rituals – demonstrations, marches, rallies, petitions and so forth – many who feel that Christian worship has been caught in a 'cultic trap' of ethical and political irrelevance. Their criticisms, implied or

explicit, should be listened to by the churches, as should the feelings of
those who, despairing of Christian worship, have sought in the rites of
eastern religions a truer encounter with the mystery of the holy than they
have found in their home churches. For authentic Christian worship must
be simultaneously a meeting with the holy living God and an alignment
with God's call for justice, compassion and peace.

Some contemporary theologians, supported by numerous sociologists
of religion, have argued that religion in the modern world has been
'privatized' and this process has deeply affected the nature of worship.
Privatization means that religion is removed from the public realm and
concerns itself almost entirely with the individual and domestic activity.
Religion and worship, it is suggested, have capitulated to modern
individualism and become in fact 'what man does with his solitariness',
with a strong emphasis on personal morality and family life. On the face of
it, this privatized worship should seem incompatible with the still
flourishing worship of civil religion, but the contrary is in fact the case: the
two fit together very neatly in societies dominated by the ideology of
bourgeois individualism. 'Extremely privatized religion', writes the
German Roman Catholic theologian Johann Baptist Metz, 'has been, as it
were, specially prepared for the domestic use of the propertied middle-
class citizen. It is above all a religion of inner feeling. It does not protest
against or oppose in any way the definitions of reality, meaning or truth,
for example, that are accepted by the middle-class society of exchange and
success. It gives greater height and depth to what already applies even
without it.'[9] Peter Berger's argument that privatized religion can no longer
provide a comprehensive structure of meaning for social life because it has
evacuated the public realm and only addresses itself to minor enclaves,
particularly the domestic, needs to be qualified.[10] The very fact that
organized religion now makes few, and not notably successful, attempts to
intervene in the public sphere, makes it more amenable to being used to
legitimate and sanctify the practices of the public realm. This is why
privatization is a trap for Christian worship. Privatized worship is partial
and unprophetic and distorted; its concern with issues of personal morality
and domestic life goes happily with conferring an outward veneer of
religious respectability on the proceedings of the public realm. But true
Christian worship is a matter both for individual and community, both for
the public and the private realms.

Closely associated with privatization is the belief that worship is not
about participation in outward, objective realities, but concerned only
with inward, subjective, individual and ultimately incommunicable truths.
The 'historicising' of the worship of Israel and of the church which led to
worship being understood as the celebration and renewal of an encounter
in history between God and mankind was not exactly reversed – that
would have been to focus worship on the cycles of nature rather than the
events of history.[11] Cross, resurrection, incarnation, if they are events at
all, are seen as events within the individual's subjectivity and existence; it is
the inner, rather than the outer, drama with which worship is concerned.
So Angelus Silesius the hymn writer could sing:

Though Christ a thousand times
In Bethlehem be born,
If he's not born in thee
Thy soul is still forlorn.

The cross on Golgotha
Will never save thy soul
The cross in thine own heart
Alone can make thee whole.[12]

This emphasis leads to a considerable reserve towards communal worship; it is in danger of losing its raison d'être as a result of the extreme subjectivizing of faith.

The decline in the numerical strength and influence of the churches together with the linked processes of privatization and subjectivization leads not uncommonly to worship becoming sectarian. Congregations who know themselves to be, in Berger's term, 'cognitive deviants' have a strong temptation to withdraw to the security of operating as inturned sects, striving for their own survival and without a basic concern for the world 'outside' or for the broader community. The existence and worship of such congregations, which are hardly more than religious clubs, gatherings of the like-minded, are tolerated and indeed encouraged even in societies which are inherently irreligious, just as the Roman Empire tolerated various *religiones licitae* on the grounds that they did not interfere with the rites of the civil religion and did not press any disturbing universal claims, or proselytise too vigorously. The early church found that it could not operate within the limits imposed upon a *religio licita*, and called down persecution upon itself. Nor could it go along with the social divisions of society, in particular that between Jew and Gentile, because to do so would be a denial of the universality of the Gospel and would have allowed the church to fragment into a variety of little sects the boundaries of which followed the social divisions of the time. William Temple's comment that the church exists for the sake of those who never darken its doors is also true of the church's worship, and worship can never provide an adequate sense of meaning if it allows itself to degenerate into being the self-conscious and contrived ritual of a club.

C—INTERPRETATION

Most of the developments and problems which we have outlined in the previous section are symptoms or effects of the pervasive social process called secularization. Put baldly, secularization is the process whereby religion and religious ideas and rituals come to play a less and less significant role in the life of a society. The influence of the church is dramatically reduced, particularly in the economic, political and cultural spheres; in matters of personal morality it sometimes continues to have a greater say, for a time at least. Religious interpretations of reality come to have less and less formative influence on people's consciousness, and decisions are taken increasingly without reference either to religious authorities or to theological notions. As Peter Berger puts it, 'Probably for the first time in history, the religious legitimations of the world have lost their plausibility, not only for a few intellectuals and other marginal individuals, but for broad masses of entire societies.'[13] The world has been evacuated of the sacred, or the sacred only lurks here and there in dark crevices. In Max Weber's terms, the world has been disenchanted, and any approach which puts the holy or the sacred at the centre of its concern, as does Christian worship, finds itself in an invidious situation of uncertainty and confusion. Secular man has 'come of age'. He is free from clerical, churchly, or religious control, and accepts a new responsibility for shaping his world and guiding its progress into the future. Starting in Western Europe, the process of secularization has spread throughout the world and affected almost all societies and cultures to a greater or lesser extent. Even in the United States, where the churches continue to occupy a far more significant and central role than is the case in Europe, they have only managed to do so, the argument runs, because they have themselves become secularized. We may suspect that some secularization theorists want to have it both ways, and would not willingly acknowledge that any case – Poland, for instance – could falsify their theory. This is not the place to enter into the contemporary discussion about secularization among sociologists, important as it is; it is enough for our present purposes to note that the displacement of religion and worship from the centre of the stage in most societies since the Enlightenment raises hard questions for worship: in particular, how can worship survive in a society in which the majority of people find it meaningless, objectionable, or simply quaint?[14]

For long it was assumed among Christians that secularization was unambiguously antagonistic to the Christian faith and therefore to Christian worship. This belief in an inherent opposition and incompatibility between Christian worship and secularization depended on some fundamental, and seldom examined, assumptions about the nature of Christian worship. Foremost among these assumptions was this: Christian worship depends on a religious *a priori*, a general agreement within a society and culture that religion is an important dimension of life, and worship a major manifestation of religion. Christianity then proceeds to press its specific claims against those of the other religions on offer, and Christian worship tries to assert its claim to be the truest, or best, or purest form of worship. Christianity belongs to the class of religions, and claims to be the crown of all religion; Christian worship is one among many forms of response to the Holy, but claims to be 'worship in spirit and in truth' while the other kinds of worship are more or less defective in comparison. But when religion is regarded as an optional matter of no great importance, and worship a peculiar, eccentric and perhaps infantile activity in a world come of age, we are involved in a different ball-game. The first response on the part of Christian theologians was to see secularization as the great enemy, which must be met by the various religions and their forms of worship standing shoulder to shoulder against the assaults of secular modernity. Once secularization was repulsed, there would be an opportunity to give renewed attention to the differences between the various faiths and their cults; meanwhile they were allies in a struggle against the common foe.

The growth in the 1930s and 40s of what is rather loosely called 'dialectical theology' led many theologians to look with suspicion on 'religion' and oppose very sharply Christianity and the religions. Religion, Karl Barth proclaimed, is unbelief, it is false, it is man's striving to reach God. Christianity is misunderstood if it is seen as a religion; its essence is God's gracious reaching out for man in Christ. It belongs to a separate category entirely from 'the religions'. Theologians such as Gogarten and Bonhoeffer, in addition to Barth, spoke of the temptations, dangers and distortions of religion, perhaps influenced more than a little by their experience of the religious pretensions of Nazism in Germany. This suspicion of religion on the part of deeply committed Christian theologians opened the way for them to begin a much more positive theological assessment of the secular. So far from being the irreconcilable opponent of all religion and all worship, secularization comes to be seen as the ally of Christianity in its conflict with false religion and false worship. Secularization is capable of purifying and reforming worship. Arendt Th. van Leeuwen in his book *Christianity in World History* (London, 1964) argues that secularization is rooted in the Judaeo-Christian tradition, its effects are fruits of the Gospel, and its spread throughout the world is continuous with the Christian mission. Others, most notably Harvey Cox in *The Secular City* (London, 1965), saw secularization as something which should be welcomed, encouraged, celebrated and spread as an inherently Christian movement of liberation and maturing. Because secularization is understood as making possible a more human and responsible life for man before God, because it opens up new perspectives and presents new opportunities for Christianity, but above all because it is interpreted by thinkers such as Cox and van Leeuwen as the work of God in history, it should be welcomed with confidence and Christians should ally themselves with the process of secularization.

All that glitters is not gold, and the sparkle which attracted some theologians to pronounce that secularization carried the divine hallmark has now become tarnished; even Harvey Cox has long ceased to celebrate the Christian mysteries of the secular city. More discriminating and chastened judgements of secularization are now being made. But even those who continue to give a more or less unqualified welcome to the new secular age acknowledge that the place of worship is highly problematic in a secular society and that this raises crucial questions for the Church.

In an important article, 'Ghetto or Desert: Liturgy in a Cultural Dilemma'[15] Charles Davis argues that the problem of worship in the modern secular age is unsolved. Modern culture is dynamic and aggressively secular; worship is at the margin, irrelevant to the fundamental concerns of the society, out of date in a culture that is no longer Christian. Davis suggests that public worship as we know it presupposes a common culture, shared by all, and is itself 'a rich cultural form' which brings to focus a unified living culture. But today Christian worship – or any form of worship, for that matter – is at variance with the culture in which it is set. Worship is a nostalgic anachronism, harking back to the time when it was the expression of a rich and lively Christian culture. It finds it impossible to relate to the dominant secular culture, which is more lively, fruitful and open by far than the deviant and atavistic Christian (or religious) sub-culture. Secularization has produced a form of society which has no place for worship; particularly for those Christians who gave an unqualified welcome to the process, this involves a profound theological and practical dilemma; is it possible to envisage a form of the Christian faith which has no place for worship, or can Christian worship take on a shape which is relevant and appropriate to a secular society? Underlying this dilemma is the problem of the relation between culture and society on the one hand and Christian worship on the other. We will shortly have to raise some questions about Charles Davis's formulation of this relationship, but few would disagree with his argument that the place and nature of Christian worship in a secular age is a major problem for Christians, and one which admits of no easy solution.

D—RESPONSE

Charles Davis suggests that there are two, and only two, responses possible to the crisis of worship in a secularized society. These he labels 'the ghetto' and 'the desert'.

1. *The Ghetto*. Since liturgy has to have a social and cultural setting to which it is integrally related and it is impossible for it to be 'some kind of pure expression of the Christian faith', it may remain central to the life of small deviant and anachronistic communities, largely cut off from the dominant secular culture and devoting a great deal of their energies to the process of boundary maintenance. Such ghetto religious communities exist – for instance, the Amish people in Pennsylvania, or the Closed Brethren in north east Scotland – nourishing a world-view, a life-style, and a form of worship radically at variance with those of the surrounding community, with which they have as little contact and interaction as possible. Davis finds this option unattractive. Christian culture, he believes (making an astoundingly unqualified judgement), is now decadent and inferior to secular culture, in crucial respects *less Christian* than its secular setting. Rather strangely, Davis does not press beyond his somewhat dubious identification of Christianity and a lively culture to examine other theological and practical objections to the ghetto – that a ghetto existence involves an abdication of responsibility for the life of the world, a repudiation by implication of the universality of the Gospel, and a sinful obsession with group survival. Nor does he consider the alternative notion of the 'counter-culture' as developed by writers such as Theodore Roszak,[16] and put into practice in Europe and America in such a bewildering variety of ways, some of them bizarre, but others of considerable importance. What Davis might dismiss as a ghetto, turned in

on itself and engrossed with questions of its own survival, may turn out, on closer acquaintenance, to be quite different: a counter cultural community, passionately concerned for the world and its life and culture, not cutting off communications with the world but witnessing *to* and *against* the society and culture in which it is set. This model of a group which deviates from the values and assumptions of the dominant culture but is dedicated to the transforming of the world rather than conforming to the world may be an attractive alternative to the ghetto.

2. *The Desert.* Davis's preferred possibility is the desert, the situation in which the believer finds himself an almost isolated wanderer in a cultural desert. The Christian culture of the past is dead; the future Christian culture has yet to be born; meanwhile the believer has no appropriate cultural forms in which to express his faith and worship. Liturgy, or public worship, is impossible, but impossible because Davis has defined it as an expression of a generally accepted cultural and religious synthesis which no longer exists. The believer in the desert longs for the future, when liturgy becomes possible once again because a new and lively synthesis of Christianity and culture has emerged, when 'the present secular culture will be redeemed and rendered open to Christian faith'. Meanwhile the believer lives between the times, wandering in the desert, without liturgy or public worship, until a return to the promised land becomes possible. But although there are no appropriate forms of liturgy available, the believer cannot live without worship, so privately and in small groups believers will soldier on, sometimes using antiquated or despised forms inherited from the past, sometimes developing a variety of experimental forms of worship for themselves. And in all this the dominant motive is the search for a new synthesis of culture and worship, which is certain to be substantially different from any earlier synthesis. 'The movement for the renewal of worship,' he writes, 'coincides with the mission of Christians to transform secular culture, preserving indeed its proper character and its gains, but opening it to a higher level.'[17]

The central problem raised in Davis's analysis is the relation of worship and culture. Clearly they are connected, and sometimes in history it is clear that worship has indeed been a major vehicle and shaper of culture. But the relation is not as direct and simple as Davis suggests. Although there have been periods when liturgy has been a vital and central cultural expression, and other periods when there has been a creative and conscious interaction between culture and worship, for much of its history and particularly at the beginning, Christian worship has been structured and practised as the way of giving glory to God, and any cultural role it may have had has been regarded as of little consequence. Neither the second century Christian participants, nor the pagan official Pliny, nor the Emperor Trajan to whom he was reporting could have thought early Christian worship a *cultural* form – Pliny regarded it as a 'superstitious contagion' posing a very minor threat to the official cult because the Christians regarded the civil cult and culture as basically idolatrous; the Christians themselves probably regarded it as their duty and delight.[18]

Most forms of Christian worship have been shaped in detail and in general primarily by the attempt to be faithful – to the God who is worshipped, to Scripture, to theological orthodoxy. They have not been understood as expressions of cultural responsibility. Liturgical reforms which are primarily attempting to be up-to-date, or 'with-it', are not misguided because they are seeking a premature and superficial synthesis between Christian worship and contemporary culture, as Charles Davis would suggest, but because they have been seduced into giving cultural considerations priority over the Christian integrity of worship.

Davis's argument is spoiled by his assumption that there is, or can be, such a thing as a 'Christian culture', and by his nostalgia for the mediaeval synthesis and for the idea of Christendom which is now irrecoverable. What we are saying is this: the effect of liturgy upon culture is vast and varied, but for the most part indirect, unconscious and unintended. And although it is obvious that culture influences liturgy very deeply it must not become simply a cultural expression. Christian worship must always combine catholicity – the sense of being the worship of the one Church all down the ages and throughout the globe – with indigenization – the sense that Christian worship has a home, albeit a temporary camp for a pilgrim people, in every culture, society and age. The way forward, we would suggest, is neither that of the ghetto nor the desert, but the attempt in faithfulness to the tradition and its sources and sensitive interaction with the culture and the political, social and intellectual issues of today, to seek ways of giving glory to God which are appropriate to *this* time and *this* place.[19]

Davis picks up Peter Berger's argument that Christians have become a marginalised minority of 'cognitive deviants'. Religion, he accurately reports 'has been relegated to the margins. It has no real part to play in thinking and decision-making even in quite minor matters.'[20] The 'plausibility structure', which used to sustain mass Christianity, has collapsed. To be a group of deviants at the margin of things is not easy; subtle and threatening pressures to conform are there all the time; an uncomfortable sense of loneliness and isolation from the mainstream of things is a common experience; it becomes increasingly hard to sustain beliefs, values and practices which diverge from those of the majority and are commonly regarded as quaint and unimportant – and almost certainly false as well. But the margin is not a strange place for Christians; it is not only a problem, but a place of opportunity too. Indeed, one could argue that the margin is a more proper place for Christians to be, than at the centre of things. After all, Jesus himself was a marginalized person, who 'suffered outside the gate in order to sanctify the people through his own blood' (Hebrews 13:13). The margin, it would appear, is the place of illumination, revelation, insight, the place where we can discern the depth of what God is doing in the life of the city or the camp. It is also the place of redemption, the place outside the city from which the salvation of the city flows. And the Letter to the Hebrews suggests that it is the place where we meet the Lord and share in his work – and keep the company he keeps, for he chooses to associate particularly with those whom society has marginalized: 'therefore let us go forth to him outside the camp, and bear the abuse he endured. For here we have no lasting city, but we seek the city which is to come. Through him then let us continually offer up a sacrifice of praise to God, that is, the fruit of lips that acknowledge his name' (Hebrews 13:13–15).

E—CHRISTIAN WORSHIP TODAY AND TOMORROW

Christian worship is today in a state of crisis. This is the situation which we have tried to analyse in this chapter. Some see nothing but the acids of modernity eating away the substance of worship, leaving only some flakes of rust behind. Others believe that the crisis is a challenge to renewal, in which worship may be liberated, renewed and purified. As in all crises, there is both danger and opportunity, and the Christian is called to respond in faith asking what God is doing and saying to his Church in the modern situation. The prophetic tradition reminds us that God may reject and destroy forms of worship when they become covers for injustice, meaningless survivals from the past or impersonal routines. But destruction goes often with purification and renewal. The same process that challenges and erodes forms of worship opens up the possibility of the recovery of vital but long forgotten elements in the worship tradition, the rebirth of long dormant symbols and images, and the development of new and living symbols, words and forms. A crisis is no time for timidity, and Christians should be adventurous in their worship, confident that God is at work amidst the threats and opportunities of the modern age.

In a secular society Christians see worship as continuing to perform vital functions. In the first place it is a way in which life is given meaning, and depth. Worship does not belong in a separate order from everyday life, and does not provide a bolt-hole from the pressures of existence. It must be rooted in ordinary life, providing an interpretation of that life which sustains and invigorates it by giving it depth. And worship is the celebration of life. In Christian worship the vertical – our encounter with God – and the horizontal – our encounter with the neighbour – are held together. To emphasise one at the expense of the other is to distort the cruciform shape of Christian worship. But worship which holds together the vertical and the horizontal is capable of transforming life. As Panikkar puts it:

> People eat. It is the eating that has to be transformed by the sacramental presence and thus the Eucharist has to regain its symbolism of being a meal. People dance and amuse themselves. Christian worship has here again to recover its aspect of celebration and festivity. People are born, come of age, get married, adopt a profession and die. The sacraments have to sanctify and consecrate these most universal and elemental human acts. The sacraments of Initiation, Maturity, Marriage, etc., must not be simply ceremonies and traditional ritualisms, but have a real bearing and meaning for these important

moments of human existence; in a word, they must really shape
them ... Worship has to permeate human life once again and
render it more meaningful, enhancing the significance of those
acts and also giving the necessary strength (grace) for one to live
up to such a human calling.[21]

Only too often, however, the actuality of worship conveys precisely the
contrary message to that intended – 'celebrations' expressing gloom and
solemnity rather than joy, the Lord's Supper less a symbolic fellowship
meal than a parody of the cafeteria, food eaten in haste and isolation from
the community. Some worship neither soars to the heights nor penetrates
to the depths but skates nervously over the surface of life. And the sign of
these distortions is the driving of a wedge between worship and life. When
worship is safely confined in a strange and unreal world of its own, boxed
into a special compartment from which it cannot impinge on the rest of
life, it quickly dies of asphyxia.

But worship does not sanctify things as they are. It is not a way of
conforming to the world but of transforming the world. It is not in the
business of maintaing the social equilibrium or sacralising the social order.
Worship disturbs the status quo, it is a standing challenge to the injustices
and oppression of the earthly city because worshippers are looking to the
city whose builder and maker is God, and in worship they are already
anticipating the life of that city.

Worship provokes the quest for understanding. It does not simply
reflect experience, but formulates, modifies and interprets experience in the
light of the encounter with the living God. As Mary Douglas puts it:

> Ritual is not merely like the visual aid which illustrates the
> verbal instructions for opening cans and cases. If it were just a
> kind of dramatic map or diagram of what is known it would
> always follow experience. But in fact ritual does not play this
> secondary role. It can come first in formulating experience. It
> can permit knowledge of what would otherwise not be known at
> all. It does not merely externalize experience, bringing it into the
> light of day, but it modifies experience in so expressing it.[22]

The trouble is that we have such trivial understandings of what worship is –
as if it were 'instructions for opening cans', or a controlled way of passing
on a self-contained and satisfactory pattern of theological understanding
or a device for conserving a religious culture, or a means for solidifying
patterns of community, order and authority. But worship is the encounter
with the living God! Michael Polanyi, chemist and philosopher, speaks of
Christian worship as a 'continual attempt at breaking out, at casting off,
the condition of man, even while humbly acknowledging its
inescapability'. It nourishes a 'heuristic hunch'.

> It resembles not the dwelling within a great theory of which we
> enjoy the complete understanding, nor an immersion in the

pattern of a musical masterpiece, but the heuristic upsurge which strives to break through the accepted frameworks of thought, guided by the intimations of discoveries still beyond our horizon. Christian worship sustains, as it were, an eternal, never to be consummated hunch: a heuristic vision which is accepted for the sake of its unresolvable tension. It is like an obsession with a problem known to be insoluble, which yet follows, against reason, unswervingly, the heuristic command: 'Look at the unknown!' Christianity sedulously fosters, and in a sense permanently satisfies man's craving for mental dissatisfaction by offering him the comfort of a crucified God.[23]

Worship also fosters, as it questions, Christian practice within the context of a fellowship that is both pastoral and prophetic; it stimulates a thirst for the Kingdom of God and his righteousness by providing an authentic anticipation of that Kingdom; it makes the worshipper dissatisfied with himself and his society; it mediates the forgiveness and grace upon which effective and purposive action depends; it sustains that vision without which the people perish and alerts us to attempts to subvert that vision; it nourishes those who live as pilgrims seeking that city whose builder and maker is God.

NOTES

1. Charles Davis 'Ghetto or Desert: Liturgy in a Cultural Dilemma' in *The Temptations of Religion*, London 1973, p. 125.
2. Raymond Panikkar, *Worship and Secular Man*, London 1973, p. 16.
3. Documentation and discussion of the points made in this paragraph may be found in S. S. Acquaviva, *The Decline of the Sacred in Industrial Society*, Oxford 1979.
4. Civil religion has been a central concern of sociologists at least since the time of Durkheim. The most interesting current discussion concerns American civil religion. See Robert N. Bellah, *The Broken Covenant: American Civil Religion in Time of Trial*, New York 1975, Russell E. Richey and Donald G. Jones, eds., *American Civil Religion*, New York 1974, and Gail Gehrig 'The American Civil Religion Debate' *Journal for the Scientific Study of Religion* 20, 1981, 51–63.
5. On political ritual in the Soviet Union see Christel Lane, *The Rites of Rulers: Ritual in Industrial Society – The Soviet Case*, Cambridge 1981.
6. Cited in Bruce Read, *The Dynamics of Religion*, London 1978, 107.
7. Peter Berger, *The Social Reality of Religion*, Harmondsworth 1973, 86.
8. Mary Douglas, *Purity and Danger*, London 1966, p. 62.
9. J. B. Metz, *Faith in History and Society*, London 1980, p. 45.

10. Peter Berger, *Social Reality*, pp. 137–8.
11. On this see Eugene H. Maly, 'The Interplay of World and Worship in the Scriptures', *Concilium* 2 No 7 (1971).
12. Johann Schefflet, otherwise known as Angelus Silesius, a seventeenth century German hymn writer, quoted in George Appleton, *Journey for a Soul*, London 1974, pp. 37–8.
13. Berger, *Social Reality*, p. 130.
14. On secularization see David Martin, *A General Theory of Secularization*, Oxford 1978, Bryan Wilson, *Religion in Secular Society*, Harmondsworth 1969, Robin Gill, *Social Context of Theology*, London 1975, part three, and the literature cited in these books.
15. In Charles Davis, *The Temptations of Religion*, London 1973, pp. 93–125.
16. Theodore Roszak, *The Making of a Counter Culture*, London 1970, and *Where the Waste Land Ends*, London 1973.
17. Davis, *The Temptations of Religion*, p. 124.
18. *The Letters of Pliny the Younger*, Book 10 ep. 97.
19. A useful critique of Davis's essay to which the above paragraphs are somewhat indebted is J. G. Davies, *Every Day God*, London 1973, pp. 253–246.
20. David, *Temptations of Religion*, p. 97.
21. Panikkar, *Worship and Secular Man*, p. 59.
22. Mary Douglas, *Purity and Danger*, 64.
23. Michael Polanyi, *Personal Knowledge*, London 1958, pp. 198–9.

FURTHER READING

Raymond Panikkar, *Worship and Secular Man*, London 1973.
Peter Berger, *The Social Reality of Religion*, Harmondsworth 1973.
J. G. Davies, *Every Day God*, London 1973.

FOR DISCUSSION

1. How would you assess the impact of secularization on worship?
2. In what ways may Christian worship relate to the rituals of civil religion?
3. 'There is no modern form of worship, because worship itself is outdated in the modern world and Christian faith a state of deviancy from contemporary culture' (Charles Davis). Discuss.

INDEX